Television News and Human Rights in the US & UK

Does the CNN Effect exist? Political communications scholars have debated the influence of television news coverage on international affairs since television news began, especially in relation to the coverage of massive human rights violations. These debates have only intensified in the last 20 years, as new technologies have changed the nature of news and the news cycle. But despite frequent assertion, little research into the CNN Effect, or whether television coverage of human rights violations causes state action, exists. Bridging across the disciplines of human rights studies, comparative politics, and communication studies in a way that has not been done, this book looks at television news coverage of human rights in the US and UK to answer the question of whether the CNN Effect actually exists.

Examining the human rights content in television news in the US and UK yields insights into what television news producers and policy makers consider to be human rights, and what, if anything, audiences can learn about human rights from watching television news. After reviewing 20 years of footage using three different types of content analyses of American television news broadcasts and two different types of British news broadcasts, and comparing those results with human rights rankings and print news coverage of human rights, Shawna M. Brandle concludes that despite rhetoric from both countries in support of human rights, there is not enough coverage of human rights in either country to argue that television media can spur state action on human rights issues. More simply, the violations will not be televised.

A welcome and timely book presenting an important examination of human rights coverage on television news.

Shawna M. Brandle is an Assistant Professor of Political Science at Kingsborough Community College, New York. Her interests include media and international relations.

Routledge Studies in Global Information, Politics and Society

Edited by Kenneth Rogerson, *Duke University*
and Laura Roselle, *Elon University*

International communication encompasses everything from one-to-one cross-cultural interactions to the global reach of a broad range of information and communications technologies and processes. *Routledge Studies in Global Information, Politics and Society* celebrates—and embraces—this depth and breadth. To completely understand communication, it must be studied in concert with many factors, since, most often, it is the foundational principle on which other subjects rest. This series provides a publishing space for scholarship in the expansive, yet intersecting, categories of communication and information processes and other disciplines.

"Shawna M. Brandle's innovative and meticulous content analysis of US and British TV news documents the shockingly sparse coverage of human rights issues around the world that leaves the general public clueless about the frequency and severity of human rights violations and decision-makers free of pressure to do more than pay lip service to these problems. While crime and terrorism in the West tend to be over-covered, human rights violations are rarely televised according to the research presented here. This is an important book that is especially recommended for the fields of communication, journalism, political science, and human rights studies."

—**Brigitte Nacos,** *Columbia University, USA*

"In this timely new work, Professor Brandle reminds us there are few things more important than human rights. By short-changing news coverage of human rights, media organizations fail to discourage the violence and also limit public outrage over under-covered atrocities. This book is a crucial study of how little we are told about a recurring global danger."

—**Stephen Farnsworth,** *Professor of Political Science and Director of the University of Mary Washington's Center for Leadership and Media Studies, USA*

Television News and Human Rights in the US & UK

The Violations Will Not Be Televised

Shawna M. Brandle

Routledge
Taylor & Francis Group

LONDON AND NEW YORK

First published 2016
by Routledge

2 Park Square, Milton Park, Abingdon, Oxfordshire OX14 4RN
711 Third Avenue, New York, NY 10017

Routledge is an imprint of the Taylor & Francis Group, an informa business

First issued in paperback 2017

Library of Congress Cataloging in Publication Data
Names: Brandle, Shawna M.
Title: Television news and human rights in the US & UK : the
    violations will not be televised / Shawna M. Brandle.
Description: New York, NY : Routledge, 2016. | Series:
    Routledge studies in global information, politics and society |
    Includes bibliographical references and index.
Identifiers: LCCN 2015029508 | ISBN 9781138908413 (hbk) |
    ISBN 9781315694467 (ebk)
Subjects: LCSH: Human rights in mass media. | Human rights—Press
    coverage—United States. | Human rights—Press coverage—Great
    Britain. | Television broadcasting of news—Political aspects—United
    States. | Television broadcasting of news—Political aspects—Great
    Britain.
Classification: LCC P96.H852 U57 2015 | DDC 070.4/49323044—dc23
LC record available at http://lccn.loc.gov/2015029508

ISBN: 978-1-138-90841-3 (hbk)
ISBN: 978-0-8153-7061-1 (pbk)

Typeset in Sabon
by Apex CoVantage, LLC

For Bobby, who would be pleased to know my homework is no longer almost done.

Contents

Figures

Tables

Series Editor's Foreword

In the 24-hour cacophony of endless information flows, it is tempting to think that every person has a voice and every event is somehow documented, in some small way, even if they are not heard or seen by anyone else. If we discover something, we can simply "search online" to learn about it.

Shawna Brandle is a voice of caution in this world of diminishing self-reflection and questioning. She invites us to consider that many of us seem to have adopted traditional news values: we (as a society and the broadly defined media that document it) are often interested only in those things that are about prominent people and the conflicts between them, and only when their activities are proximate or unusual.

This tension is especially pronounced in the area of human rights. Professor Brandle deftly navigates the difficulties that human rights monitors face in spreading their messages. Her insights are not only valuable to media scholars but bridge a gap between them and those examining the politics and ethics of global human rights violations

Ken Rogerson

Acknowledgments

This project has been a long time in the making and would not have been possible without the help and generosity of so many people, though all errors, omissions, and faults are my own.

Many thanks are due to Kathleen Dickson and the staff of the British Film Institute for their assistance both in and out of country, Louise North and the staff of the Written Archives Center of the BBC for their assistance and warm hospitality, and the Ralph Bunche Institute and Fried Memorial Fellowship for their generous research support.

My special thanks to my advisor, George Andreopoulos, and reader, Brigitte Nacos, for their insightful suggestions while I wrote my dissertation on which this book is based. Invaluable practical support was provided by Meghan Metzler, whose Excel advice improved this project and my own skills exponentially, Garrett Eisler and Naaborle Sackeyfio for their assistance in obtaining research materials, and Brian Hasbrouck and John McMahon for their coding assistance. The comments of Patricia Stapleton and Janet Reilly on countless outlines and drafts improved this project immeasurably.

I owe my greatest debt of thanks to my family, whose support and patience have been unending, especially krf, e, and p.

1 Introduction

As technological advancements continue at rapid speeds, it is easy to think that everything has changed. Letters are replaced by e-mails, landline telephones are replaced with mobiles and Internet telephony, and print and television news are dinosaurs that somehow continue to limp on despite having gone instinct years ago.

This last point, however, is not borne out by the evidence. Audiences may have declined, they may have aged, and they may also seek additional sources of news, but over the last 20 years, television has continued to be the biggest source of news for Americans. The Pew Research Center compiled data from its "Where People Got News Yesterday" surveys from 1990 onward, which revealed that television news still has the highest percentage of news consumers of any type of news source, as shown in Figure 1.1.[1] Television news still matters.

Television reaches a mass audience, beaming moving pictures from around the world into everyone's living rooms. By 1960, 90 percent of American homes had a television set; 98 percent had televisions by 1978.[2] Nielsen reports that in 2009, more than half of American homes had at least three televisions and that, on average, there are more televisions in American homes—2.86 per home—than there are people, 2.5 per home.[3] The most recent numbers available show further increase in the reach of television: Nielsen estimates that in 2014, there were 116.3 million homes with at least one television in them and, "that nearly 296 million persons age 2 and older live in these TV homes."[4] Since its spread into American homes, television has become the primary way people get information about the world around them. This level of penetration of the daily lives of citizens combined with the advent of cable, satellite, and digital technology allowing for faster news cycles and 24-hour news channels gave birth to the idea of the CNN Effect. Although it is named for CNN, the 24-hour Cable News Network, and inspired by that network's round-the-clock coverage of the Persian Gulf War and US military intervention in Somalia, the CNN Effect has been a broad theory: television news coverage, either broadcast or cable, of major issues would force government action, a sort of humanitarian "if they see it, they will come" argument.

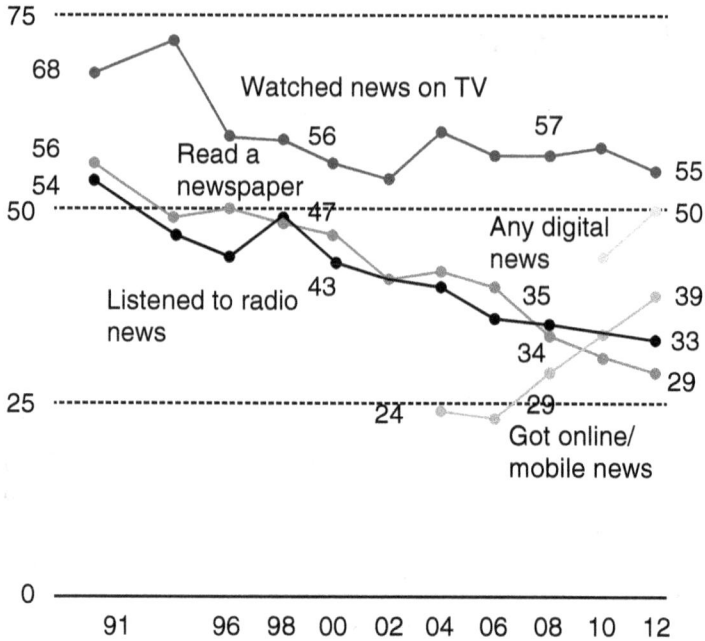

PEW RESEARCH CENTER 2012 News Consumption Survey.
Q9, Q11, Q13, Q17, Q20 Q21, Q70, Q75, Q82, Q87.

Figure 1.1 Where People Got News Yesterday

I began this project as a test of the CNN Effect with the intention of examining the human rights content of television news in the US and UK as a way of determining whether human rights television news coverage could drive human rights policy or the other way around, and whether this would be the same across two different countries with two different media systems. During the long process of collecting and analyzing data, however, it became apparent that there is not very much television coverage of human rights at all in either country. There is, in fact, so little human rights coverage on television news that it is impossible to support the idea of a CNN Effect on human rights issues. The violations, it seems, are not being televised.

In 1970, Gil Scott-Heron recorded "The Revolution Will Not Be Televised," a spoken word poem about the numbing power of television, referencing musical acts, political figures, and popular advertising campaigns as a way of pointing out that they are a distraction from the revolution, which will be live. Since then, the phrase has been adapted and remixed in various ways by musicians, filmmakers, and intellectuals to the point that it has become part of popular culture, divorced from Scott-Heron's original usage. Artists ranging from Public Enemy to Elvis Costello have used the phrase for their own purposes, and this book is titled in the same vein. There is no doubt that there are tremendous human rights violations occurring every day in many places around the world, as well as within the US itself. But these issues are not covered by television news in either the US or the UK—the violations are simply not televised.

That is not to say, however, that this study has not revealed important data. Examining the small amount of human rights content in television news in the US and UK yields insights to what television news producers and policy makers do and do not consider to be human rights, what types of human rights stories get covered, and what, if anything, audiences can learn about human rights from watching television news. Although sources for news abound today, with multiple print, television, and especially Internet outlets available, television news still holds a tremendous market share. Thus discovering what human rights information is conveyed by television is an important task, which is pursued in this study through four different cuts at the television news data.

First, Chapter 2 briefly reviews the relevant communication studies and international relations literatures to build the foundation for the content analyses by defining terms and highlighting the most salient points for comparison between the media and human rights systems in the US and UK. Chapter 3 consists of a content analysis of all of the stories containing the phrase human rights from one US network nightly news broadcast from 1990–2009, which illustrates the amount of human rights coverage in the US in the post-Cold War period and examines both the issues and the countries that are covered in the context of human rights in the US. Objective rankings of human rights conditions throughout the world are analyzed to see what could be getting coverage but is not. Chapter 4 begins the comparative part of this study by analyzing one month of transcripts/shooting scripts for evening news broadcasts in the US and UK in 1990 to see what, if any, kinds of stories might be covering human rights issues without explicitly using the phrase human rights. Comparisons are made to rankings of human rights conditions during that time period as well as to American and British print news to see both what violations are occurring and what print journalists find to be newsworthy. Chapter 5 avoids the potential shortcomings of transcripts and shooting scripts by viewing the actual broadcasts as audiences would have seen them. One week of evening news broadcasts for the US and UK from 1990–2009 are analyzed in conjunction with human rights ranking data to see which stories are covered in each country, how deeply stories are covered, and how that coverage differs from the US to the UK. Chapter 6 takes a case study approach, analyzing all of the television coverage of China, Somalia, and Sudan over time to see what share of each country's coverage is devoted to human rights. Chapter 7 concludes the study, summarizing the results from the four different television news content analyses and expounding on their implications for media and human rights in the US and UK.

Each of the four different ways of looking at human rights coverage in television news shows a slightly different part of a very small picture, proving definitively that the human rights violations will not be televised.

Notes

1 "In Changing News Landscape, Even Television is Vulnerable." Pew Research Center, Washington, DC (September 27, 2012). http://www.people-press.org/2012/09/27/in-changing-news-landscape-even-television-is-vulnerable/.
2 "Number of TV Households in America." http://www.tvhistory.tv/Annual_TV_Households_50–78.JPG
3 "More than half the homes in the US have three or more television sets." July 20, 2009. http://www.nielsen.com/us/en/insights/news/2009/more-than-half-the-homes-in-us-have-three-or-more-tvs.html
4 "Nielsen estimates 116.3 million TV homes in the US, up 0.4 percent." May 5, 2014. http://www.nielsen.com/us/en/insights/news/2014/nielsen-estimates-116–3-million-tv-homes-in-the-us.html

2 Human Rights and the Media in the US & UK

Before examining the human rights content and impact of television media in the US and UK, theoretical lenses, definitions, and local context need to be carefully specified. This chapter will explore the relevant schools of international relations theory: the Constructivists and, more specifically, the theories of NGO action and influence. The meaning of human rights, including its historical and legal origins and possible differentiation from international humanitarian law, is clarified; related terms such as genocide and crimes against humanity are also defined. This chapter also explores the differing contexts of the American and British approaches to human rights. Theories from the field of communications studies and political science are examined to shed light on the concepts of framing, the CNN Effect, and the direction of causality of media influence, followed by a survey of the existing literature on human rights in the media. Finally, the chapter offers a sketch of the broadcasting systems of the US and UK to further contextualize the results of the content analyses that make up the bulk of this study.

International Relations Theory

There is a growing body of literature that is exploring the role of media and communications in international relations both theoretically and empirically. The non-state constructivists focus on the actions, norms, and values of states and non-state actors. The evolution of a norm begins with norm entrepreneurs convincing states to abide by a specific norm, and as states do so, a cascade occurs, where an evolving norm becomes an established norm, the expected and appropriate behavior for all states (Finnemore & Sikkink 1998). Thomas Risse (2000) uses the example of public human rights commitments made by human rights–violating states who, nevertheless, wish to appear to be playing by the rules of civilized states. This leads to the self-entrapment of the state in those commitments, which empowers domestic resistance, transnational advocacy networks, and NGOs to achieve changes in state action.

Norm entrepreneurs cannot influence states *qua* states but must seek to convince the individuals who comprise those states, either as bureaucrats, elected representatives, or citizens who will subsequently pressure their governments; additionally, norm entrepreneurs themselves are either individuals or groups, networks, or organizations that consist of individuals (Florini 1996). It is therefore important to empirically examine the processes by which individuals are influenced, with one such process being the news media. Jeffrey T. Checkel (1997) argues that in some political systems, such as liberal and corporatist systems, society can wholly or partially constrain state options to drive state behavior in the direction of adopting international norms. Analyzing media coverage of immigration issues in German newspapers, Checkel finds some support for claims of its influence.

More recent work has sought to acknowledge the complex interrelationships between states, non-state actors, and flows of information. Miskimmon, O'Loughlin, and Roselle's (2014) work on strategic narratives adapts international relations theories to the real world, where information and communication are real forms of power with real effects. Monroe Price explores the essential role media flows have in shaping international affairs (2002) and the way states are influenced by information as well as the way they seek to control that information (2015).

Social Movements, NGOs, and the Outside Strategy

Social movements and NGOs have also been explored both theoretically and empirically. Keck and Sikkink (1998) map out the relationships between individuals and domestic NGOs in developed and underdeveloped countries, as well as the transnational actors, conferences, and technologies that help bring them together into transnational advocacy groups. Media coverage is a vital part of the information and symbolic politics that network activists use. The authors describe the boomerang process, whereby third-world actors (NGOs, groups, or individuals) provide facts and/or testimony to more powerful first-world allies, who in turn exchange their greater financial, media, and political resources for the information and the international credibility of working directly with the third-world groups. First world and international actors (state officials, NGOs, groups, or individuals) may advocate for change in the original state's policies or for their own government to pressure the original state. NGOs need to be able to "mobilize their own members and affect public opinion via the media" (23) by "cultivat[ing] a reputation for credibility with the press, and packag[ing] their information in a timely and dramatic way to draw press attention" (22). Snow et al. (1986) argue that social movement organizations (SMOs) perform interpretive actions in constructing, maintaining, and aligning frames or interpretive schema to create meaning. Moreover, they contend that these actions are so vital, those SMOs that cannot frame effectively will cease to exist.

Most social movements, transnational actors, and NGOs seek to change government policy, either their national government's or another state's. To that end, they pursue strategies that can be loosely classified into two categories: inside strategies of directly trying to influence policy makers, such as lobbying, and outside strategies of protest politics or attempting to influence the public, which then pressures policy makers. Ruud Koopmans (2004) argues that social movements are now less dependent on direct confrontations with policy makers via protests; the media coverage of protests is what influences authorities the most. "Authorities will not react to—and will often not even know about—protests that are not reported in the media" (368). Koopmans further argues that any response policy makers choose to make to social movements will likely be a public one via the mass media. So pursuing media coverage becomes an essential goal of NGOs and other social movements: "movements need the news media for three major purposes: mobilization, validation, and scope enlargement" (Gamson and Wolsfeld 1993 116, see also Nelson 2006 on the importance of the mass media to human rights NGOs).

This is not, however, an uncontested point. Thrall (2006) concludes that despite wide consensus on the necessity of mediated outside strategies as a necessary goal, as well as a way to level the playing field between smaller, poorer social movements and larger, better-resourced interest groups, empirical evidence is to the contrary. Investigating TV and print news, Thrall finds that the overwhelming majority of news coverage of interest groups is devoted to the largest and most well-resourced groups, while the smaller groups, which would need the advantages of media coverage more to make up for their lack of resources, are seldom successful in getting into the news. Tresch and Fischer (2008) attribute this lack of coverage not to the social movements themselves, which, regardless of their size and resources, all tend to pursue outside strategies, but to a media bias, whereby journalists prefer high-ranking state actors and public officials or established NGOs that have the resources to prepare press releases and maintain staff dedicated to assisting the media. Interestingly, Tresch and Fischer find that the more established and better-resourced social movements and NGOs are the ones most likely to pursue, and achieve greater success with, traditional inside strategies of lobbying.

Human Rights Defined

Before the human rights content of the media can be examined, the term must be clarified. "Human Rights are, literally, the rights that one has simply because one is a human being." (Donnelly 10) Dignity, equality, and the worth of the individual are the core of international human rights (Mertus 2008 5). As Alyson Brysk summarizes, "Human rights may be conceived as a set of entitlements to the social prerequisites to human development: protection, security, freedom, and community" (Brysk 2005 23). At the same time, human rights are a minimalist framework, as emphasized by Weiss, Forsythe, Coate, and Pease (2007) as "fundamental entitlements of persons constituting means to the end of minimal human dignity" (132). Donnelly further states, "we do not have human rights to all things that are good, or even to all important good things."(10). Though they are often enshrined in public statements and international agreements, including the Charter of the United Nations, the definition of human rights is seldom elaborated. So what are human rights, specifically?

The most commonly referred to list of human rights is the Universal Declaration of Human Rights (UDHR), which, with the International Covenant on Civil and Political Rights (ICCPR) and the International Covenant on Economic, Social, and Cultural Rights (ICESCR), is considered the International Bill of Rights. Paul Gordon Lauren (2003) traces the process of participation, negotiation, and consultation with as many religious and cultural groups as could be obtained at the time to come up with the most comprehensive list possible that would apply to all peoples everywhere. The UDHR contains 30 articles with provisions protecting nondiscrimination, the protection of life, liberty, and the security of person, protection against slavery and torture, equal protection under the law, equal rights of men and women in marriage, rights to work, social security, rest and leisure, adequate standard of living, education, privacy, and the freedom of assembly and association (Donnelly 24).

The UDHR was drafted and signed in 1948 as a nonbinding declaration of the United Nations General Assembly. The legal classification was a tactical move on the part of the drafters to gain widespread state support for a comprehensive list covering all human rights, be they civil, political, economic, cultural, or social in nature, which could then be built into a legally binding treaty. The politics of the Cold War intervened, however, and it would be almost twenty years before a binding treaty on human rights could be agreed to and opened for signature by the UN General Assembly in 1966 and then only after it was split into two separate treaties, the ICCPR, supported by the US and Western countries, and the ICESCR, supported by the USSR and Eastern Bloc countries (Lauren 236–246). In the generational approach to classifying human rights, civil and political rights are considered the oldest, or first-generation rights, while economic, social, and cultural rights are considered second-generation rights, with a third generation, that of group rights, receiving less widespread acceptance (Sriram et al. 37–40).

Since the end of the Cold War, both the ICCPR and the ICESCR have received widespread ratification across the East-West divide. Article 5 of the Vienna Declaration from the 1993 World Conference on Human Rights reaffirms, "All human rights are universal, indivisible and interdependent and interrelated," but the distinction between civil and political rights on the one hand and economic, cultural, and social rights on the other still retains significant importance in several countries, particularly in the US, which has refused to ratify the ICESCR and where the language of civil and political rights are much more resonant with the state as well as the public.

The drafting and signing of the ICCPR and ICESCR initiated a period of (relatively) rapid codification of more specific human rights treaties. Although largely based (and frequently explicitly referencing) the UDHR, these treaties were issue specific, much more detailed, and designed to be legally binding documents from the start (Lauren 246). Treaties on eliminating racism, eliminating discrimination against women, preventing torture, protecting the rights of the child, migrant workers, and persons with disabilities, and protection of all persons from enforced disappearance all spell out specific definitions for their issues and have received widespread state signature and ratification.[1]

Crimes Against Humanity and Genocide

Two areas related to human rights have received extensive codification and jurisprudence: crimes against humanity and genocide. However, their definitions, limitations, and interactions with the existing human rights treaties and other relevant international law are still constantly debated, even among academics and jurists. A brief exploration of their statutory definitions will clarify both the meanings of the terms, as well as point to why there may be significant confusion among non-experts.[2]

Crimes against humanity first appeared in the Charter of the International Military Tribunal at Nuremberg in 1945 and were defined as:

> murder, extermination, enslavement, deportation, and other inhumane acts committed against any civilian population, before or during the war; or persecutions on political, racial or religious grounds in execution of or in connection with any crime within the jurisdiction of the Tribunal, whether or not in violation of the domestic law of the country where perpetrated.
>
> (IMT Article 6(c))

This phrasing, particularly the expanded international jurisdiction over the rights of individuals, prefigures the human rights treaties that were to be developed in the ensuing decades. Decades after 1945, crimes against humanity would come to be interpreted as customary international law applying to all states, regardless of their treaty affiliations, and the nexus between crimes against humanity and armed conflict was discarded as unnecessary in the 1990s, as evidenced by the Tadic decision (Cassese 2001 251). More recently, as the culmination of "considering that systematic gross violations of human rights directed against civilians may qualify as crimes against humanity" (Meron 2000 265), the Rome Statute of the International Criminal Court, which entered into force in 2002, defined crimes against humanity as:

> any of the following acts when committed as part of a widespread or systematic attack directed against any civilian population, with knowledge of the attack:
>
> (a) Murder;
> (b) Extermination;
> (c) Enslavement;
> (d) Deportation or forcible transfer of population;
> (e) Imprisonment or other severe deprivation of physical liberty in violation of fundamental rules of international law;
> (f) Torture;
> (g) Rape, sexual slavery, enforced prostitution, forced pregnancy, enforced sterilization, or any other form of sexual violence of comparable gravity;
> (h) Persecution against any identifiable group or collectivity on political, racial, national, ethnic, cultural, religious, gender as defined in paragraph 3, or other grounds that are universally recognized as impermissible under international law, in connection with any act referred to in this paragraph or any crime within the jurisdiction of the Court;
> (i) Enforced disappearance of persons;
> (j) The crime of apartheid;
> (k) Other inhumane acts of a similar character intentionally causing great suffering, or serious injury to body or to mental or physical health.
>
> (Rome Statute of the International
> Criminal Court, Article 7(1))

Arguably the most universally agreed upon (though still violated) human right and one of the greatest achievements of the human rights movement is the prohibition against genocide. Originally conceived of at the Nuremberg Tribunal as a subset of crimes against humanity, genocide came into its own with the Genocide Convention of 1948 (Cassese 2001 252). Genocide is defined as "a criminal act intended to destroy an ethnic, national or religious group, which is targeted for destruction as such" (Mann 17). The *dolus specialis* is what separates genocide from run-of-the-mill crimes against humanity: without the special intention for the act to destroy the group in whole or in part, the act cannot be considered genocide; crimes against humanity require merely the intent to "subject a person or group to discrimination, ill-treatment, or harassment, so as to bring about great suffering or injury to that person or group on religious, political, or other such grounds" (Cassese 2001 252). The Genocide Convention also does not require a link with armed conflict for it to be triggered. Crimes of genocide can occur during peace, wartime, or any degree in between (Meron 2000 264) and have been interpreted by judicial decisions at the ICTR and ICTY to include single acts (meaning no repeated pattern is necessary) and sexual violence. Furthermore, it is widely considered to be a part of customary international law, binding on all states, from which no derogation is permitted (Othman 2005 252). The prohibition against genocide is not merely that states must not commit the act, they are also required to prevent and punish genocide and to enact relevant domestic law to be able to do so (Sriram et al. 50, 53).

International Humanitarian Law

International humanitarian law (IHL), alternatively known as the law of armed conflict or law in war (Kennedy 2006 83), is closely related to international human rights law (IHRL) but conceptually distinct, at least in the legal and academic literature. IHL officially encompasses both Hague Convention Law, or how war should be carried out, and Geneva Law, which spells out the commitments of states during armed conflict for the protection of civilians, the security of belligerent populations, the treatment of the wounded, sick, and shipwrecked, and the treatment of prisoners of war (Best 116–179), though more emphases is usually placed on the Geneva law. Unlike IHRL, which is supposed to apply to all humans equally at all times by virtue of their being human, IHL only enters into force during times of war and is based on the principle of distinction, of civilian from combatant, uniformed soldier from guerilla, and *levee en masse* from illegal opposition to occupation (Best 1994 128–232; Kennedy 2006 117–122). Even the difficult question of what exactly constitutes war or conflict sufficient to trigger the applicability of IHL must be decided for each conflict, whereas human rights law applies at all times, unless a state makes a clear announcement of derogation, which can only apply to derogable human rights (which notably do not include the right to life and not to be tortured, among others) (Meron 2000 267, Droege 2007). IHL is also predicated on the interactions of states with each other, while IHRL "was designed to protect the individual from abuse at the hands of the state" (Leebaw 2007 225).

Causes of the Blur With Human Rights

David Kennedy argues that the development of modern warfare, where the clear demarcation of battlefield and soldier by geography and uniform and of periods of conflict from post-conflict are increasingly inapplicable, has caused humanitarians to intentionally blur the line between law in war and human rights law in order to extend the protections of the law in war to all internal conflicts and violence regardless of whether they truly fit the legal criteria (Kennedy 2006 112–114). Although Common Article 3 of the 1949 Geneva Conventions does address armed conflict not of an international nature, states are often loathe to admit that this threshold has been reached, for example, when Russia argued in the case of two attacks by the Russian air force during the conflict in Chechnya (Tamura 2011). Further muddying the water is the fact that newer treaties draw from both IHRL and IHL sources, including "the Convention on the Rights of the Child, the Rome Statute of the International Criminal Court, and the Optional Protocol to the Convention on the Rights of the Child on the Involvement of Children in Armed Conflict 2000," among others (Droege 2007 317).

The changing nature of warfare and the challenge of determining exactly what constitutes armed conflict sufficient to trigger IHL is only one factor blurring the line between IHL and IHRL. Many treaties include both types of law as sources, creating overlap in the two frameworks that is not easy to delineate. This lack of clarity results in differences of opinion among jurists and courts, who may come up with conflicting answers to questions such as if IHRL applies at all times, then which law, IHL or IHRL takes precedence? So far, two responses have been put forth: either the *lex specialis*, where IHL takes precedence over IHRL as the more specific law to the context of armed conflict or, complementarity, where the two sets of laws are seen as additive. This "belt-and-suspenders approach" says that "the norm that better protects the individual, whether it is drawn from international human rights law or international humanitarian law, is to be applied" (Schabbas 593). The International Court of Justice (ICJ), in its Advisory Opinion on Nuclear Weapons in 1996, endorsed the *lex specialis* approach, because IHRL was insufficient to determine whether a loss of life could be arbitrary, as defined by Article 6 of the ICCPR (Meron 2000 266). This interpretation is criticized, however, on the grounds that it is unclear whether IHL would always take precedence (Tomuschat 2010 17). It is also criticized on the grounds that the entire advisory opinion was decided on the issue of the justness of self-defense/recourse to war, which falls purposely outside the realm of IHL, meaning that IHL was not the applicable law either (Schabas 595). In 2004, in its decision on the wall in occupied Palestinian territory, the ICJ laid out three possible options for the relationship of IHL to IHRL: "some rights may be exclusively matters of international humanitarian law; others may be exclusively matters of human rights law; yet others may be matters of both these branches of international law" (Tomuschat 18), but the decision failed to specify what rights fall into what categories in what contexts. Increasingly, jurists and commentators are moving in the direction of applying whichever body of law provides more protection to the victims, placing more emphasis on closing whatever gaps exist to ensure human protection.

All of the preceding codifications, both in IHL and IHRL, are state-centric: they see the state as the primary guarantor of international human rights, as well as, ironically, the primary violator. Over time, however, these treaties have been interpreted more and more expansively to account for human rights violations perpetrated by non-state actors, such as insurgent groups, private corporations, and even individuals (Brysk 2005).

Human Rights in the US and UK

The definitions of human rights explored earlier are drawn from the literature on various international treaties and norms. Possibly more important for the present study are the ways in which those definitions have been operationalized in the national context. Examining the way human rights are conceived of in the US and UK sheds significant light on what the term means in each country, which, contrary to the foregoing legal definitions, can vary widely. Within their national contexts, the US and UK differ on such points as their involvement in regional institutions; the speed at which they sign and ratify agreements; the attachment of reservations, understandings, and declarations; the types of rights included in the domestic understanding of human rights; the timing of the rising prominence of human rights; the conceptualization of human rights as a foreign or domestic issue; and the institutionalization of human rights.

Schmitz & Sikkink (2002) argue that "Europe and the Americas feature today the most advanced human rights institutions" (524). The US, however, is not very active in the regional human rights arrangements of the Americas:

> The US has played a marginal role in both the Inter-American Commission on Human Rights and the Inter-American Court of Human Rights, not ratified the "American Convention on Human Rights" and neither signed nor ratified the "Additional protocol to the American Convention on Human Rights in the Area of Economic, Social and Cultural Rights"
>
> (Felice 2006 83)

The UK, by contrast, is subject to several layers of regional human rights legislation, monitoring, adjudication, and enforcement. The UK is party to the Council of Europe's European Convention of Human Rights (ECHR), which covers civil and political rights, and is enforceable by the European Court of Human Rights. The ECHR has also been interpreted by the European Union's European Court of Justice as "stating human rights principles [are] common to the legal systems of the member states" and therefore legally enforceable (Jones 2004 248). This means that in addition to its own domestic legislation, the UK is subject to both EU and Council of Europe legislation and adjudication.

The US has a history of being slow to sign and ratify international treaties; for example, it only ratified the ICCPR in 1992. Thus American ratification was almost 15 years after the US signed the treaty, which was a full 10 years after the ICCPR was opened for signature. The US only ratified the CAT and ICERD in 1994, 10 and almost 30 years after they were opened for signature, respectively. Furthermore, the reservations, understandings, and declarations the US attaches to its ratifications are significant, simultaneously declaring the treaties to be non-self-executing,[3] while generally refusing to enact any implementation legislation or accept any obligations beyond current US law and practice. The US defends these attachments on the grounds that existing US law already protects the relevant rights as far as or further than the treaties would, when read according to the US reservations, declarations, and understandings (RUDs) (Nash 1995). Notable sticking points for the ICCPR include the US protection of hate speech and war propaganda under the First Amendment and of the use of the death penalty for offenders under 18. Critics of the US approach to the ICCPR have said that such RUDs are an abuse of the process: "By adhering to human rights conventions subject to these reservations, the United States, it is charged, is pretending to assume international obligations but in fact is undertaking nothing" (Henkin 1995 344). The UN Human Rights Commission found that the US RUDs for the ICCPR go too far, "making them incompatible with the object and purpose of the covenant, and therefore in violation of international law" (Mertus 2008 36). In contrast, the UK has a much better signature and ratification record of international human rights treaties, with far fewer reservations, understandings, or declarations.

The United States also has a very limited view of which human rights are immediate, actionable rights and which are perhaps not human rights at all. Contrary to the indivisibility of the whole of human rights proposed by the UDHR, the US has always had a tremendous preference for civil and political rights as opposed to economic, social, and cultural rights, and this preference includes both the US government and most of the large US-based human rights NGOs, such as Human Rights Watch, who until recently did not include economic, social, and cultural rights because they were perceived to be resource-intensive and/or nonjusticiable. The US did sign the ICESCR in 1977 but has yet to propose it for ratification, let alone actually ratify it more than 30 years later. "Claims of a 'right' to employment, health care, and housing seemed to run counter to the American ethos of individualism, personal responsibility, hard work, and individual initiative" (Felice 2006 80). The US does not see economic, cultural, and social rights as legally enforceable rights; rather, they are characterized more as social goods that should be achieved only if possible in either the domestic or foreign policy arenas.

Although economic, cultural, and social rights as rights are contested in the UK, they are infinitely more accepted as human rights there than in the US. The UK ratified the original European Social Charter of 1962 and signed the revised version, though it has yet to ratify it (The United Kingdom and the European Social Charter). The UK also ratified the ICESCR and complies with reporting requirements to the UN's Committee on Economic, Social, and Cultural Rights, which notes continuing improvements in several areas over time between reports (Felice 87–90). As Felice puts it, "The US limits, while the EU states expand, state responsibility to guarantee sufficient resources to all citizens as the ultimate guarantor of the right to subsistence" (91). The ECJ, the European Court of Human Rights, and the CESCR, to which the UK is subject, have all ruled that economic, social, and cultural rights are concrete goals toward which states must work immediately, regardless of resource constraints.

Kathryn Sikkink (1993) discusses the difference in human rights ideas between the US and UK. First, the idea of human rights gained prominence later in the US than it did in the UK. For the US, generally, human rights are thought to be issues that occur in the rest of the world, especially in the third world, while the UK's conception of human rights is more open to consideration of human rights issues at the European and even domestic levels. The US views human rights as a foreign concept, as something that happens "out there" instead of at home. In fact, the most common discussion of rights in the domestic sense is about civil rights or constitutional rights, which are of much greater salience to the US public. These types of issues, such as nondiscrimination or the right to free speech, for example, are also human rights. What is interesting is that they are not considered to be human rights by the US public or US government in the domestic arena. For the most part, human rights only enter the discussion when the topic is foreign: human rights happen outside the country, constitutional and civil rights happen within it (Mertus 2008 231). The US (in)famously used the Final Act of the Helsinki Agreement as a way to criticize the USSR, while simultaneously ignoring its own monitoring and reporting obligations under the agreement.

In addition to being more tightly integrated to various international and regional treaties and monitoring systems, the UK is also more receptive than the US to human rights at the domestic level. The UK has recently been involved in a process of "rights brought home" (Petley 2009 78), which means both making human rights apply explicitly within the UK as human rights and doing so through UK domestic legislation, specifically the Human Rights Act (HRA) of 1998, as opposed to only through the EU or Council of Europe. Subsequently, human rights have entered the domestic discourse in academia, the media, and government documents in issues as wide-ranging as the privacy of celebrities, the adoption of children (Welbourne 2002), the delivery of public services (Gavrielides 2008), and the protection of the elderly and sick in care homes (The Human Rights of Older People in Healthcare 2007).

Human rights have been further institutionalized in the UK by the creation of the Joint Committee on Human Rights, which is consists of six peers and six members of Parliament. The JCHR has responsibility for "scrutiniz[ing] legislation for compliance with the *Human Rights Act 1998* and the UKs international human rights commitments" (Tolley 2009). The HRA is not without criticism. It does not have the force of a constitutional document, and its ultimate power of judicial review creating a declaration of incompatibility does not change or nullify the law in question; that remains the prerogative of the government (Sypnowich 2008 106). Fearing an overwhelming increase in rights-based claims, some have proposed replacing it with a British Bill of Rights or a British Bill of Rights and Duties (Amos 2009), though to date, no such bill has been presented. In any case, Tolley argues that "Both Houses of Parliament in the post-HRA era have shown greater awareness of the human rights issues at stake in proposed legislation than any time before" (Tolley 49).

Having defined human rights and its related terms, as well as how those terms are understood in the US and UK, I now turn to examining the literature on the influence of the media.

The Influence of the Media

For years, political scientists and media analysts have insisted on the important role of the media in politics, based on the logics of agenda-setting and framing. Iyengar and Kinder's experiments in 1987 with slight alterations on television newscasts showed that individuals significantly change their perception of the importance of issues based on television news. Iyengar (1991) uses similar experimental methodology to show that television news content contributes to individuals' assessment of who is responsible for policies, programs, or problems such as poverty, racial inequality, and terrorism. Robert Entman (2003) further explores this framing power of the news media, which goes beyond the agenda-setting of putting issues that are frequently mentioned into the conscious thought of viewers and further influences the way those viewers will think about the issue.

At the beginning of the 20th century, Walter Lippmann (2007) was already pointing out the tremendous influence of the mass media on public opinion, especially of the emerging technology of the moving image (35), and especially on issues that are not part of the public's daily experience, the unseen environment (101), such as foreign policy. This theme is picked up by Page and Shapiro (1992), who stress the influence of not just the mass media but television specifically:

> The American public has learned a great deal about the United States and the world through the mass media, especially television. Facts about foreign countries and international events, about US social problems and resources and policy alternatives, have been conveyed through the media. The mass media, in fact, are the chief means by

which most other major sources of political information actually reach the public.

(358)

The information that reaches the public is of paramount importance, since that is how individuals decide what issues are important as well as how they feel about those issues. Democratic governments seek to be responsive to their citizens' preferences, which are formed in large part by media coverage and political elites (Aldrich et al. 2006). Gabriel Almond (1950) saw a very limited role of public opinion on foreign policy action; he divided public opinion on foreign policy into three groups: the mass public, which is neither informed nor capable of exerting influence; the attentive public, which is informed but has little influence; and the elite public, which is both informed and influential. Richard Sobel (2001) builds on Almond's work but argues that public opinion has played a larger role in constraining possible US government action on foreign military interventions since Vietnam. Sobel closely tracks benchmark events, foreign policy decisions, and public opinion polling data before and after the benchmarks to show how policy makers operated within the realm of options acceptable to the general public. It is important to note that Sobel does not claim public opinion directly determined specific foreign policy action, rather it merely defined the parameters of what government officials might do (See also Hurwitz and Peffley 1987; Gelpi 2006).

Media & Human Rights

Most research on the media refers to print media. Patrick Rossler (2004) reviews the few comparative empirical studies of television news and his own comparative study of television news in the US and nine European countries, finding that "universal regionalism," or the tendency for the media to cover its home country's closest neighbors either geographically or strategically, is strong in all ten systems.

Additionally, most research on media coverage and influence of foreign policy focuses directly on foreign intervention or military action[4]; very few studies look at media coverage of human rights. Early works of content analysis of news for human rights issues, such as Hanson and Miller's (1987) examination of US television news coverage of human rights in Central America and Geyer and Shapiro's (1988) analysis of public opinion data on human rights with the story indexes that contain human rights from the major newspapers, news magazines, and *CBS Evening News* found very little coverage of human rights in mainstream print and television media. Ovsiovitch (1993) asserts the importance of media on issues of human rights and analyzes television and print news in the US, finding that there is relatively little coverage of human rights in US media and that most of that coverage refers to two regions of the world, Latin America and Eastern Europe. Writing about the problem of limited news coverage of human rights, he hints at what would come to be called the CNN Effect:

> News coverage of human rights shapes public opinion, influences foreign policy development, and serves as an informal means of documenting abuse. Yet this information is incomplete, thus skewing the public's perception of human rights around the world. If this information is, in fact, helping to set the political agenda, government officials will focus attention primarily on those regions receiving media coverage. Human rights in Africa and Asia will be all but forgotten.
>
> (685)

Ovsiovitch's methodology has some limitations: his methodology uses pre-prepared indexes of stories to identify human rights stories and not the stories themselves, and the study relies primarily on the counting of stories, thereby missing the opportunity to find meaning in the content of the stories. It also analyzes stories from 1978–1987, and therefore cannot say anything about media and human rights in the post-Cold War period. Ramos, Ron, and Thoms (2007) looked explicitly at media coverage of human rights from 1986–2000, finding that coverage increases for more repressive countries, relatively wealthier countries, and places that receive Amnesty International attention. The work is admirable in that it is comparative, encompassing American and European news sources, but it is limited in only addressing print media, and using counts and statistics, not detailed story analyses. In contrast, Caliendo et al. (1999) delve deeper into content, looking for themes, continuities, and tone of coverage. After examining only American print news and, even more restrictively, only one paper, the *New York Times*, they conclude that there is more coverage of human rights in the news than Ovsiovitch found, but less than they expected to find, citing the media's preference for reporting stories when there are a high number of deaths associated with an event or issue. Heinze and Freedman (2010) find similar results from their study of American and British newspaper coverage of human rights and also note that the amount of coverage does not correlate with the severity of human rights violations as measured by Amnesty International reports; their study, while interesting, only spans three months at the end of 2006 and looks only at print news.

The Direction of Causality

If media does exert an influence on elite and/or mass opinion that then influences or constrains government discourse or action, there is still a question of the direction of causality: Does media coverage drive government discourse and policy action or is the news media instrumen-talized by government elites so that the influence is exerted from the gov-ernment to the public through the media? Herman and Chomsky (1988) argue that mass media organizations are so beholden to both their cor-porate owners and the government sources who provide information that the mass media becomes little more than a propaganda machine for the economic and political elites to control the population and generate con-sent to justify their continued rule. Bennett et al. (2007) invoke less of a conspiracy theory while expanding on the same basic ideas: mass media journalists seek the most reliable information by using established elites as a shorthand for reliability (they are also easier to find). The media's preference for relying upon existing contacts with governmental elites makes it difficult for journalists to pursue stories that do not have elite sources. In addition, journalists become more deferential to existing elites in order to maintain their continued access to information. These prob-lems are exacerbated as the issue gets geographically more remote from the journalist; the harder it is for the journalist to access an area on his or her own, the more dependent he or she will be on official government sources. Mermin's (1997) study of television news coverage leading up to US intervention in Somalia is consistent with the approach that journal-ists take their cues from official sources: he finds that broadcast news only begins significant coverage of the famine in Somalia after impor-tant government officials, such as Senators Nancy Kassebaum and Paul Simon, began talking about it.

The belief that the government leads the media's coverage of human rights is not the only theory of causal direction. Other scholars, in fact, argue the opposite: the media can exert an independent influence on gov-ernment discourse and policy action, which is most commonly known as the CNN Effect. The name reflects the idea that improvements in media technology and real-time reporting "disrupted traditional patterns of media deference to foreign policy elites and expand[ed] the power of the news media" (Robinson 2005). Real-time news coverage provides information not just to the general public but also to policy makers and journalists, some of whom admit to "using CNN as a kind of wire service for monitoring fast-breaking stories" (Minear 1996 et al. 35). The CNN Effect is not universally recognized, however. Eytan Gilboa (2005a) sur-veys the existing literature on the CNN Effect using methodological cri-tiques of the studies that claim television media coverage does influence government policy (Zaller and Chiu 1996; Miller 2002) to conclude there is insufficient evidence in support of the existence of the CNN Effect. Yet in the same essay, Gilboa finds similar problems with authors claiming that there is no evidence, so his conclusion cannot be taken as an abso-lute. Additionally, all of the studies Gilboa considers, as well as the over-whelming majority of studies of the phenomenon, deal with intervention, conflict, and war; few in general and none in Gilboa (2005b) examine human rights. Even among scholars who believe in the CNN Effect, there is still disagreement over the level of influence the media can have on government (see, for example, Kriesi and Jochum 2007, on the significance of influence). The questions of whether the CNN Effect exists, as well as how much influence it can exert, are therefore not settled.

A third possibility exists between the first two arguments on causality and seems most plausible. Rather than claim definitively that media coverage influences government or government controls media coverage, Baum and Potter (2008) and Entman (2003) call for a more nuanced view. Unidirectional causality does not make sense where the actors are so intricately linked. It is most likely that on different issues at different times, government elites, elites outside the government, journalists, and the public will have varying degrees of influence on what the media covers and on what that media coverage influences. Baum and Potter argue that the causality debate is a waste of time, since

> a clearer understanding of the media-opinion-foreign policy nexus emerge when, rather than exploring static snapshots of bilateral relationships between foreign policy actors, we consider them together as coequal players within a market that produces foreign policy outcomes through dynamic interaction.
>
> (42)

Television News in the US and UK

Having surveyed the general literature in communication studies about the potential importance of mass media, I turn now to the news broadcasting and regulatory systems in the US and UK.

Hallin and Mancini (2004) set out a framework to classify different political-media systems based on the development of media markets, political parallelism, development of journalistic professionalism, and the degree and nature of state intervention in the media system; they use this framework to analyze the economically advanced democratic countries of Western Europe and North America, finding three models of media systems, Mediterranean or Polarized Pluralist, Northern European or Democratic Corporatist, and North Atlantic or Liberal. Both the US and the UK are classified as North Atlantic/Liberal, but the authors concede significant differences between the two, especially in regards to ownership and regulation. First, broadcasting in the UK is required by law to be impartial and balanced in news and public affairs issues (216), while the Fairness Doctrine in the US was abandoned in the late 1980s, and the US has "shifted considerably toward a pure market model of broadcasting" (230). The regulatory agencies in the two countries differ significantly in influence and independence. The Independent Television Commission

(ITC), though weaker than its predecessor, the Independent Broadcasting Authority (IBA), still had much more influence over programming schedules and advertising than the Federal Communications Commission has in the US (231); since the passage of the Communications Act of 2003, British television has been under the purview of Ofcom, which while weaker still than the ITC, still dwarfs the regulatory activity of the FCC in the US, such as with its wide-sweeping research into television content (Gardam 2005 47). Commercial pressures are much stronger on the US networks than on the publicly supported BBC, raising questions about journalistic independence and how well the public interest is served (Hallin and Mancini 2004 247). Journalists in the two countries also tend to define professionalism differently. British journalists fall more in the category of social responsibility journalism, where the mark of a good journalist is one who makes informed judgments and presents news in light of those judgments, while North American norms of professionalism are closely tied to "objectivity," where journalists are supposed to present both sides of an issue, regardless of their personal opinion (226).

Ownership, regulation, and competition are the biggest differences between the American and British broadcasting systems. In their earliest days, radio and television broadcasting were seen to need at least some state intervention in both countries because of a technological necessity: spectrum scarcity. There was only so much bandwidth that could be given out, and with that bandwidth came the idea of responsible use and an obligation to serve the public interest. The difference between the two country's television systems and regulatory practices is largely a result of how that obligation has been defined and operationalized.

Ownership and Funding in the US and UK

The US and UK responded differently to the question of ownership in light of the potential power of broadcasting technology combined with spectrum scarcity. The US adopted a private system: "private ownership, created through government licensing" (Conrad 2010 242). Three networks "enjoyed a virtual monopoly of nationwide television for three decades, during which a collective prime-time share of 90 per cent was not uncommon" (Kung-Shankleman 2000 26). US television networks and the news programs they broadcast are funded by advertising and sponsorship sales. The UK, on the other hand, adopted public service broadcasting, creating a public corporation, the British Broadcasting Corporation, which covered first radio and then both radio and television (McNair 2003 11). In the UK, broadcasting was "deemed to be too important to be left to the whims of the market place" (Harrison 2000 44). The BBC was designed to be a public service, "free from the direct influences of both government and commerce" (Crisell 1999 61) as the result of the Sykes and Crawford committee reports, which cautioned against radio broadcasting being controlled by either government or private interests, respectively (McNair 2003 108), with a Charter obligation to educate, inform, and entertain. The BBC is funded by an annual licensing fee that is paid by all television owners to prevent the targeting of mass audiences at the expense of unprofitable minorities (Crisell 1999 62), which has been defined in terms of taste preferences as well as ethnicity and class. The BBC does not carry advertising on its domestic channels.

Regulation in the US and UK

US regulation of television in general and of television news specifically has been far less stringent than in the UK and has been much more market-focused. In the early days of television in the US, competition between the very limited number of channels was backed up by the Federal Communications Commission (FCC) and the Fairness Doctrine. The FCC was created in 1934 as the regulatory arm of the Federal Communications Act to "set standards and obligations for broadcasters to obtain and keep their licenses" (Conrad 2010 242). All licensees were required to act in the public interest, but no law ever defined the term—that was (remains to this day) up to the FCC. The Fairness Doctrine required licensees "(1) to devote a reasonable amount of their broadcast time to the discussion of controversial issues of public importance, and (2) to cover those issues fairly, affording reasonable opportunities for the presentation of opposing viewpoints" ("The Fairness Doctrine" 1980 1028). But as early as the 1960s and '70s, the FCC was facing suits over its use of the Fairness Doctrine as a violation of First Amendment constitutional guarantees to freedom of speech ("The First Amendment and Regulation of Television News" 1972). Criticism of the doctrine sharpened as the technological grounding for differential regulation of print and broadcasting media was deemed to have evaporated. With cable and satellite television, more channels were becoming more widely available. By 1987, the FCC had abandoned the Fairness Doctrine (Hershey Jr. 1987), and with the Telecommunications Act of 1996, Congress made the FCC significantly deregulate broadcast media ownership and licensing (Conrad 2010 245).

Regulation of broadcasting in the UK has historically been much more stringent, though it has been liberalized significantly and progressively since the 1980s. In addition to spectrum scarcity, increased regulation of broadcast media was justified in the UK because it was deemed to be more influential than print media and because it developed in the age of increased state involvement in many industries, as opposed to the print media's development during the laissez-faire 19th century (Goodwin 1999 131).

As part of its independence from both government and private ownership, the BBC has had to walk a careful line of impartiality, especially when it comes to controversial issues. If the BBC was to be the voice of the nation, and "the nation was recognized to contain diverse elements (diverse politically, socially, and geographically), the BBC would have to be an 'impartial arbiter,' independent of commercial and political interests" (McNair 2003 37). The perception that the BBC was being partial or was a creature of one of the parties or of the current government would not only destroy its credibility, but it could also endanger its revenue, the license fee; so from its earliest days, the corporation voluntarily accepted the importance of impartiality and balance in its broadcasting policy; this voluntary acceptance was finally written into the BBC License in 1996 (Barendt 1998 108). Neither independence nor impartiality has been absolute: on certain occasions informally and formally on others, such as the Broadcasting Act of 1996, the government has asserted control over who or what the BBC can discuss. For example, during the troubles in Northern Ireland, the BBC received notice from the secretary of state, in accordance with the Broadcasting Act of 1996, that certain groups, including the IRA, INLA, Sinn Fein, Republican Sinn Fein, and the Ulster Defence Association were to be banned (Petley 2009 149). The BBC responded to this and other previous bans by having actors or announcers read the words from banned individuals, though bans are thought to have at least partly affected the likelihood of covering banned stories:

> The BBC claimed, on the basis of its obligation to be impartial and to inform, the right to include Sinn Fein, the protestant extremists, and sometimes the IRA as voices that needed to be heard, while the government claimed the political right to exclude from the BBC voices which they thought had to change in order to win a right to a voice. The government always interpreted exposure as endorsement. "Publicity", said Mrs. Thatcher famously, "is the oxygen of terrorism . . ." The Broadcasting Ban was imposed. This meant that when members of terrorist groups appeared on television, their voices could not be heard and actors had to read their words. This ban did nothing to reduce public interest in paramilitary personalities. It did, however, constitute a humiliation to the public service broadcasters, as it was little more than a visible badge of government power. It also meant that television executives did not make programmes about Northern Ireland if they could help it.
>
> (Curran and Seaton 2009 211)

The Independent Broadcasting Authority (IBA) was established to regulate independent television shortly after its creation in much the same manner and with similar rules as the BBC's board of governors was to oversee the BBC:

> The authority was also required to ensure "balanced programming", "due impartiality" in the treatment of controversial issues, and a

high quality in programme production as a whole. To enforce its rec-
ommendations the IBA could determine the broadcasting schedule,
prohibit the transmission of particular programmes, or even revoke
the franchises of offending companies.

(Curran and Seaton 2009 180)

Particularly when it came to news, then ITV "was subject to the same
constrains in coverage as the BBC's news and current affairs service"
(McNair 2003 109).

The 1990 Broadcasting Act eliminated the IBA in favor of the Independent Television Commission, a greatly weakened regulator (Crisell
1999 65). Unlike the IBA, the ITC had no power to preview a program
and either block its broadcast or demand it be moved in the schedule to
preemptively promote more impartial coverage of controversial issues via
previewing broadcasts; the ITC had only retrospective power to sanction
broadcasters after the fact (Barendt 1998 115). Post-facto ITC sanctions
for violating the program code were somewhat significant, ranging from
"warnings, the imposition of fines and/or on-screen apologies to, ultimately, loss of the licence to broadcast" (Petley 2009 150).

Regulation of broadcasting has been continually scaled back over the
last 30 years in the UK on similar grounds as in the US—technological
change ameliorates spectrum scarcity, so minority views no longer need
protection. More and more viewpoints can have their say as more and
more channels become available. Further to this approach to deregulat-
ing broadcasting, the Communications Act of 2003 replaced the ITC
with the Office of Communications (Ofcom), which assumed the duties
of the ITC, as well as responsibility for radio and "fixed line telecoms,
mobiles, postal services, plus the airwaves over which wireless devices
operate" ("What Is Ofcom?"). Perhaps ironically for a regulator, Ofcom's
main brief is to "roll back regulation promptly when regulation becomes
unnecessary" (Curran and Seaton 2009 394).

As of 2005, the biggest change to come out of the latest round of
BBC Charter renewal negotiations has been the apparent abandonment
of measuring the quality of British television in any objective manner
other than by market share. "Government and regulatory authorities
alike have abandoned the last vestiges of a belief that they have a role
in ruling on the quality of programming in anything more than market
terminology" (Gardam 2005 49).

Competition in US and UK

Thus "the overriding aim of US media policy has always been to further
public interest by encouraging competition" (Kung-Shankleman 2000
25). According to Lucy Kung-Shankelman, contrary to the trends in other
industries, "increased competition has increased costs for broadcasters

across the board," in all media systems, due to the increased costs of talent and broadcasting rights to sports events (33). In the US, competition for network news means competition for advertising revenues between the networks and the increasing number of cable and satellite news providers, including 24-hour channels like Fox News and CNN. Though the evening network news broadcasts still soundly defeat their cable news competitors, it would be naïve to think they are not actively monitoring and trying to adapt to what is happening on Fox, CNN, and the rest of the cable news channels now widely available in the US.

As a public corporation, the BBC started out insulated from competition, but the public service monopoly it enjoyed was quickly changed into a duopoly with the introduction of Independent Television (ITV) in 1955. ITV was funded by advertising, but as the only television channel allowed to accept advertising at the time, it was a very comfortable position (Crisell 1999 62). ITV and the BBC soon found that the duopoly form of competition could serve them well, as they were not in direct competition for funding but able to balance each other's schedules with similar types of programming required by the public service obligations that fell equally on both of them. For example, "it was found that documentaries and current events programmes achieved their maximum audience only if they were shown at the same time" (Curran and Seaton 2009 164). Additional public service broadcasters came online in subsequent years, including second channels for BBC and ITV and Channels Four and Five, but they were folded into the same regulatory system, a functional expansion of the duopoly.

But the duopoly could not last forever. Partly as the result of regulatory changes initiated by the Conservative Party to increase competition and introduce market reforms to all public services and partly as a result of changes in technology, such as the advent of new terrestrial television channels, increased spectrum from digital television broadcasting, and the take-up of cable and, much more widely, of satellite television, competition has come in a large way to the broadcasting system in the UK, with hundreds of channels now available. More important than any financial competition, since the BBC is still license-fee funded, is the effect that competition has had on the internal structure and culture of the BBC: the corporation is much more concerned with maintaining audience share, demonstrating efficiency, and justifying its receipt of the license fee in the face of the periodic reviews that are part of its Charter renewal process (Kung-Shankleman 2000 86–95). Where Conservative attempts to statutorily increase competition or strip the license-fee monopoly from the BBC during several Charter renewals failed, Tory appointments to the BBC's board of governors, such as Marmaduke Hussey as chairman of the corporation in 1986, succeeded in shifting the BBC to a more market-focused approach (Goodwin 1999 137). This market-oriented legacy continues through the present day, as the next Charter renewal, a maximum of 10 years away, is always on the horizon. Director General John Birt's attempts to pursue other revenue streams and "introd[e] tighter financial disciplines in the form of producer choice and the 'internal market'" in the late 1990s are only one example of market-oriented reforms (Crisell 1999 68).

While the BBC faces competition from private broadcasters such as BSkyB's Sky News, a 24-hour news channel, as well as its own rolling news channel, BBC 24 (Harrison 2000 28), it still has the overwhelming share of the market for news broadcasts, with neither BBC 24 nor Sky News gaining more than 1 percent of the multichannel audience, excluding international crises like September 11 or the war in Iraq (McNair 2003 15). In fact, satellite, cable, and other digital broadcasters have not really stolen audiences from the core of British broadcasting. Although subscribers may be using digital, cable, or satellite connections to view television programming, the public service broadcasters who are subject to license renewal (the BBC, ITV, Channels 4 and 5) "amounted for 72 per cent of total television viewing" in 2004 (Gardam 2005 57), leaving only 28 percent of the audience for the remaining hundreds of channels available.

In a comparative study, the importance of the type of broadcasting system cannot be overstated, as the difference in media system has been shown to create differences in the very news covered. In their 2008 study of pure market (US), pure public (Finland, Denmark), and heavily public but market-influenced (UK) media systems, Curran, Iyengar, Brink Lund, and Salovaara-Moring (2009) found that hard news and international news were covered much more frequently in pure public and heavily public systems than in the pure market system, because networks in the market system competed with each other by playing more entertainment shows than news and more local and domestic news than international, and because increased competition led these networks to save money by cutting their overseas bureaus. Increased competition, whether in purely market or partly market systems, leads to decreased hard news and increased infotainment (Harrison 2000 27). Hallin and Mancini (2004) argue that increased commercialization in European systems leads to homogenization and globalization of media, making them increasingly similar to the American media system (38–40).

Having reviewed the relevant sections of the international relations and communications studies literatures and defined the terms that will be involved in the content analyses as carefully as possible, this study now turns to explaining the methodology that will be used to examine the British and American television news for human rights content.

Notes

1 See the International Convention on the Elimination of All Forms of Racial Discrimination (ICERD 1965), the International Covenant on the Elimination of All Forms of Discrimination Against Women (CEDAW 1979), the Convention

Against Torture and Other Cruel, Inhuman or Degrading Treatment or Punishment (CAT 1984), Convention on the Rights of the Child (CRC 1989), the International Convention on the Protection of the Rights of All Migrant Workers and Members of Their Families (ICRMW 1990), the Convention on the Rights of Persons with Disabilities (CRPD 2006), and the International Convention for the Protection of All Persons from Enforced Disappearance (2006).

2 See Chapters 3 and 5 for an analysis of misused terms by television journalists.

3 Non-self-executing treaties require implementation legislation to be passed before they can be considered part of the law of the land.

4 Though there is the likelihood of overlap in these issues, it is the direction of the investigation that is the point. Media influence and public opinion projects tend to look at a war or military intervention, addressing human rights issues as incidentals, if they come up at all (See, for examples, Livingston 1997 on Somalia; Jentleson & Britton 1998 on post-Cold War interventions; Sobel 2001 on Vietnam, the Gulf War, and Bosnia; Boaz 2005 and Kollmer and Semetko 2009 on the Iraq War; and Lai and Reiter 2005 for the use of force by the United Kingdom from 1948–2001).

Bibliography

Abdela, L. (2007). "Anyone here been raped and speaks English?": Workshops for editors and journalists on gender-based violence and sex-trafficking. *Gender and Development*, 15(3), 387–398.

Aldrich, J. H., Gelpi, C., Feaver, P., Reifler, J., & Sharp, K. T. (2006). Foreign policy and the electoral connection. *Annual Review of Political Science*, 9, 477–502.

Almond, Gabriel. *The American People and Foreign Policy*. Harcourt Brace, New York, 1950.

Amos, M. (2009). Problems with the human rights act 1998 and how to remedy them: Is a bill of rights the answer? *The Modern Law Review*, 72(6), 883–908.

Andreopoulos, G. J., Kabasakal Arat, Z. F., & Juviler, P. H. (2006). *Non-State Actors in the Human Rights Universe*. Bloomfield, CT: Kumarian Press.

Apsel, J. The complexity of destruction in Darfur: Historical processes and regional dynamics. *Human Rights Review*, 10(2) (June 2009), 239–259.

Barendt, E. (1998). "Impartiality and Broadcasting." In J. Seaton (ed), *Politics and the Media*. Oxford, UK: Blackwell Publishers.

Barnett, M. N., & Finnemore, M. (1999). The politics, power, and pathologies of international organizations. *International Organization*, 53(4), 699–732.

Barnett, S., & Seymour, E. (2000). From Callaghan to Kosovo: CHANGING TRENDS IN BRITISH TELEVISION NEWS 1975–1999. Retrieved on September 15, 2015 from http://www.ofcom.org.uk/static/archive/itc/research/callaghan_to_kosovo.pdf

Baum, M. A. (2002). Sex, lies, and war: How soft news brings foreign policy to the inattentive public. *American Political Science Review*, 96, 91–110.

Baum, M. A. (2004). Going private: Public opinion, presidential rhetoric, and the domestic politics of audience costs in U.S. foreign policy crises. *The Journal of Conflict Resolution*, 48(5), 603–631.

Baum, M. A., & Potter, P. B. K. (2008). The relationships between mass media, public opinion, and foreign policy: Toward a theoretical synthesis. *Annual Review of Political Science*, 11(1), 39–65.

BBC's *Journalism After Hutton: The Report of the Neil Review Team.* 2004. http://downloads.bbc.co.uk/aboutthebbc/insidethebbc/howwework/reports/pdf/neil_report.pdf

Bennett, W. L., & Entman, R. M. (2001). *Mediated Politics: Communication in the Future of Democracy.* Cambridge: Cambridge University Press.

Bennett, W. L., Lawrence, R. G., & Livingston, S. (2007). *When the Press Fails: Political Power and the News Media from Iraq to Katrina.* Chicago: University of Chicago Press.

Best, G. (1994). *War and Law Since 1945.* Oxford: Clarendon Press.

Boaz, C. (2005). War and foreign policy framing in international media. *Peace Review, 17*(4), 349–356.

Boyle, E. H., & Hoeschen A. (2001). Theorizing the form of media coverage over time. *The Sociological Quarterly, 42*(4), 511–527.

Boyle, E. H., McMorris, B. J., & Gomez, M. (2002). Local conformity to international norms: The case of female genital cutting. *International Sociology, 17*, 5–34.

Brysk, A. (2002). *Globalization and Human Rights.* Berkeley: University of California Press.

Brysk, A. (2005). *Human Rights and Private Wrongs: Constructing Global Civil Society.* New York: Routledge.

Bull, H. (1995). *The Anarchical Society: A Study of Order in World Politics.* New York: Columbia University Press.

Caliendo, S., Gibney, M., & Payne, A. (1999). All the news that's fit to print? *Harvard International Journal of Press/Politics, 4*(4), 48.

Caliendo, S. M., & Gibney, M. P. (2006). American print media coverage of human rights violations. *Conference Papers—American Political Science Association,* 1–17.

Campbell, V. (2006). A journalistic deficit? A comparative content analysis of British television news coverage of the 1994 and 2004 European election campaigns. *Journalism Studies, 7*(4), 593–609.

Cassese, A. (2001). *International Law.* Oxford: Oxford University Press.

Checkel, J. T. (1997). International norms and domestic politics: Bridging the rationalist—constructivist divide. *European Journal of International Relations, 3*(4), 473–495.

Checkel, J. T. (1998). The constructivist turn in international relations theory. *World Politics, 50*(2), 324.

Checkel, J. T. (2001). Why comply? Social learning and European identity change. *International Organization, 55*(3), 553–588.

Chomsky, N., & Chomsky, N. (2002). *Media Control: The spectacular achievements of Propaganda.* New York: Seven Stories Press.

Clark, A. M., & Friedman, E. J. (1998). The sovereign limits of global civil society. *World Politics, 51*(1), 1.

Conrad, M. (2010). The new paradigm for American broadcasting—changing the content regulation regime in the age of new media. *International Review of Law, Computers & Technology, 24*(3), 241–249.

Crisell, A. (1999). 'Broadcasting: Television and Radio' in J. Stokes and A. Reading (eds), *The Media in Britain: Current Debates and Developments.* New York: Macmillan.

Curran, J., & Seaton, J. (2009). *Power without Responsibility: The Press, Broadcasting, and New Media in Britain.* New York: Routledge.

Curran, J., Iyengar, S., Brink Lund, A., & Salovaara-Moring, I. (2009). Media system, public knowledge and democracy. *European Journal of Communication, 24*(1), 5–26.

Desyllas, M. C. (2007). A critique of the global trafficking discourse and US policy. *Journal of Sociology and Social Welfare, 34*(4), 57–80.

Donnelly, J. (2003). *Universal Human Rights in Theory and Practice*, 2nd ed. Ithaca, NY: Cornell University Press.

Dover, C., & Barnett, S. (2004). *The World on the Box: Changing Trends in International Factual Coverage on British Terrestrial Television*. London: International Broadcasting Trust.

Droege, C. (2007). The interplay between international humanitarian law and international human rights law in situations of armed conflict. *Israel Law Review Israel Law Review, 40*(2), 310–355.

Dustin M., & Phillips A. (2008). Whose agenda is it? Abuses of women and abuses of 'culture' in Britain. *Ethnicities, 8*(3), 405–424.

Eke, C. (2008). Darfur: Coverage of a genocide by three major US TV networks on their evening news. *International Journal of Media and Cultural Politics,* 4(3), 277–292.

Entman, R. M. (2003). *Projections of Power: Framing News, Public Opinion, and U.S. Foreign Policy*. Chicago: University of Chicago Press.

Entman, R. M. (2008). Theorizing mediated public diplomacy: The U.S. case. *Harvard International Journal of Press Politics, 13*(2), 87–102.

Esser, F., & Pfetsch, B. (2004). *Comparing Political Communication: Theories, Cases, and Challenges*. Cambridge: Cambridge University Press.

Felice, W. F. (2006). Human rights disparities between Europe and the United States: Conflicting approaches to poverty prevention and the alleviation of suffering. *Cambridge Review of International Affairs, 19*(1), 79–104.

Finnemore, M., & Sikkink, K. (1998). International norm dynamics and political change. *International Organization, 52*(4, International Organization at Fifty: Exploration and Contestation in the Study of World Politics), 887–917.

Finnemore, M., & Sikkink, K. (2001). TAKING STOCK: The constructivist research program in international relations and comparative politics. *Annual Review of Political Science, 4*(1), 391.

Florini, A. (1996). The evolution of international norms. *International Studies Quarterly, 40*(3, Special Issue: Evolutionary Paradigms in the Social Sciences), 363–389.

Franks, S. (2004). The world on the box: International issues in news and factual programmes. *Political Quarterly-London then Oxford- Macmillan then Blackwell, 75*(4), 425–428.

Gamson, W. A., & Wolfsfeld, G. (1993). Movements and media as interacting systems. *The Annals of the American Academy of Political and Social Science, 528*(1), 114–125.

Gardam, T. (2005), What's good on television? *The Political Quarterly, 76,* 46–59.

Gavrielides, T. (2008). Human rights and customer satisfaction with public services: A relationship discovered. *The International Journal of Human Rights the International Journal of Human Rights, 12*(2), 189–204.

Gelpi, C., & Mueller, J. (2006). How many casualties will Americans tolerate? *Foreign Affairs,* (Jan/Feb).

Geyer, A., & Shapiro, R. (1988). Human rights. *Public Opinion Quarterly, 52,* 3.

Gibney, M., Cornett, L., Wood, R., & Haschke, P. (2015). *Political Terror Scale 1976–2012*. Retrieved on March 30, 2015 from the Political Terror Scale Web site: http://www.politicalterrorscale.org/

Gilboa, E. (2002). Global communication and foreign policy. *Journal of Communication, 52*(4), 731.

Gilboa, E. (2003). Television news and U.S. foreign policy. *Harvard International Journal of Press/Politics, 8*(4), 97.

Gilboa, E. (2005a). The CNN effect: The search for a communication theory of international relations. *Political Communication, 22*(1), 27–44.

Gilboa, E. (2005b). Global television news and foreign policy: Debating the CNN effect. *International Studies Perspectives, 6*(3), 325–341.

Goldstein, J., Keohane, R. O., & Social Science Research Council (U.S.). Committee on Foreign Policy Studies. (1993). *Ideas and Foreign Policy: Beliefs, Institutions, and Political Change.* Ithaca, NY: Cornell University Press.

Goodwin, P. (1999). 'The Role of the State in Shaping the Media.' In J. Stokes & A. Reading (eds), *The Media in Britain: Current Debates and Developments,* Houndsmills, UK: Macmillan.

Hafez, K. (2002). Journalism ethics revisited: A comparison of ethics codes in Europe, North Africa, the Middle East, and Muslim Asia. *Political Communication, 19*(2), 225–250.

Hafner-Burton, E., & Ron, J. (2009). Seeing double: Human rights impact through qualitative and quantitative eyes. *World Politics, 61*(2), 360–401.

Hallin, D. C., & Mancini, P. (2004). *Comparing Media Systems: Three Models of Media and Politics.* Cambridge: Cambridge University Press.

Hanson, J., & Miller, C. (1987). The moral dilemma of reporting human rights: US television networks' coverage of Central America, 1977–1980. In S. Thomas (ed), *Culture and Communication.* Norwood, NJ: Ablex Publishing.

Harrison, J. (2000). *Terrestrial TV News in Britain: The Culture of Production.* Manchester, UK: Manchester University Press.

Heinze, E., & Freedman, R. (2010). Public awareness of human rights: distortions in the mass media. *International Journal of Human Rights, 14*(4), 491–523.

Henkin, L. (1995). U.S. ratification of human rights conventions: The Ghost of Senator Bricker. *American Journal of International Law, 89*(2), 341–350.

Herman, E. S., & Chomsky, N. (1988). *Manufacturing Consent: The Political Economy of the Mass Media.* New York: Pantheon Books.

Hershey, R. D., Jr. (1987). F.C.C. votes down fairness doctrine in a 4–0 decision. *The New York Times,* Aug. 5.

Huang, J. (2012). The ICC and Darfur. *Eyes on The ICC, 9*(1), 63–93.

Hubbert, J. (2014). The Darfur Olympics: Global citizenship and the 2008 Beijing Olympic Games. *Positions, 22*(1), 203–236.

Hurwitz, J., & Peffley, M. (1987). How are foreign policy attitudes structured? A hierarchical model. *APSR, 81*(4), 1099–1120.

Iguyovwe, R. (2008). The inter-play between international humanitarian law and international human rights law. *Commonwealth Law Bulletin, 34*(4), 749–789.

Iyengar, S. (1994). *Is Anyone Responsible?: How Television Frames Political Issues.* Chicago: University of Chicago Press.

Iyengar, S., & Kinder, D. R. (1987). *News That Matters: Television and American Opinion.* Chicago: University of Chicago Press.

Iyengar, S., & Kinder, D. R. (1988). *News That Matters: Television and American Opinion.* Chicago: University of Chicago Press.

Jakobsen, P. V. (2000). Focus on the CNN effect misses the point: The real media impact on conflict management is invisible and indirect. *Journal of Peace Research, 37*, 131–144.

Jentleson, B. W., & Britton, R. L. (1998). Still pretty prudent: Post-cold war American public opinion on the use of military force. *Journal of Conflict Resolution, 42*(4), 395–417.

Jones, C. A. (2004). Regulating political advertising in the EU and USA: A human rights perspective. *Journal of Public Affairs, 4*(3), 244–255.

Journalism, Media and the Challenge of Human Rights Reporting. 2002. International Council on Human Rights Policy, Versoix, Switzerland. *Human rights of older people in healthcare.* Retrieved March 1, 2013, 2013, from http://www.publications.parliament.uk/pa/jt200607/jtselect/jtrights/156/156i.pdf

Keck, M. E., & Sikkink, K. (1998). *Activists Beyond Borders: Advocacy Networks in International Politics.* Ithaca, NY: Cornell University Press.

Kennedy, D. (2006). *Of War and Law.* Princeton, NJ: Princeton University Press.

Kolmer, C., & Semetko, H. A. (2009). Framing the Iraq war: Perspectives from American, U.K., Czech, German, South African, and Al-Jazeera news. *American Behavioral Scientist, 52*(5), 643–656.

Koopmans, R. (2004). Movements and media: Selection processes and evolutionary dynamics in the public sphere. *Theory and Society, 33*(3/4, Special Issue: Current Routes to the Study of Contentious Politics and Social Change), 367–391.

Kriesi, H., Tresch, A., & Jochum, M. (2007). Going public in the European Union. *Comparative Political Studies, 40*(1), 48–73.

Krippendorff, K. (2004). *Content Analysis: An Introduction to Its Methodology.* Thousand Oaks, CA: Sage Publications.

Kuhn, R. (2007). *Politics and the Media in Britain.* Houndmills, UK: Palgrave Macmillan.

Küng-Shankleman, L. (2000). *Inside BBC and CNN: Managing Media Organisations.* London: Routledge.

Lambert, R. (2002). *Independent Review of BBC News 24.* Department of Culture, Media and Sport, Broadcasting Policy Division. http://webarchive.national archives.gov.uk/+/http://www.bbccharterreview.org.uk/pdf_documents/independentreviewnews24.pdf

Lai, B., & Reiter, D. (2005). Rally 'Round the union jack? Public opinion and the use of force in the united kingdom, 1948–2001. *International Studies Quarterly, 49*(2), 255–272.

Lauren, P. G. (2003). *The Evolution of International Human Rights: Visions Seen,* 2nd ed. Philadelphia: University of Pennsylvania Press.

Leebaw, B. (2007). The politics of impartial activism: Humanitarianism and human rights. *PPS Perspectives on Politics, 5*(2), 223–239.

Leipold, G. (2000). Campaigning: A fashion or the best way to change the global agenda? *Development in Practice-Oxford, 10*, 453–460.

Lewis, J., Williams, A., & Franklin, B. (2008). A compromised fourth estate? *Journalism Studies, 9*(1), 1–20.

Lippmann, W. (2007). *Public Opinion.* Miami, FL: BN Pub.

Livingston, S. (1997). *Clarifying the CNN Effect: An Examination of Media Effects According to Type of Military Intervention.* Cambridge, MA: Joan Shorenstein Center on the Press, Politics and Public Policy, John F. Kennedy School of Government, Harvard University.

Lloyd, J., & Seaton, J. (2006). *What Can Be Done? Making the Media and Politics Better*. Malden, MA: Blackwell, in association with the *Political Quarterly*.

Lustgarten, A., & Debrix, F. (2005). The role of the media in monitoring international humanitarian law during military interventions: The case of Kosovo. *Peace & Change, 30*(3), 359–397.

Mann, M. (2005). *The Dark Side of Democracy: Explaining Ethnic Cleansing*. New York: Cambridge University Press.

McNair, B. (2003). *News and Journalism in the UK*. London: Routledge.

Mermin, J. (1997). Television news and American intervention in Somalia: The Myth of a media-driven foreign policy. *Political Science Quarterly, 112*(3), 385–403

Meron, T. (2000). "The Humanization of Humanitarian Law." *The American Journal of International Law*, 94(2), 239–278.

Mertus, J. (2008). *Bait and Switch: Human Rights and U.S. foreign policy*. New York: Routledge.

Miller, D. (2002, March). *Measuring media pressure on security policy decisionmaking in liberal states. The poisoning hypothesis*. Paper presented at the annual convention of the International Studies Association, New Orleans.

Minear, L., Scott, C., & Weiss, T. G. (1996). *The News Media, Civil War, and Humanitarian Action*. Boulder, CO: L. Rienner.

Miskimmon, A., O'Loughlin, B., & Roselle, L. (2014). *Strategic Narratives: Communication Power and the New World Order*. New York: Routledge.

Monasebian, S. (2006). *Media Matters: Reflections of a Former War Crimes Prosecutor Covering the Iraqi Tribunal*. Cleveland, OH: Case Western Reserve University School of Law.

Moravcsik, A. (2000). The origins of human rights regimes: Democratic delegation in postwar Europe. *International Organization, 54*(2), 217–252.

Nacos, B. L. (2002). *Mass-Mediated Terrorism: The Central Role of the Media in Terrorism and Counterterrorism*. Lanham, MD: Rowman & Littlefield.

Nacos, B. L., Shapiro, R. Y., & Isernia, P. (2000). *Decisionmaking in a Glass House: Mass Media, Public Opinion, and American and European Foreign Policy in the 21st Century*. Lanham, MD: Rowman & Littlefield.

Nacos, B. L., & Torres-Reyna, O. (2007). *Fueling Our Fears: Stereotyping, Media Coverage, and Public Opinion of Muslim Americans*. Lanham, MD: Rowman & Littlefield.

Nash, M. L. (1995). *Contemporary Practice of the United States Relating to International Law, The American Journal of International Law*, 74(2), 418–432.

Nelson, A. (2006). The news media in the arena of human rights. In G. J. Andreopoulos, Z. F. Kabasakal Arat, & P. H. Juviler (Eds.) *Non-State Actors in the Human Rights Universe* (227–248). Bloomfield, CT: Kumarian Press.

Neuendorf, K. A. (2002). *The Content Analysis Guidebook*. Thousand Oaks, CA: Sage Publications.

Neuman, J. (1996). *Lights, Camera, War: Is Media Technology Driving International Politics*. New York: St. Martin's Press.

New News, Future News: The challenges for television news after Digital Switch-over (2007). Retrieved March 30, 2015 from http://stakeholders.ofcom.org.uk/binaries/research/tv-research/newnews.pdf

Norris, P. (1997). *Politics and the Press: The News Media and Their Influences.* Boulder, CO: L. Rienner Publishers.

Othman, M. (2005). "Justice and Reconciliation." In E. Skaar, S. Gloppen, & Astri Suhrke (eds), *Roads to Reconciliation*. Lanham, MD: Lexington Books.

Ovsiovitch, J. S. (1993). News coverage of human rights. *Political Research Quarterly, 46*(3), 671.

Padania, S., Coleman, S., & Georgiou, M. (2007). *Reflecting the Real World 2: How We Connect with the Wider World. A Report Looking at How UK Television and Media Portray Developing Countries.* London: International Broadcasting Trust.

Page, B. I., & Shapiro, R. Y. (1992). *The Rational Public: Fifty Years of Trends in Americans' Policy Preferences*. Chicago: University of Chicago Press.

Peksen, D., Peterson, T. M., & Drury, A. C. (2014). Media-driven humanitarianism? News media coverage of human rights abuses and the use of economic sanctions. *International Studies Quarterly, 58*(4), 855–866.

Petley, J. (2009). What rights? Whose responsibilities? *Soundings-London- Lawrence and Wishart, 43*, 77–88.

Price, M. (2002). *Media and Sovereignty: The Global Information Revolution and Its Challenge to State Power.* Cambridge: Massachusetts Institute of Technology.

Price, M. (2015). *Free Expression, Globalism, and the New Strategic Communication.* New York: Cambridge University Press.

Ramos, H., Ron, J., & Thoms, O.N.T. (2007). Shaping the northern media's human rights coverage, 1986–2000. *Journal of Peace Research, 44*(4), 385–406.

Richiardi, S. (2005). Déjà vu. *American Journalism Review*, Feb./Mar. Retrieved February 20, 2015 from http://ajrarchive.org/Article.asp?id=3813

Riffe, D., Lacy, S., & Fico, F. (1998). *Analyzing Media Messages Using Quantitative Content Analysis in Research.* New York: Routledge.

Risse, T. (2000). "Let's argue!": Communicative action in world politics. *International Organization, 54*(1), 1–39.

Risse-Kappen, T. (1991). Public opinion, domestic structure, and foreign policy in liberal democracies. *World Politics, 43*(4), 479–512.

Risse-Kappen, T., & Sikkink, K. (1999). The socialization of international human rights norms into domestic practices: Introduction. In T. Risse-Kappen, S. C. Ropp, & K. Sikkink (Eds.) *The Power of Human Rights: International Norms and Domestic Change.* New York: Cambridge University Press.

Robinson, P. (2000). World politics and media power: Problems of research design. *Communication Abstracts, 23*(5), 227–232.

Robinson, P. (2005). The CNN effect revisited. *Critical Studies in Media Communication, 22*(4), 344–349.

Rossler, P. (2004). 'Political Communication Messages: Pictures of Our World on International Television News. In F. Esser and B. Pfetsch (eds), *Comparing Political Communication: Theories, Cases, and Challenges.* Cambridge: Cambridge University Press.

Rotberg, R. I., & Weiss, T. G. (1996). *From Massacres to Genocide: The Media, Public Policy, and Humanitarian Crises.* Washington, DC: Brookings Institution.

Ruggie, J. G. (1998). What makes the world hang together? Neo-utilitarianism and the social constructivist challenge. *International Organization, 52*(4,

International Organization at Fifty: Exploration and Contestation in the Study of World Politics), 855–885.

Schabas, W. A. (2007). Lex specialis? Belt and suspenders?: The parallel operation of human rights law and the law of armed conflict, and the conundrum of jus ad bellum. *Israel Law Review Israel Law Review, 40,* 592–613.

Schmitz, H. P., & Sikkink, K. (2005). "Do International Human Rights Treaties Improve Respect for Human Rights?" *Journal of Conflict Resolution, 49,* 925–953.

Scott, M. (2008). *Screening the World: How the UK Portrayed the Wider World in 2007–8.* London, UK: International Broadcasting Trust.

Scott, M., Rodriguez Rojas, S M., & Jenner, C. (2010). *Outside the Box: How UK Broadcasters Portrayed the Wider World in 2010 and How International Content Can Achieve Greater Impact with Audiences.* London, UK: International Broadcasting Trust.

Seaton, J. (1998). *Politics and the Media: Harlots and Prerogatives at the Turn of the Millennium.* Oxford, UK: Blackwell Publishers.

Semetko, H. A. (2009). Media and public diplomacy in times of war and crisis. *American Behavioral Scientist, 52*(5), 639–642.

Shaw, M. (1996). *Civil Society and Media in Global Crises: Representing Distant Violence.* New York: Pinter.

Shaw, M. (2000). Media and public sphere without borders? News coverage and power from Kurdistan to Kosovo. In B. L. Nacos, R. Y. Shapiro, & P. Isernia (Eds.) *Decisionmaking in a Glass House: Mass Media, Public Opinion, and American and European Foreign Policy in the 21st Century.* Lanham, MD: Rowman & Littlefield Publishers.

Sikkink, K. (1993). Human rights, principled issue-networks, and sovereignty in Latin America. *International Organization, 47*(3), 411–441.

Skaar, E., Gloppen, S., & Suhrke, A. (2005). *Roads to Reconciliation.* Lanham, MD: Lexington Books.

Slantchev, B. L. (2006). Politicians, the media, and domestic audience costs. *International Studies Quarterly, 50*(2), 445–477.

Smith, J., Edge, L., & Morris, V. (2006). *Reflecting the Real World?: How British TV Portrayed Developing Countries in 2005.* London: International Broadcasting Trust.

Snow, D. A., Rochford, E. B., Jr., Worden, S. K., & Benford, R. D. (1986). Frame alignment processes, micromobilization, and movement participation. *American Sociological Review, 51*(4), 464–481.

Sobel, R. (2001). *Public Opinion in American Foreign Policy: From Vietnam to the Nineties.* New York: Oxford University Press.

Sriram, C. L., Martin-Ortega, O., and Herman, J. (2010). *War, Conflict, and Human Rights: Theory and Practice.* New York: Routledge.

Stimson, J. A. (2004). *Tides of Consent: How Public Opinion Shapes American Politics.* New York: Cambridge University Press.

Stokes, J. C., & Reading, A. (1999). *The Media in Britain: Current Debates and Developments.* Houndmills, UK: Macmillan.

Sypnowich, C. (2008). Taking Britain's human rights act seriously. *The University of Toronto Law Journal, 58*(1), 105–117.

Tamura, E. (2001). "The *Isayeva* Cases of the European Court of Human Rights: The Application of International Humanitarian Law and Human Rights Law in Non-International Armed Conflicts" *Chinese Journal of International Law*, 10(1), 129–140.

"The Core International Human Rights Bodies and their monitoring bodies." (2015). Retrieved September 15, 2015 from http://www.ohchr.org/EN/Professional Interest/Pages/CoreInstruments.aspx

The fairness doctrine and claims of systematic imbalance in television news broadcasting: American security council education foundation *v*. FCC (1980). *Harvard Law Review*, 93(5), 1028–1038.

The first amendment and regulation of television news (1972). *Columbia Law Review*, 72(4), 746–771.

Thrall, A. T. (2006). The myth of the outside strategy: Mass media news coverage of interest groups. *Political Communication*, 23(4), 407–420. *UK and European social charter*. Retrieved March 1, 2013 from http://www.coe.int/t/dghl/ monitoring/socialcharter/countryfactsheets/UK_en.pdf

Tolley, M. C. (2009). Parliamentary scrutiny of rights in the United Kingdom: Assessing the work of the joint committee on human rights. *Australian Journal of Political Science*, 44(1), 41–55.

Tomuschat, C. (2010). Human rights and international humanitarian law. *European Journal of International Law European Journal of International Law*, 21(1), 15–23.

Tresch, A., & Fischer, M. (2008). Political actors in search of media attention: An analysis of mobilisation and communication strategies in seven European countries. *Conference Papers—American Political Science Association*, 1, 1–18.

Weiss, T. G., Forsythe, D. P., Coate, R. A., and Pease, K.-K. (2007). *The United Nations and Changing World Politics*. Boulder, CO: Westview Press.

Weiss, T. G. (2007). *The United Nations and Changing World Politics*. Boulder, CO: Westview Press.

Welbourne, P. (2002). Adoption and the rights of children in the UK. *International Journal of Children's Rights*, 103, 269–289.

What is ofcom? Retrieved March 1, 2013 from http://www.ofcom.org.uk/about/ what-is-ofcom/

Wheeler, N. J. (2002). *Saving Strangers: Humanitarian Intervention in International Society*. New York: Oxford University Press.

Zaller, J., & Chiu, D. (1996). Government's little helper: U.S. press coverage of foreign policy crises, 1945–1991. *Political Communication*, 13(4), 385–406.

3 Content Analysis I
US Phrase Search

Determining whether or not the CNN Effect exists on human rights issues begins with analyzing all of the human rights content of television news. Chapter 3 is the first of several different approaches to measuring human rights content of television news: a large-scale transcript analysis applied to the American case[1] by searching ABC *World News* transcripts from 1990–2009 on LexisNexis.[2] It is important to note that any Lexis-Nexis transcript search must be conducted carefully, as duplicate stories are sometimes generated by the search results, especially in the earlier years of this study.[3] In total, 824 stories that include the phrase "human right!"[4] were analyzed for topic, country, category of human rights, and type of story.

So Few Stories

Immediately, one point is very clear: 824 is a very small number of stories. From 1990–2009, there were 7,305 nights when evening news could have been broadcast.[5] Eight hundred twenty-four stories is far less than one story per night, and there were only three years (1994, 1995, and 1998) in which there were enough human rights stories to average one story per week. If each nightly broadcast is conservatively assumed to have 14 stories, then these 824 stories may be said to represent 0.8 percent of stories broadcast during the time period. Less than 1 percent of the stories broadcast during this time period contained the phrase human rights. The very small number of stories containing the phrase human rights is consistent with the conclusions from Ovsiovitch (1993), Ramos, Ron, and Thoms (2007) and Caliendo, Gibney, and Payne (1999), and Heinze and Freedman (2010). Figure 3.1 shows the number of stories broadcast that contain the phrase human rights by year. The trend line of the data illustrates a gradual decline over the time period.

Eight hundred twenty-four is an extremely small number of stories for a 20-year period. It is theoretically possible, albeit highly unlikely, that there are very few stories that contain the phrase human rights because there just happened to be very few human rights issues that occurred during those two decades. A comparison with the *New York Times* coverage from the same 20-year span puts this possibility to rest. Table 3.1 lists the

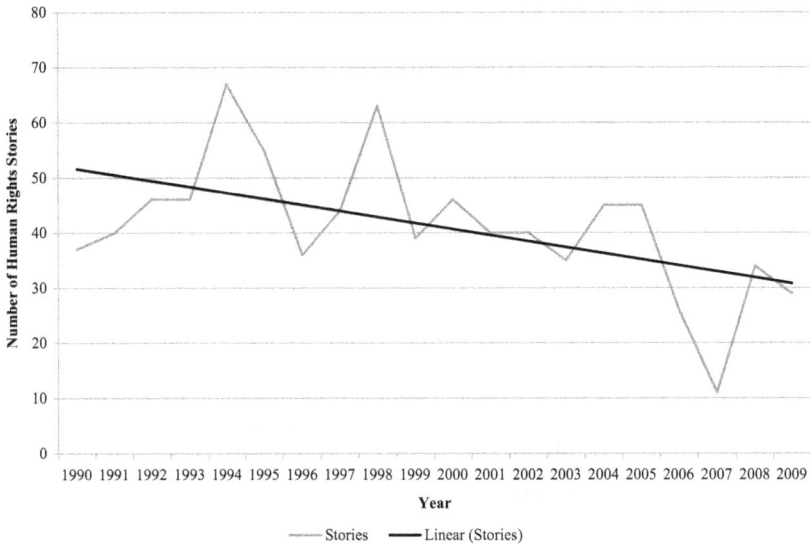

Figure 3.1 Human Rights Stories by Year, 1990–2009

Table 3.1 Human Rights Stories 1990–2009, *World News* and *New York Times*

Stories that contain the phrase "human rights"

Year	ABC World News	New York Times, Front-Page Stories	New York Times, All Stories
1990	37	98	1234
1991	40	96	1145
1992	46	76	1151
1993	46	99	1295
1994	67	146	1336
1995	55	98	1165
1996	36	84	1138
1997	44	117	1337
1998	63	130	1437
1999	39	145	1561
2000	46	146	1580
2001	40	124	1470
2002	40	111	1433
2003	35	133	1309
2004	45	132	1259
2005	45	167	1331
2006	26	142	1398

(*Continued*)

Table 3.1 (Continued)

Stories that contain the phrase "human rights"			
Year	ABC World News	New York Times, Front-Page Stories	New York Times, All Stories
2007	11	133	1211
2008	34	153	1330
2009	29	117	1459
Total	824	2447	26579
Average	41.2	122.4	1329.0

number of stories that contain the phrase human rights for each year for *ABC World News* and the *New York Times.*

From 1990–2009, there were 26,579 stories printed in the *New York Times* that contained the phrase human rights. That means there were literally tens of thousands of human rights issues that received the attention of print journalists during this time, yet there were only 824 stories broadcast on ABC. The *New York Times* printed an average of 1,329 stories per year that contained the phrase human rights, while ABC *World News* averaged only 41.2 stories per year. There are plenty of violations happening every year that gain the attention of print media, they are just not being televised.

It is slightly unfair to do a word count–based comparison between a television news program such as ABC's *World News* and a large newspaper such as the *New York Times* because the edition of the *New York Times* is much longer and contains many, many more words than the corresponding television news broadcast for a given day. Because television news broadcasts are limited in time, it is much fairer to compare their content to that of just the first page of a newspaper; this data is also listed in Table 3.1. Even by this more generous measure, however, television news still lags behind significantly in human rights coverage. From 1990–2009, the *New York Times* had 2,447 front-page stories that contained the phrase human rights, for an average of 122.3 stories per year, approximately three times the annual average of ABC *World News* stories that contain the phrase human rights.

What Gets Covered?

The very small amount of human rights coverage makes it difficult to argue in favor of a CNN Effect on human rights issues, but the sheer count of human rights stories only tells part of the story. What types of issues are covered in these human rights stories is a much more interesting question. A review of the issues that received repeat coverage in a year helps contextualize the rest of the chapter: What does television news cover when it covers human rights? Major coverage here is defined as an issue that had at least four stories of any type in the year of which 40 were identified from 1990–2009. Table 3.2 shows the issues that received major coverage each year.

The main issues covered in these 824 human rights stories can be divided neatly into two periods: before 2001 and after. Up to and including 2001, every single year included major issues focusing on China's human rights policies, particularly as they relate to arrested dissidents or whether the US

Table 3.2 Major Coverage of Human Rights Stories, 1990–2009

1990	**USSR:** ending of Cold War; Paris summit; anniversary of Helsinki Accords
	China: fallout from Tiananmen Square, including continued hiding of Fang Zhili and his eventual emigration; Ge Xun goes to Beijing to find his friend; general follow-up stories
	Iraq: reports of atrocities in Kuwait that may or may not be reliable; debate over what the UN, US, or others will do about it
1991	**China:** whether to renew Most Favored Nation (MFN) status despite human rights violations; use of prison labor for exported goods; second anniversary of Tiananmen crackdown
	Iraq & Kuwait: conduct of invasion and rebuilding; alleged human rights violations committed by Kuwait
1992	**US:** evolving policy on Haitian refugees
	Bosnia: atrocities during the war
	China: whether to renew MFN despite human rights violations
1993	**Haiti:** Aristide removed; military government and violence; US response
	Bosnia: rape in the war; peace negotiations
	China: release of dissidents; whether or not to renew MFN despite human rights violations; use of prison labor for exports
1994	**Haiti:** Aristide has not returned; embargo not working; international observers expelled; US invasion
	China: prison labor; political prisoners; MFN status; delinking human rights and trade
	Rwanda: ethnic killings; conditions of refugees
	Indonesia: Clinton attends APEC meeting in Jakarta amid questions of Indonesia's human rights policies
1995	**China:** American Harry Wu's arrest and detention in China and his release; Hillary Clinton attends Beijing Conference on Women's Rights
	Russia: fighting affecting civilians in Chechnya
	Bosnia: atrocities including rape used as weapons of war; UN abandons Srebrenica and Zepa, with massacres following

(Continued)

Table 3.2 (Continued)

1996	**China:** doctor alleges orphanages selected children to die; MFN status extended despite HR concerns; questions of Hong Kong transition
	Bosnia: NATO provides guards for investigators into atrocities in Bosnia but not for the evidence itself
1997	**China:** US VP visits Beijing; organ sales from executed prisoners; Jiang Zemin comes to US, struggle over MFN
1998	**China:** President Clinton visits China and speaks about HR candidly; China subsequently hosts some protests but then cracks down again
	Cuba: Pope John Paul II visits Cuba
1999	**Kosovo:** NATO bombing; fate of refugees
	China: US signs trade deal and supports Chinese application to WTO; crackdowns on religious groups and dissidents
2000	**China:** US considers and approves Permanent Normal Trading Relations with China
2001	**China:** China campaigns for and gets the 2008 Olympics; increasing religious repression, particularly of Falun Gong; detaining and then releasing Chinese-born American scholars
	Global War on Terror (GWOT): military action in Afghanistan; questions of treatment and trial of detainees
2002	**Israel & Palestine:** attack on Palestinian refugee camp Jenin leaves many Palestinians dead; suicide bombings called crimes against humanity.
	GWOT: civilian casualties in Afghanistan; treatment of detainees
2003	**GWOT:** treatment of detainees; invasion and occupation of Iraq
2004	**GWOT:** Abu Ghraib abuse scandal; transition to independent governing authority in Iraq
	Sudan: ethnic cleansing in Darfur
2005	**GWOT:** CIA interrogation techniques questioned; trial of Saddam Hussein
	Vatican: death and funeral of Pope John Paul II
2006	**GWOT:** Saddam's trial and plans for execution; tribunals for Gitmo detainees struck down by Supreme Court; torture denied; secret prisons discovered
	China: Yahoo's cooperation helps China track dissidents; Hu Jintao's visit to the US
2007	**GWOT:** CIA secret prisons admitted; waterboarding outlawed; refugees from Iraq face dire conditions
2008	**China:** protests leading up to the Olympics; reactions at the Olympics
2009	**GWOT:** NATO agrees to send troops to Afghanistan for training missions; Afghan elections; release of young Afghan detainee from Guantanamo

should tie its trading relationship to China's human rights record. Starting in 2001, however, the Global War on Terror (GWOT), especially the treatment and trial of detainees in various locations, became the most frequent major issue of human rights stories. The GWOT was the only human rights major issue covered in 2003, 2007, and 2009. As a major issue, China's human rights policies did not disappear; they surfaced again in 2006, and the lead up to and protests at the Beijing Olympics were the only human rights issues to receive major coverage in 2008.

Looking again at Table 3.2, a pattern appears over time: there are fewer major stories per year as time progresses. Taken together, the decreasing trend line of the total number of stories from 1990–2009 and the declining number of issues to receive major coverage can both be seen to grow out of the existence and subsequent fading away of the New World Order proclaimed by President George H. W. Bush in 1991. With the end of Cold War politics as the dominant frame for both states and the media, human rights was one of several policy goals/media frames that was put into practice. Human rights, however, seems to have been displaced from prominence in the policy and media worlds by more dominant frames; even the stories that receive repeat coverage in later years are related to the GWOT, which has been the most dominant frame in American politics since September 11, 2001.

Location, Location, Location

Analyzing the countries covered in human rights stories can shed light on the nature of television coverage of human rights. All stories were coded for whether they were domestic stories pertaining to the US, international stories not directly involving the US, or both international and involving the US. The results are displayed in Figure 3.2. A significant portion of the human rights stories, 315 stories or 38 percent of the total, were coded as international, not involving the US. The smallest share of the human rights stories were domestic, only 115 stories or 14 percent of the total. These results are consistent with the general US approach to human rights—that they are generally considered foreign, something that does not happen in the US but instead happens in other countries. Domestic human rights issues are generally framed differently in the US, frequently as civil liberties, civil rights, or constitutional rights; these issues receive coverage, and sometimes prominent coverage as domestic news on television, but not as human rights.

A plurality of the human rights stories, almost half of the total, were coded as both international and involving the US. Three hundred ninety-four stories, or 48 percent of the total human rights stories, involved the US at least partially, and this is also consistent with communications studies literature that says news outlets are more likely to cover stories that involve their home countries for at least two reasons: news producers may have more access if their own government is involved, and news producers may believe that it is of greater interest to their audience since their own government is at least tangentially involved. Stories

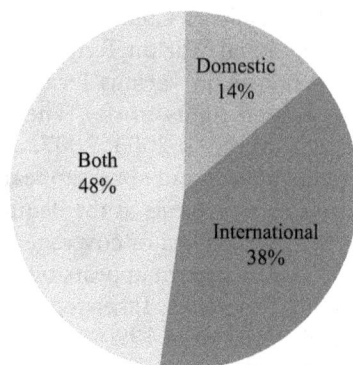

Figure 3.2 Domestic and International Human Rights Stories in the US, 1990–2009

that do not involve the home country at all, whether they are human rights stories or not, are less likely to get coverage.

Just looking at the content of the broadcasts cannot answer the question of whether the countries that are most-frequently featured as locations in human rights stories are the ones with the worst records. To answer that question, the television news content would need to be compared to a measure of the actual human rights issues occurring in the world. Luckily, there are two different data sets that seek to do exactly that: the Political Terror Scale and the Cingranelli-Richards (CIRI) Human Rights Data Project. The Political Terror Scale (PTS) (Gibney, Cornett, Wood, and Haschke 2015) ranks states for the level of political violence and terror according to annual reports from Amnesty International and the US State Department's Country Reports on Human Rights Practices, with 1 being the best human rights record and 5 being the worst human rights offenders. Table 3.3 lists the 25 countries with the worst average PTS scores from 1990–2009 and the number of human rights stories that mentioned each country. Five of these worst offender countries were not mentioned in a single human rights story in the entire 20-year period.

The CIRI data (Cingranelli, Richards, and Clay 2014) use the same source material, annual reports from the US State Department and Amnesty International, but are more directly focused on human rights and code for several different human rights. CIRI also does not rate countries in years where there are periods of or complete collapse of political authority,[6] thereby making the CIRI numbers an even more specific rating of human rights concerns around the world, since they exclude periods of interstate and civil war from their calculations. Two composite indexes provide an overview of the wide range of human rights CIRI codes: the Physical Integrity Rights Index, which combines ratings from the Torture, Extrajudicial Killing, Political Imprisonment, and Disappearance indicators and is scored out of 8 possible points and the new Empowerment

Table 3.3 The States With the Worst PTS Averages Versus Number of Mentions in Human Rights Stories, 1990–2009

Country		PTS Average, 1990–2009	Number of Human Rights Stories
1	Iraq	4.93	68
2	Colombia	4.8	6
3	Sudan	4.8	19
4	Afghanistan	4.75	23
5	Democratic Republic of the Congo	4.6	5
6	North Korea	4.5	2
7	*Burundi*	*4.4*	*0*
8	Myanmar	4.35	4
9	Somalia	4.35	2
10	*Sri Lanka*	*4.25*	*0*
11	Algeria	4.1	1
12	Israel & Palestine	4.1	37
13	*Angola*	*4.08*	*0*
14	India	4.08	3
15	Liberia	4	1
16	Brazil	3.98	2
17	Pakistan	3.93	7
18	Rwanda	3.93	10
19	*Chad*	*3.88*	*0*
20	China	3.83	221
21	USSR/Russia	3.83	35
22	Turkey	3.83	2
23	*Ethiopia*	*3.78*	*0*
24	Indonesia	3.75	15
25	Iran	3.75	5

Key: Countries in shaded rows are not in the list of the 20 most-frequently featured countries in human rights stories.

Rights Index, which combines ratings for the Foreign Movement, Domestic Movement, Freedom of Speech, Freedom of Assembly & Association, Workers' Rights, Electoral Self-Determination, and Freedom of Religion indicators and is scored out of 14 possible points. For all measures, lower scores in the CIRI dataset indicate a worse human rights record, while higher scores indicate fuller respect for human rights. Table 3.4 lists the

Table 3.4 The States With the Worst CIRI Physical Integrity and Empowerment Index Averages versus Number of Mentions in Human Rights Stories, 1990–2009

Country	CIRI Physical Integrity Index Average, 1990–2009 (0–8)	Number of Human Rights Stories	Country	CIRI Empowerment Index Average, 1990–2019 (0–14)	Number of Human Rights Stories
India	0.20	3	North Korea	0.10	2
North Korea	0.20	2	Saudi Arabia	0.30	4
Colombia	0.58	6	Burma	0.55	4
Sudan	0.60	19	Sudan	0.65	19
Iraq	0.61	68	China	0.80	221
Democratic Republic of Congo	1.00	5	Iraq	1.00	68
Iran	1.22	5	Vietnam	1.20	3
Burma	1.25	4	United Arab Emirates	1.30	2
Indonesia	1.40	15	Iran	1.50	5
Burundi	1.41	0	Cuba	1.55	18
Pakistan	1.50	7	*Syria*	1.75	0
Sri Lanka	1.50	0	Afghanistan	2.07	23
China	1.60	221	*Turkmenistan*	2.11	0
Afghanistan	1.64	23	Libya	2.20	1
Philippines	1.80	1	*Oman*	2.20	0
Turkey	1.85	2	*Uzbekistan*	2.28	0
Angola	1.89	0	Democratic Republic of Congo	3.10	5
Ethiopia	1.89	0	*Belarus*	3.11	0
Mexico	2.10	13	*Laos*	3.45	0
Bangladesh	2.20	1	*Equatorial Guinea*	3.50	0

Key: Countries in shaded rows are not in the list of 20 most-frequently featured countries in human rights stories.

20 countries with the lowest average Physical Integrity Index and Empowerment Index scores from 1990–2009 and, again, in both the physical integrity rights and empowerment rights composite indexes, many of the states with the worst human rights records are featured in very few human rights stories. Four of the 20 worst offenders for physical integrity rights and 7 of the 20 worst offenders for empowerment rights were not featured as locations in a single one of the 824 human rights stories from 1990 to 2009.

The 824 human rights stories featured 75 countries[7] as prominent parts of the story. When ranked by number of mentions, the top-20 countries[8] account for 90 percent of the stories. Table 3.5 lists the 20 most-frequently covered countries and their average PTS from 1990–2009. The shaded countries in Tables 3.3 and 3.4–14 of the 25 states with the worst PTS scores, 13 of the 20 states with the worst CIRI Physical Integrity scores, and 14 of the 20 states with the worst CIRI Empowerment Rights scores do not get mentioned within the 20 most-frequently mentioned human rights story countries as listed in Table 3.5.[9] This data makes it clear that the severity of human rights conditions in a country does not translate directly into media coverage, even in stories that include the phrase human rights, and this makes it hard to argue that there is a comprehensive CNN Effect on human rights issues. What kind of effect could possibly be extrapolated from an extremely small pool of human rights stories that ignores whole chunks of the worst human rights offending states? The worst violations are simply not being televised.

War means media coverage, and heightened media coverage means the opportunity to seek additional angles to stories, one of which could be human rights issues, so it is not surprising to see several countries that have had military relations with the US rank highly in the top-20 list. Three countries on the top-20 list, Yugoslavia/Successor States, Haiti, and Kuwait, are there because of stories mentioning human rights that relate to American military action in those locations; similarly, three other countries from the top-20 list, Iraq, Afghanistan, and Pakistan, are hotspots in the US GWOT.

China is overwhelmingly the most featured country in US television news human rights coverage, despite the existence of 19 other countries with worse PTS averages, 12 other countries with worse CIRI Physical Integrity scores, and 4 other countries with worse CIRI Empowerment Rights scores from 1990–2009. The 221 stories involving China represent 27 percent of the total human rights stories from 1990–2009. That is more than three times the number of stories of the other non-US countries.

Story Content: Type, Description, and Focus

The type and content of these stories reveal much more than just a simple count of the involved locations. What human rights information could

Table 3.5 Top-20 Countries in Human Rights Stories

Country	Stories Mentioning that Country	Percentage of Total Human Rights Stories	PTS Average, 1990–2009	CIRI Physical Integrity Rights Index, Average 1990–2009 (0–8)	CIRI New Empowerment (0–14)
1. US (international)	398	48%	1.85	6.15	12.00
2. PRC (216) & Hong Kong (5)	221	27%	3.83	1.6	0.80
3. US (domestic)	115	14%	1.85	6.15	12.00
4. Iraq	68	8%	4.93	0.61	1
5. Yugoslavia(2) & Successor States: Bosnia (31), Kosovo (10), Serbia (6), Croatia (2) Macedonia(1)	52	6%	3.93(Y), 3(B), 2(K), 2.25(S), 2.25(C), & 2.11(M)	3.6(Y), 6.44(B), 6(K), 3.4(S), 5.83(C), 6.12(M)	6.4(Y), 7.22(B), 9(K), 5.86(S), 9(C), 11.53(M)
6. Haiti	39	5%	3.4	3.15	8.95
7. Israel & Palestine	37	4%	4.1	2.9 (Israel)	7.6 (Israel)
8. Russia & USSR & Chechnya	35	4%	3.89	2.6	4.85
9. Afghanistan	23	3%	4.75	1.64	2.07
10. Vatican	23	3%	–	–	–
11. Sudan	19	2%	4.8	0.6	0.65
12. Cuba	18	2%	2.93	3.65	1.55
13. UK & Northern Ireland	17	2%	1.6	6.55	12.20
14. Indonesia & East Timor	15	2%	3.75 & 2.3	1.4 & 6.13	4.35 & 11.5
15. Mexico	13	2%	3.3	2.1	10.25

16. Kuwait	13	2%	2.33	5.16	4
17. Rwanda	10	1%	3.93	2.25	5.70
18. Chile	9	1%	2.03	5.05	12.00
19. South Africa	8	1%	3.6	3.35	10.50
20. Pakistan	7	1%	3.93	1.5	4.7
Total	1140				

Key:

Countries whose relations with the US are linked to GWOT

Countries where the US military saw action 1990–2009 (not related to GWOT) audiences viewing these 824 stories obtain? The answer is not very much. The small number of human rights stories is compounded by the lack of information in most of the stories. First, the type of story sheds light on the amount of information that could possibly be transmitted. A short Video Over Sound On Tape (VOSOT) has less detail and information in it than a longer, full package but more than a teaser before a program break, and live two-ways are often used for further analysis from the reporter as a way to follow up on a story. In addition to the amount of information each type of story can convey, story type can also indicate the priority of the story for producers: VOSOTs take fewer resources to produce, while full packages and live two-ways require more substantial planning and commitment. Placement in headline introductions and teasers before program breaks indicate that producers believe the story to be one of the major stories of the day and of sufficient interest to entice viewers to stay with the program. So what types occurred most in the human rights stories? Table 3.6 lists the story types of human rights stories.

Most of the human rights stories were full packages, which initially indicates significant dedication to these stories. But a deeper look is required to see how much human rights information those full-package stories contained.

Was each story containing the phrase human rights really about human rights? A story could theoretically include the phrase human rights with either a lot, some, or no description of human rights issues. To put it another way, to what extent could these stories form the basis for a substantive discussion of human rights? Stories were coded for the amount of human rights detail, description, and focus they contained. Most of the stories coded as human rights stories were lacking in description or examples of human rights. Figure 3.3 breaks down the human rights stories by how much human rights description they included.

Most of the 824 human rights stories were human rights in name only. Three hundred stories contained no description of human rights at all, while only 266 contained a clear description of human rights. Examples

Table 3.6 Story Type of Human Rights Stories

Type of Story	Number of Stories	Percentage
VOSOT	155	19%
Full Package	623	75%
Live Two-Way	14	2%
Headline/Intro	15	2%
Restatement at End	3	0%
Teaser Before Break	14	2%

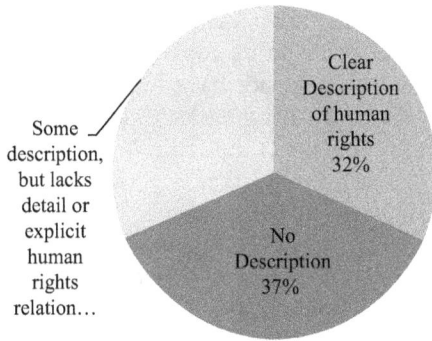

Figure 3.3 Human Rights Descriptions

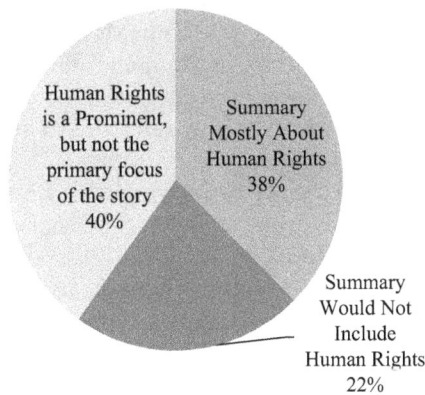

Figure 3.4 Human Rights Focus

of these stories include the VOSOT from April 7, 2008, where Hillary Clinton says, "I believe the Bush administration has been wrong to downplay human rights"; the full-package story on November 19, 1993, where President Clinton says, "My policy is to try to engage China, to be very firm on the human rights issue, to be very firm on the weapons proliferation issue"; and the November 19, 2000, full package on the end of Alberto Fujimori's rule in Peru where "Union-led protestors have been demanding a return of human rights." These three stories, and the other 297 coded as no description, include the phrase human rights but offer no details, no examples or illustrations or additional information that helps to explain any human rights issues.

Even if there is no clear example, illustration, or definition of human rights issues in a story, it could theoretically still be focused on human rights, so stories were coded for whether human rights was the primary focus of the story, one of several prominent foci of the story, or not a focus of the story at all. Figure 3.4 displays the results.

The September 23, 2001, full package about the life and death of composer Isaac Stern is an excellent example of a story that can include the phrase human rights but does not have human rights as a focus of the story and does not include any human rights detail. The only human rights information in the story is the claim "He fought for human rights and artistic freedom," with no further explanation or relation to human rights or human rights issues. Although it contains the phrase human rights, this story simply does not have enough human rights information or focus to inform or interest the audience about human rights. There are 162 stories like this. Twenty percent of the total human rights stories have neither detail about nor focus on human rights!

A different way to determine if a story contained human rights information was to see whether the phrase human rights was used substantively and descriptively or simply in the unofficial or official title of a person, place, or group, such as "Tom Malinowski, Human Rights Watch," "human rights lawyers," or "human rights activist." Figure 3.5 displays stories by whether or not they included the phrase human rights in a formal or informal title as the only reference to human rights.

Thirty-five percent of the total human rights stories are only human rights stories because the formal or informal title of a person, place, or group is spoken during the story. A further 8 percent only use the title in a captioned headline for a speaker; the title is not even audible during the story, so someone who happened to be looking away from the screen at that point would miss it. Together that's 353 stories or 43 percent of the total human rights stories that are only human rights stories because of a formal or informal title.

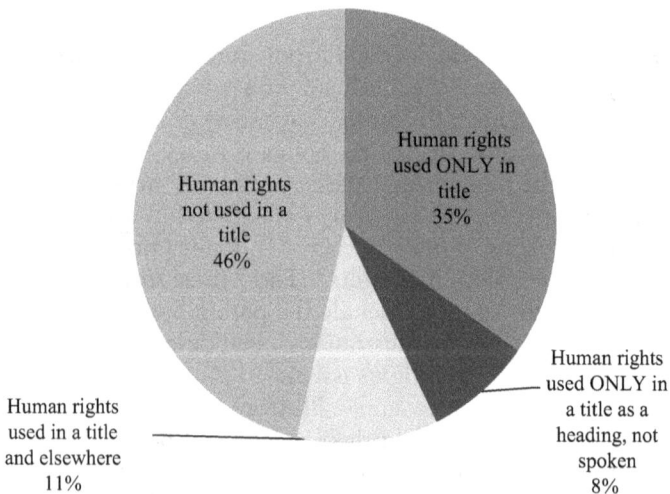

Figure 3.5 Human Rights Used in Title

The February 19, 2005, VOSOT about fox hunting in Britain is a prime example of how the title of a person or institution can make a story include the phrase human rights while at best only being related to human rights in a distant way:

> BOB WOODRUFF (Voice-Over): To a controversial sport in England now. Four people have been arrested for fox hunting. It's the first weekend of a new law banning hunting with hounds. Hunters unhappy with the ban say they will take their case to the European Court of Human Rights.

There is no detail, description, or explanation of why this would be a human rights issue; on the face of it, foxes are not human and the UDHR does not contain a stated unalienable right to hunt foxes. A very long line could be drawn from a person appealing their arrest under an unfair law on human rights grounds, but it would be a stretch and very likely beyond the interest or ability of most viewers. The story itself provides no easily accessible detail about or focus on human rights.

Returning to what appeared to be a high proportion of full-package stories in the total human rights stories pool, the 75 percent of human rights stories that are full packages do not contain as much information as first assumed based solely on the type of story. One hundred eighty-eight of the full-package human rights stories had no description of human rights; this equals 23 percent of all human rights stories and 30 percent of the full packages that have no detail or description of human rights. One hundred fifty two of the full packages, or 24 percent of those full packages, amounting to 18 percent of all human rights stories, did not include human rights in a summary of the story. Two hundred sixty-six of the full-package stories, or 43 percent of the full-package stories and 32 percent of the total human rights stories, had the only inclusion of human rights as part of the formal or informal title of a person, place, or group. Therefore, despite a high number of human rights stories being full packages, many of those full packages did not include any information or focus on human rights.

Story Content: Category

Human rights are a large framework encompassing many different issues, so the human rights stories were coded for the kind of human rights they covered, as shown in Table 3.7.

The largest number of stories by far were in Category 18, Not Applicable/Not Specified/Unclear, coming in at 343 stories or 42 percent of the total. This is entirely consistent with the lack of human rights information in many of the human rights stories; if there is no human rights information in a story, it cannot possibly be classified as a specific issue

Table 3.7 Categories of Human Rights in Human Rights Stories

Categories of Human Rights	Number of Stories	Percentage of Stories
18. Not Applicable/Not Specified/ Unclear	343	42%
2. Civil & Political Rights	241	29%
12. Humanitarian Law, Laws of War, Crimes Against Humanity, War Crimes Tribunals	77	9%
5. Torture and Other Cruel, Inhuman, or Degrading Treatment or Punishment	42	5%
4. Women's Rights	29	4%
17. GLBTQ	17	2%
13. Genocide	16	2%
6. Children's Rights	15	2%
11. Refugees & Asylees	14	2%
1. Racial Discrimination	11	1%
10. Abolition of Death Penalty	10	1%
3. Economic, Cultural, and Social Rights	4	0%
15. Slavery and Slavery-Like Practices	4	0%
14. Rights of the Elderly	1	0%

area of human rights. The second most popular category was Category 2, Civil and Political Rights. This is not surprising given the US's preference for civil and political rights as the dominant conception of human rights. Two hundred forty-one stories, or 29 percent of the total human rights stories, were classified as civil and political rights. These 241 stories are more than the sum of all the other stories that could be categorized by one type of human right; all of the other categories, except 18, Not Applicable/Not Specified/Unclear, add up to 240 stories.

The category results are also revealing in what did not show up at all. From the coding instrument list, which is based on all of the international human rights treaties and prominent nontreaty norms, several categories did not have even one story: Rights of Migrant Workers/Families, Protection Against Enforced Disappearance, the Rights of Disabled Persons, and the Rights of Indigenous Groups.

It is perhaps unusual to see a category such as Humanitarian Law/Laws of War/Crimes Against Humanity/War Crimes on a list of human rights issues, as these issues are usually considered part of other frameworks, namely international humanitarian law or international criminal law. This academic and legal distinction appears to be completely lost on television news journalists and producers, as humanitarian law and crimes against humanity stories were covered as human rights stories. This is likely due to several reasons. First, as discussed in Chapter 2, IHL and IHRL are distinct, but they also overlap, and the borders and overlap between these issues are complex and difficult to understand, even for those who spend years studying them. The quick-paced, event-driven nature of the television news medium does not allow for teaching the fine points of categories of international law to the audience, who would likely not be interested anyway. Second, another journalistic imperative may be at play as well: if it bleeds, it leads—those issues that can include compelling video images of mangled bodies or crying victims are more likely to get coverage, which would likely contribute to the blurring of international relations' theoretical boundaries. Third, and finally, even the policy makers seen and heard in these stories do not seem to acknowledge the difference, so why should journalists, producers, or the audience? Further compounding this issue is the expansive mission of organizations, such as Human Rights Watch, that deal in humanitarian law areas as well as in human rights issues strictly defined. The inclusion of the name of Human Rights Watch alone can trigger a story to be coded as human rights, whether it is about humanitarian law or human rights strictly defined. For all of these reasons, the category was included here and was actually a very frequent category among the human rights stories—the third most frequent, with 9 percent of the coded stories.

A New Frame: The GWOT

Since the Global War on Terror (GWOT) was proclaimed in 2001, it has become a dominant frame for both policy makers and journalists, and human rights stories are no exception. Table 3.8 displays the number of human rights stories since 2001 that had a predominantly GWOT frame.

In every year since 2001, the GWOT frame appeared in at least 20 percent of the human rights stories for that year, excluding 2008 when human rights stories were all about the lead up to the Beijing Olympics. In 2003 and 2004, more than half the human rights stories were GWOT-related and 49 percent of 2005's human rights stories were GWOT-related. This is not necessarily surprising, as both the GWOT in general and specifically the treatment and legal rights of detainees from the GWOT became major news issues in the US. It is interesting to note that this is an area where the issues at hand, political rights of detainees and treatment of detainees that may amount to torture, are simultaneously clear-cut human rights issues as well as constitutional or civil liberties issues, the latter of which would not necessarily have been caught by this manner of data collection. Chapter 5's analysis of 20 weeks of

Table 3.8 GWOT Human Rights Stories

Year	GWOT	Not GWOT	Percentage GWOT of That Year's Human Rights Stories
2001	8	32	20%
2002	15	25	38%
2003	21	14	60%
2004	26	19	58%
2005	22	23	49%
2006	9	17	35%
2007	4	7	36%
2008	2	32	6%
2009	7	22	24%
Total	114	191	

footage will shed light both on coverage about the GWOT and about the possibility of human rights coverage that doesn't include the phrase human rights.

State Department and NGO Reports

Official reports from government offices and NGOs are often released with an eye toward garnering media coverage, and this study found evidence of some limited success. The State Department's release of their annual report on human rights received a story every year from 1990 to 2002, one story in 2004 about the annual report, and one story in 1994 about a (non-annual) State Department report on Haiti. Although the annual reports continued to be issued, and their releases continued to be introduced at official events, no stories were found for 2003 or 2005–2009.

Many human rights NGOs devote a significant part of their resources to researching reports and seeking to disperse the results widely, including by providing expert commentary to news programs. Kenneth Roth and John Sifton from Human Rights Watch, Cheryl Jacques and Elizabeth Birch from the Human Rights Campaign, and Stephen Bright from the Southern Center for Human Rights are just a few examples of NGO representatives who appeared in multiple stories. NGOs also publish their official reports, the release of which they hope will trigger news coverage. This study uncovered 28 stories that mention reports written by various NGOs, as displayed in Table 3.9.

At least one NGO report is included in every year, except 1990, 1994, 2006, and 2007. Considering both the number and the research and

Table 3.9 NGO Reports in Human Rights Stories

NGO	Mentions of Reports
Human Rights Watch	14
Amnesty International	12
Freedom House	1
ICRC	1
Save the Children	1
Total	29*

*One story mentioned reports by HRW and Amnesty International, so they were each credited with one story, which is why there are 29 NGO mentions in 28 stories.

report output of these organizations, 29 mentions of their reports is not a very high number. Human Rights Watch had the largest number of its reports mentioned, but it must be remembered that Human Rights Watch has a decided advantage in being caught by this method of data collection, because the inclusion of its name alone is enough to trigger being categorized as a human rights story. Amnesty International is also frequently introduced as "human rights organization Amnesty International" or "human rights group Amnesty International," which would partially account for its prominence in this method of collecting human rights stories. It may be that NGO reports are getting more television coverage than is indicated here, but that must be investigated in a future study.

Conclusions

Analyzing the 824 stories containing the phrase human rights that were broadcast from 1990–2009 yields several conclusions. First and foremost, there is very little television news coverage of human rights as human rights and that which is broadcast is often not very detailed or focused on human rights—human rights do not get televised in the US. The 824 stories that contained the phrase "human rights" contain no thematic coverage; there is no in-depth coverage of human rights that could offer definitions and explanations of the human rights framework to a general audience that lacks specialized training or education in human rights. So what is being covered, and what does it mean?

Big Bad China

One of the biggest results from this study is that China is the absolute bête noire of American television news stories involving human rights. More than one quarter of the human rights stories from this period involve China. In

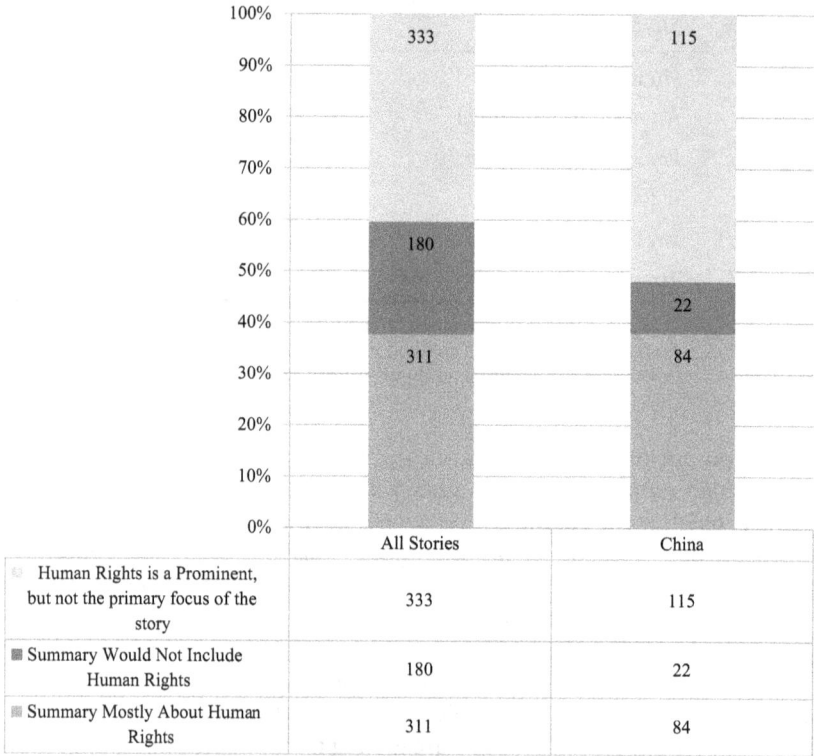

	All Stories	China
○ Human Rights is a Prominent, but not the primary focus of the story	333	115
■ Summary Would Not Include Human Rights	180	22
▨ Summary Mostly About Human Rights	311	84

Figure 3.6 Human Rights Focus: All Stories Versus China Stories

addition to the frequent mention of China in association with human rights, stories involving China are more likely to feature human rights as at least a prominent, if not the primary, focus of the story, as shown in Figure 3.6.

Despite China stories tending to feature human rights as a prominent theme more than the general pool of human rights stories, the China stories (42 percent) are more likely than the human rights stories as a whole (36 percent) to not include any detail or description about human rights, as shown in Figure 3.7.

If the phrase "human rights record" is uttered, it is more than likely to be preceded by the word "China's" or some variation of that phrase with China included,[10] though this frequency of mention does not coincide with an increased likelihood of providing descriptions of human rights. Television news in the US covers human rights stories that relate to China more than human rights stories that relate to any other country in the world. These human rights stories relating to China are more likely to be focused on human rights than the total pool of human rights stories but less likely than the total pool to include a description or definition of human rights. All three of these trends hold true across the entirety

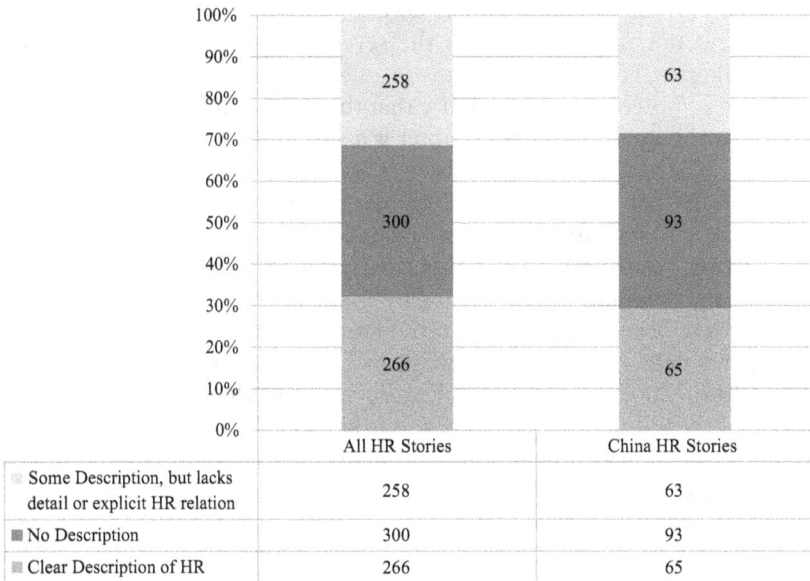

	All HR Stories	China HR Stories
Some Description, but lacks detail or explicit HR relation	258	63
■ No Description	300	93
▨ Clear Description of HR	266	65

Figure 3.7 Human Rights Description: All Stories Versus China Stories

of the time period under review. Taken together, this data indicates the existence of a hollow frame on China and human rights: policy makers speak often about, and journalists report often about, China and human rights so that a link is established between human rights and China for audiences (and future journalists and policy makers). But the frame is hollow, lacking in content: there is not much detail given about human rights in these stories, so the inclusion of human rights is more of a reflex—something policy makers say and journalists report but not something that is explored or developed in detail. A viewer would be hard-pressed to learn much about human rights in China from watching the news, despite the frequency with which the two ideas are presented together. Moreover, when these references are repeated over time, they become self-fulfilling: journalists look for the story angles that fit their existing frames of reference, and then the stories they produce reinforce the frame with which the journalists started. Chapter 6 begins with an in-depth case study of overall television news coverage of China, which confirms and then further develops these results.

What Isn't Being Broadcast Versus What Might Not Be Caught by This Methodology

So far, comparison of the countries featured in human rights stories and the PTS and CIRI data confirm for American television news what Heinze and Freedman (2010) found true of three months of American and British print news in 2006: News outlets do not cover human rights issues very much and not in proportion to the severity of the violations that are occurring throughout the world.

There is, however, the possibility that the very small number of human rights stories analyzed in this chapter is a side effect of methodology. It is conceivable that human rights issues are being covered by television news but perhaps not with the phrase human rights. If human rights are not a dominant theme for American television journalists, then it may not be used for covering human rights issues, which might mean the phrase human rights would not be used. Any usage of the phrase human rights would have been collected in the 824 stories analyzed here. But according to this data, only 10 stories that touched on Rwanda were broadcast from 1990–2009, and only 7 of those were in 1994. Considering the scope of the killings that went on, this is beyond shocking. That the international media was slow to cover the genocide in Rwanda has been well established. That in 20 years, 5 prior to and 15 after the genocide, only 10 stories were broadcast is not to be believed. It is therefore likely that stories relating to the Rwandan genocide have been broadcast but did not include the phrase human rights. And if human rights stories relating to the Rwandan genocide might be broadcast without the phrase human rights in them, then what other human rights issues did this phrase search fail to pick up? The transcript, 20-year code, and case study content analyses in the following chapters collect data differently to discover if human rights issues are being covered without the phrase human rights in the story. They also compare the American television news coverage of human rights with British television news coverage to determine whether the national media system will affect the amount or type of human rights coverage in television news.

Notes

1 A searchable electronic database of British television is not currently available; this will be an excellent area for future research, as both the tapes of news shows and the technology to create transcripts and house them in a searchable database exists. The author's next project will be grant writing to support creating such a database.

2 See Appendix I: Methodology.

3 Additional data collection by the author shows that the early 1990s in Lexis-Nexis news transcripts are particularly prone to this problem, as well as a few misdated stories. Researchers should take extra care to ensure their numbers are accurate and reliable.

4 Actual search applied in LexisNexis: "human right!" and BODY("human right!")

5 This number is an estimate, because there are nights when evening news broadcasts are suspended due to sporting events or other issues, such as weather emergencies.

6 FAQ: What human rights are included in CIRI," http://www.humanrights-data.com/p/faq.html.
7 All stories were coded for at least one location and up to three, which is why there are more featured countries than total stories. A story could have one, two, or three locations included. Locations were not in rank order, i.e., a country coded as location two for a story is counted equally to the country coded as location one for that story.
8 Countries have been collapsed to combine old states with their successor states and/or previous names, and the US is listed separately for its "Domestic" and "Both Domestic and International" categories.
9 Please see Appendix II for the complete list of countries.
10 A partial list includes ABC *World News* stories from August 10, 2008; August 7, 2008; April 8, 2008; April 7, 2008; March 24, 2008; July 31, 2001; July 13, 2001; April 1, 2001; February 26, 2001; February 21, 2001; November 15, 1999; July 23, 1991; September 4, 1991; May 26, 1994; May 28, 1993; November 5, 1992; February 25, 1992; March 2, 1992; July 21, 1992; and June 2, 1992.

Bibliography

Caliendo, S., Gibney, M., & Payne, A. (1999). All the news that's fit to print? *Harvard International Journal of Press/Politics, 4*(4), 48.

Cingranelli, D. L., & Richards, D. L. (2014). The Cingranelli-Richards (CIRI) Human Rights Data Project Coding Manual Version 5.20.14. Retrieved February 20, 2015 from http://www.humanrightsdata.com/p/data-documentation.html

Cingranelli, D. L., Richards, D. L., & Clay, K. C. (2014). *The CIRI Human Rights Dataset*. Version 2014.04.14. Retrieved February 20, 2015 from http://www.humanrightsdata.com.

Gibney, M., Cornett, L., Wood, R., & Haschke, P., (2015), *Political Terror Scale 1976–2012*. Retrieved February 20, 2015 from the Political Terror Scale website: http://www.politicalterrorscale.org/

Heinze, E., & Freedman, R. (2010). Public awareness of human rights: Distortions in the mass media. *International Journal of Human Rights, 14*(4), 491–523.

Ovsiovitch, J.S. (1993). News coverage of human rights. *Political Research Quarterly, 46*(3), 671.

Ramos, H., Ron, J., & Thoms, O.N.T. (2007). Shaping the northern media's human rights coverage, 1986–2000. *Journal of Peace Research, 44*(4), 385–406.

4 Content Analysis II
US & UK Transcript Analysis

Chapter 3 argued that a CNN Effect for human rights is unlikely because of the very small number of human rights stories and the small amount of human rights content in those stories; in effect, the violations are not televised. Since the last chapter only reviewed stories that contained the phrase human rights, it leaves open the question of stories about human rights that do not use the phrase human rights. One way to see if news programs are covering human rights issues without using the phrase human rights is to examine the entirety of news transcripts instead of just performing a phrase search. Additionally, one way to deepen the analysis is to make it comparative: to find out not only how American television news covers human rights but also how that coverage compares to the coverage in the UK. A working hypothesis of this study was that there would be more human rights coverage in the British news than in the American news, for a number of reasons. For one, the UK is more integrated into human rights mechanisms. Second, the BBC is more insulated from commercial pressures than American commercial television news. And finally, the BBC has a specific mission to educate and inform, and because British journalistic traditions allow reporters to be more advocacy-oriented, while American journalists use a different view of neutrality as not taking a side. While the data does support this hypothesis, the distance between human rights coverage in the US and the UK is not nearly so large a difference as expected. And again, in both the US and the UK it is almost impossible to argue in favor of a CNN Effect on human rights issues generally, because there are so few human rights stories broadcast in either country. Thus this data reveals that human rights violations are rarely televised in the US and are only marginally more frequently televised in the UK.

In order to answer the question left open by Chapter 3, entire broadcast transcripts[1] were collected and coded to determine whether human rights stories were covered on television news in stories that did not include the phrase human rights. February 1990 was selected as the month of that year with the highest number of human rights stories.[2] Transcripts were collected from ABC's *World News Tonight with Peter Jennings* and the BBC's *9 O'clock News*. Twenty-eight days of transcripts were coded for each country, with a total of 353 American and 380 British stories[3] having sufficient information to be coded for location.[4] While the total number of stories analyzed is small, the results are still informative. Each story was coded for location and whether it could possibly be a human rights story. Figure 4.1 shows the results, with the overwhelming majority of stories in both American and British television news having nothing to do with human rights whatsoever.

Seventy-nine percent of American news stories and 75 percent of British news stories did not even have a possibility of being about human rights issues. In the month selected for having the most human rights coverage of the year, only five British and one American story actually contained the phrase human rights. While this is a small sample size, some conclusions can be drawn. First, these results show that neither American nor British television news cover human rights very much, though the BBC does cover it a bit more.

Chapter 3 found 353 stories, or 43 percent of the total human rights stories broadcast on ABC from 1990–2009, only contain the phrase human rights in a formal or informal title. This phenomenon seems to occur in the BBC's coverage as well; two of the five stories that the BBC broadcast containing the phrase human rights in February 1990 contained the phrase human rights only in informal titles. The February 9 story referenced human rights groups who believe the threats against Salman Rushdie's life are an attack on his freedom of expression, and the

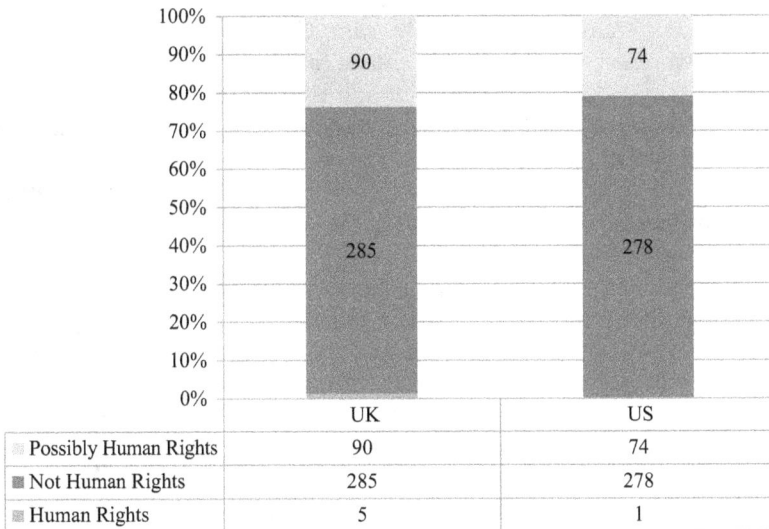

	UK	US
Possibly Human Rights	90	74
Not Human Rights	285	278
Human Rights	5	1

Figure 4.1 Possibly Human Rights Stories and Non-Human Rights Stories, UK & US

February 26 story mentioned "Vaslav [*sic*] Havel, once pilloried in the Soviet press as a subversive and a wrecker was greeted as an honoured guest with a Pravda biography hailing him an active defender of human rights."[5]

The stories broadcasted by the BBC containing the phrase human rights covered an assortment of topics and locations. These stories covered both foreign and domestic stories, from reactions around the world to the events in South Africa to the overturning of a deportation order by the High Court. The deportation story would seem highly irregular to American television news audiences, as it features footage framing immigration as a basic human right:

> Ann Owers: Immigration officers are people who are a specialised service, they see themselves very much as being guardians of the gate whose main job is to keep out people who are not entitled to be here and to get rid of people who are here without permission. They're therefore not the best people to make a decision which affects basic human rights, where there are matters of public interest to consider, those decisions are better made by people in a different department with more time to consider the case and look at all the papers.[6]

This is a strong contrast with American television news, where opinions framing deportation issues as human rights would be unlikely to be broadcast even today, let alone in 1990. Figenschou and Thorbjørnsrud (2015) found that about half of broadcast television news immigration stories in the US have a human-interest focus. Human rights did not come up as a frame in their sample. Kim, Carvalho, Davis, and Mullins (2011) examined the definitions, causes, and solutions of illegal immigration presented in American print and television news, finding frames such as "crime," "social costs," and "national security" to be the most frequent—again, human rights is not mentioned at all as a frame, as it is not how American journalists conceptualize and talk about immigration. Immigration stories often make television news in the US, but journalists reach for other frames.

During the entire month, there was one American story that did contain the phrase human rights. It is a news brief read by Peter Jennings on February 21, 1990, on a topic that did not get any coverage by the BBC: the release of the US State Department's annual report on human rights. The *New York Times* printed stories about the State Department's report in general and China's human rights record specifically as early as February 3,[7] but ABC did not address the State Department report until its official release on February 21. ABC broadcast only a short news brief summarizing how the State Department report calls out several countries, but the brief includes almost no details about the actual human rights violations, and the broadcast did not develop any of the human rights topics touched on into full stories:

> The State Department has released its annual report on human rights. This year it takes 1,600 pages to detail man's inhumanity to man. The report comes down hard on China for the violence in Tiananmen Square, cautious praise for reforms in the Soviet Union, criticism for virtually every country in the Middle East. It said Israeli actions against Palestinians were a cause of deep concern as was increasing Palestinian violence against other Palestinians. And it said Cuba refuses any shift toward democracy and criticized Nicaragua for maintaining what the report called "a repressive internal security apparatus"[8]

Two full stories from that night's broadcast cover areas named in the State Department report story: a full package on the upcoming elections in Nicaragua, and a full package on economic pressure exerted by the Soviet Union on Lithuania and other Baltic states. Yet neither the Nicaragua nor the USSR/Lithuania stories are framed in ways remotely related to human rights, even though both topics easily could have been. The Nicaragua story segued directly from the human rights story, beginning with Peter Jennings saying, "Well, there are some significant changes in Nicaragua like this Sunday's election, the first free election in a decade." But instead of focusing on any of the human rights relating to elections or political participation, the story goes on to cover the style of the campaign:

> Ortega is counting on young people to elect him. His campaign is slick and sexy. (POSTER) Talking to first time voters, their poster says, "When you do it for the first time with love, it's beautiful." And they've hired a popular Colombian rock band to draw a crowd. (BAND) The message: Daniel Ortega and Sandinista voters have more fun.[9]

The story about nascent democracy in USSR and upcoming elections in Lithuania similarly skips any human rights angles in favor of covering how Moscow is attempting to influence its republics via economic pressure. Even when the ABC correspondent asks a Lithuanian politician about freedom, the topic is quickly turned back to the economic clout Moscow wields; the obvious human rights story angle was not pursued.

The story about the State Department human rights report contained many possible leads for human rights stories but none were developed into stories that evening or in the following days, and the two stories broadcast that night about locations mentioned in the State Department human rights report ignored possible human rights angles in favor of other frames.

The Glass Is Half Empty

A more optimistic interpretation of this data is conceivable. The data could be interpreted as also meaning that 21 percent of American news stories and 24 percent of British news stories, or slightly more than one in every five stories, had a possibility of covering human rights issues. So these transcripts were read again and coded further to establish whether they actually were human rights stories that just happened to omit the phrase human rights. Stories could either contain the phrase human rights, be a human rights story without containing the phrase human rights, not be a human rights story, or come close to being a human rights story, but lack sufficient detail or human rights framing.[10] Figure 4.2 illustrates how most of the possibly human rights stories were not actually human rights stories.

For both countries, the majority of possibly human rights stories are simply not human rights stories. Sixty-one percent and 55 percent of British and American possibly human rights stories, respectively, are not human rights stories at all. They cover issues that could possibly be human rights stories but without sufficient explanatory detail to actually provide any human rights information to the viewer. For example, 29 of the British and 16 of the American potentially human rights stories that were coded as non-human rights stories are about South Africa, and all of these have one thing in common: they seem to assume that viewers have considerable knowledge of South Africa, apartheid, and its implied discrimination and human rights violations. For example, the February 1 ABC broadcast opens with a story about the possibility of Nelson Mandela and South African President F. W. de Klerk meeting, noting that "For weeks there has been speculation, in part fueled by the government that de Klerk might announce major apartheid reforms and most importantly the release of Nelson Mandela."[11] But the story did not spell out why such a meeting or reforms would be so newsworthy. The February 14 ABC story featuring Ted Koppel interviewing Nelson Mandela after his release focused on the strain on his family and what he meant by armed struggle continuing, not on describing the system that had kept him in prison or the legal structure of apartheid that denied black South Africans full citizenship and outlawed opposition groups such as the African National Congress, who were working for equal rights. In the context of limited airtime, American journalists were likely making the decision to not expand on the definition or history of apartheid, assuming their viewers would know enough of the background to be able to understand the news that was being reported. One must wonder, however, where audiences are expected to learn that information if US television news

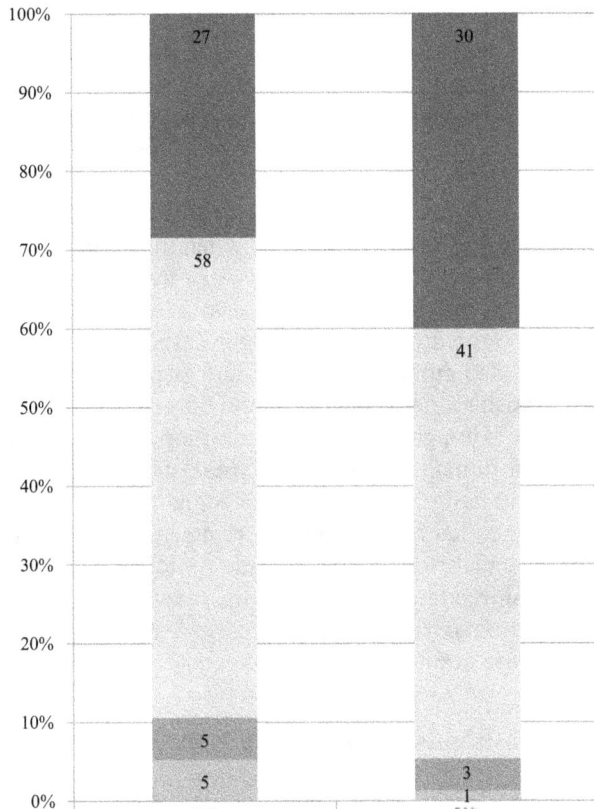

	UK	US
■ Could have been a human rights story, but not framed that way	27	30
▨ Not a Human Rights Story	58	41
■ Human Rights Story that does not contain the phrase Human Rights	5	3
▨ Human Rights Story that contains the phrase Human Rights	5	1

Figure 4.2 Human Rights Stories, UK & US

coverage continually makes decisions to limit historical context and back-ground. British television news also includes stories that have little or no background or description of human rights in stories that could have been framed as human rights stories but balances these stories that are light on historical development and context with stories that delve deeper into complex topics, so British audiences have a chance of learning the background of contemporary events, even if their only source of infor-mation is television news. American audiences who were using television news as their sole source of information would not get the same chance as their British counterparts to learn background context and historical detail either in general or about human rights issues more specifically. As a result of these journalistic decisions, most American news stories, and a few of the British stories, do not include any explanatory detail about human rights issues and thus fall short of meeting the criteria of being a human rights story. More importantly, audiences are receiving very little human rights information even when the human rights importance of the stories would be an obvious possible frame.

The 27 British and 30 American stories that were coded as close to human rights stories but lacking in sufficient human rights detail or framing are also almost all about South Africa: approximately 88 percent of the British stories (24 stories) and 80 percent of the American stories (24 stories). Though they do include more human rights information than the non-human rights stories, these stories still lack explanatory detail about human rights generally or human rights issues in South Africa and so were coded close to human rights stories. Only five British and three American stories actually include sufficient detail about human rights to be considered human rights stories even though they do not contain the phrase human rights; four of the five British and all of the three American stories are about South Africa.

Human Rights Are a Foreign Concept in the US

Human rights stories, both those that contain the phrase human rights and those that do not, were further coded to see what types of human rights issues occur most frequently. In total, 10 British stories and 4 American stories, representing 2.6 percent and 1.1 percent of the total stories for each country respectively, received the full coding. While the small number of stories precludes any meaningful quantitative analyses, the results nevertheless point to some tentative conclusions. The four stories in the American news are all foreign stories; none of them are about domestic policies or issues. This is consistent with the American approach to human rights, in that they are something foreign that happens elsewhere. There were three ABC stories that included references to constitutional rights in the domestic setting: February 4's "constitutional right to an abortion," February 20's constitutional rights regarding a child abuse case decided by the Supreme Court, and February 27's assertion that there is no constitutional right to drive as a justification for police roadblocks to prevent driving while intoxicated. Three other ABC stories referenced civil rights in the domestic setting: February 12's protests in Selma, Alabama, that referenced the civil rights movement; February 19's relating the Civil Rights Act to gender discrimination at Virginia Military Institute; and February 25's education story covering teachers learning about the civil rights movement. The overlap between most of these stories and human rights issues is clear—nondiscrimination on the grounds of race and sex are essential parts of the Universal Declaration of Human Rights (UDHR), the International Covenant on Civil and Political Rights (ICCPR), the International Convention on the Elimination of All Forms of Racial Discrimination (ICERD), and the Convention on the Elimination of All Forms of Discrimination Against Women (CEDAW). Yet a human rights frame is not applied in any of these stories occurring in the US reported by American news. The British human rights stories, on the other hand, include three different stories based in the UK: The BBC's stories on February 9 about Salman Rushdie living in secrecy following death threats against him, on February 12 about the government's possible criminalization of marital rape, and on February 21 about the High Court's ruling on improper delegation of immigration decision making. These three are all human rights stories that are primarily domestic stories. This is quite different from the American example, where no human rights stories are domestic. This difference will be investigated further in the next chapter.

Major Issues Get the Most Coverage but Few Issues Get Human Rights Frame

Overwhelmingly, the subject matter for both countries' human rights stories is South Africa; six of the British stories and three of the American stories are about the monumental changes that began in South Africa in February 1990 with the release of Nelson Mandela from prison after 27 years. The frequent recurrence of this issue area led to the recoding of all of the news stories, human rights and not human rights alike, for whether they covered one of three general "hot" topics during that time period that could be related to human rights issues: South Africa, political reforms and independence movements within the USSR, and German reunification. Table 4.1 displays the number of stories that cover each hot topic, as well as the percentage of the total stories for the month that each hot topic represents.

These three topics represent a large chunk of the coverage in both countries: one third in the UK and one quarter in the US. Twenty-one percent of all British news stories and 14 percent of all American stories were about the changes taking place in South Africa. Political reforms and independence movements within the USSR garnered 9 percent in both the US and UK, while German reunification stories represented 4 percent and 5 percent of the total stories, respectively. But most of these issue areas are not covered as human rights stories, although human rights angles could have been applied with ease to the case of South Africa and with only minimal effort in the case of the USSR and German reunification. The racial discrimination inherent in the system of apartheid, as well as high levels of political violence in South Africa connect clearly to the

Table 4.1 Number and Percentage of All Stories for Major Issues

	CIRI 1989			UK		US	
	PTS Average 1989	Physical Integrity Rights Index	New Empowerment Rights Index	Number of Stories*	Percentage	Number of Stories*	Percentage
South Africa	4	3	4	81	21%	49	14%
USSR Reforms/ Independence	2			36	9%	31	9%
German Reunification	2 (East) and 1 (West)	7 (Germany)	13 (Germany)	21	5%	13	4%
None of the Above				245	64%	261	74%

*For the UK, two stories combine South Africa and USSR Reforms/Independence and one story combines South Africa and German Reunification, so there are three additional stories in the total number of stories. For the US, there is one story that combines USSR Reforms/Independence and German Reunification, so there is one additional story in the total number of stories. Percentages are calculated out of the increased total for both cases.

UDHR, ICCPR, and ICERD, while guarantees of political participation and self-determination found in the UDHR and ICCPR relate directly to German reunification and the reform and independence movements in the USSR.

Comparing quantitative human rights rankings is another way to see if there were human rights issues occurring in the hot topic stories of February 1990, and both the Political Terror Scale (PTS) (Gibney, Cornett, Wood, and Haschke 2015) and CIRI Human Rights show that human rights issues were present in all three hot topic locations. Rankings for 1989 provide the most relevant data for the condition of human rights in the countries, as the month under review is February, which is early in 1990; the numbers for each country are included in Table 4.1. At a combined average of four, South Africa had the highest PTS score, which means of the three countries under examination here, it had the worst human rights records in 1989. Only seven countries had worse PTS average scores for 1989 than South Africa did, while 137 had lower PTS average scores and thus better human rights records. South Africa's CIRI ratings are equally low with a 3 out of 8 for the physical integrity rights composite and a 4 out of 14 on the new empowerment rights composite. The USSR had a PTS average score of two for 1989, indicating a human rights record with some problems, although there were 66 countries with higher PTS averages for the year, meaning worse human rights records; no CIRI ratings were been recorded for the USSR that year. East Germany's PTS average score of two for 1989 was the same as that of the USSR's, meaning there were some human rights concerns though not as bad as in 66 other worse ranked countries, while West Germany's average score for 1989 was a one, indicating low levels of human rights violations. CIRI only has a combined German rating, which at 7/8 for the physical integrity rights composite and 13 out of 14 for the new empowerment composite likely reflects more analysis of West Germany than the conditions in the East at the time.

Thus even though the rankings show that human rights issues were clearly a possible frame for stories about these countries, the human rights frame was selected for very few of the stories about South Africa, German reunification, or reform and independence movements in the USSR during this month in either the US or UK. Of the 21 BBC German reunification stories, only one was coded as possibly human rights, and even that one was fully coded as not a human rights story; none of the 13 ABC German reunification stories qualified to be coded as possibly human rights. The USSR stories tell a similar tale. Of the BBC's 36, only 14 were possibly human rights stories and all of them were subsequently coded as non-human rights stories, while ABC's 31 USSR reform/independence had 8 possibly human rights stories that also all turned out to be non-human rights stories. Most of these stories in both countries utilized the frame of democratic development, focusing on the potential for movement toward multi-party democracy. This frame has significant potential overlap with civil and political human rights, but the human rights frame was not represented in any of the USSR reform/independence stories in either the US or UK.

Only in the case of South Africa were there actual human rights stories, but again, these represent a very tiny share of the whole population of either BBC or ABC stories. Out of 81 South Africa stories on BBC, 60 were possibly human rights stories or contained the phrase human rights, but only 6 actually were human rights stories; and of ABC's 49 South Africa stories, 43 were possibly human rights stories but only 3 turned out to be human rights stories.

The disconnect between possibly human rights stories and stories that are actually human rights stories can largely be attributed to the lack of information in the news stories themselves, and the stories about South Africa are an excellent illustration. Very few of the stories actually took the time to explain Apartheid; it was mentioned in most of them, but seldom defined. As discussed earlier, the lack of explanations and descriptions is much more noticeable in the American stories than in the British stories. On February 2, as well as on February 11, the BBC showed lengthy stories that explained the history of apartheid; there are no such explanations to be found in the American stories. For example, both the American and British news programs on the evening of February 11 dedicated the bulk of their airtime to the release of Nelson Mandela from prison in South Africa: 13 out of 16 stories for the BBC and 8 out of 11 stories for ABC. Yet ABC offered very little background information or evidence on why this event should be so newsworthy, while the BBC spelled it out in much more depth for their audience. The BBC dedicated an entire feature story of seven shooting script pages to the entwined histories of apartheid and Mandela:

> Buerk: Doctor Milan's Afrikaaner National Party didn't invent racial discrimination but codified it, into laws designed to legislate the black majority out of constitutional existence, the doctrine of apartheid. Nelson Mandela, whose legal practice in a white area, had become itself illegal, led the campaign against it. He was arrested, stood out amongst dozens of defendants, in a vast treason trial, that lasted four years.
>
> The case against them was thin. Their defiance campaign was non-violent, their Freedom Charter calling for a democratic non-racial society would be revolutionary only in a totalitarian state. South Africa has never quite been that.
>
> The charges were finally dropped. Mandela was released into a society run by the Dompas, the black man's pass, his people classified and confined by the bureaucracy of apartheid, into an ever-lasting under class. The past became the focus of black's resentment

and resistance. They burned them, but the protests themselves were peaceful. In the background, Mandela tirelessly organized strikes and demonstrations.

It was Sharpeveill that changed everything. The Police panicked, and opened fire on a black demonstration, killing sixty-nine people. The ANC was outlawed, Mandela went underground. June 1961, while on the run, Nelson Mandela wrote to the Prime Minister and architect of apartheid, Hendrik Verwoerd. There are two alternatives before you- either you accede to our demands, and you may still save our country, or you persist with your present policies, which we will never cease to fight against . . . . "[12]

In contrast, the ABC broadcast that evening did not define apartheid at all, let alone give a history of its development and the development of the struggle against it. Instead, ABC spent most of the stories about South Africa discussing the release itself and the reactions of foreign governments, particularly the US government. In these stories, there was an absence of expansion on why Mandela's release was a momentous occasion, beyond a few short lines like Mandela "calling for an end to apartheid" and "Many whites and blacks see Mandela as the best hope for a peaceful end to apartheid."[13] Both the American and British news shows spent the bulk of their programs discussing the events in South Africa, though the BBC broadcasts offered more context and more background than their American counterparts did. Consequently, if an individual were to view a possibly human rights stories with limited or no knowledge of the issue and was depending only on that individual story for information as was the assumption for this coding, much if not all of the human rights connection to the topic would be missed in the American case. In the case of the BBC stories, however, more information and thus more human rights knowledge were provided to the British audience.

Compared to What?

Overall, television news in both the US and UK broadcast very few human rights stories in February 1990. One possible counterargument to the thesis of this book—that television news does not cover human rights issues—would be that there simply might not have been many human rights stories to cover in that month. Data from both the Political Terror Scale (PTS) and the CIRI Human Rights Index provide compelling evidence that there were many grave human rights situations throughout the world at that time. For 1989, there were 111 countries with a PTS average of two or higher, while for 1990 there were 107 with scores of two or higher. The CIRI Physical Integrity Index is scored out of eight points. In 1989, there were 42 countries, or 30.0 percent of the total countries coded for that year, that scored a three or less, while for 1990 there were

53 countries, or 39.3 percent of the total countries coded, that scored a three or less. This data illustrates that many countries had a very poor human rights record during the time under review. The Empowerment Rights Index tells a similar story: In 1989, 66 countries, or 48.1 percent of the total countries coded for this measurement scored a six or worse, with 58 countries, or 40 percent of the total countries scored, earning a six or worse in 1990. Such data indicates that not only were there many places in the world where human rights violations were likely to be occurring but that those violations were significant. Yet there was very little news coverage of human rights during this time period.

Both the Political Terror Scale and the CIRI Human Rights Index provide baselines of human rights conditions calculated based on government and nongovernment sources: annual human rights reports from the US State Department and Amnesty International, both of which are easy sources for journalists and news producers to access. Across a wide variety of topics, journalists often look to official government sources to determine the news agenda, yet, when it comes to human rights, neither ABC nor the BBC had much coverage of the worst offenders according to either the PTS or the CIRI rankings, which are based on data from the same official sources journalists and news producers could access.

Both the PTS and CIRI rankings, however, are annual scores; neither protocol includes coding at the month level. Theoretically, this means there is at least a possibility that all of the issues that could cause a country to receive a poor human rights rating from either CIRI or PTS in 1989 or 1990 could have happened in the months preceding and following February 1990 but not in February 1990 itself. If this were the case, a lack of coverage of human rights issues would be understandable. Additionally, both the PTS and the CIRI scores are calculated based on data from reports by a government and an advocacy organization. The reports that CIRI and PTS codes are generated from naturally reflect the organizations that publish the reports, and neither the State Department nor Amnesty International are composed of journalists. It is again theoretically possible that human rights issues happening during February 1990 did not receive television news coverage because they were not newsworthy—for that, a comparison to what other journalists deemed newsworthy is in order. To address the possibility that the annual nature of the CIRI and PTS data might have hidden a month that was actually uneventful in human rights terms, as well as to see what other journalists considered newsworthy, as those values might differ from the priorities of the government and NGO officials who wrote the reports CIRI and PTS use for their rankings, a comparison with newspaper coverage of human rights for that month is now in order.

Print journalism's coverage of human rights has been explored before. In 1993, Jay Ovsiovitch looked at stories from the *New York Times*, *CBS Evening News*, and *Time* magazine that mentioned human rights in their indexed story abstracts from 1978 to 1987. He found very little coverage overall and a preference in American media to define civil and political rights as human rights while leaving out economic, social, and cultural rights. Ramos, Ron, and Thoms (2007) similarly used statistical methods on the weekly news magazines *Newsweek* and the *Economist*, as well as some European and American daily newspapers from 1986 to 2000. They found an overall increase in the mention of the phrase human rights in stories over the time period studied, with the level of coverage for a country being affected by "violations of personal integrity rights, levels of economic development, population size, and Amnesty International press releases" (401). Likewise, Caliendo, Gibney, and Payne (1999) used a case study approach to look at the 50 countries with the worst PTS scores and to collect all stories featuring those countries in both 1985 and 1995. Their approach found more coverage of human rights in the *New York Times* than Ovsiovitch did but still less than would seem merited by the seriousness of human rights violations and political terror occurring in the countries under review.

These three examples of content analysis of print news coverage of human rights issues all made use of story indexes, but this chapter will diverge from that approach slightly. Instead of searching indexes, which are summaries of stories for archival purposes and would not be read by newspaper readers, I searched the actual stories themselves for the phrase "human right!" This approach casts a wide net for human rights stories while also ensuring that the stories examined are the ones readers would see explicitly connected to human rights. During February 1990, the *New York Times* published 116 articles that included the phrase human rights and the *Times* published 42.[14] In both the US and UK, significantly higher a number of stories including the phrase human rights were published were was broadcast in February 1990: 116 *New York Times* articles to ABC's 1 story and 42 stories in the *Times* against the BBC's 5.

What areas were covered as human rights stories by print journalists during February 1990? Table 4.2 shows the locations featured in stories containing the phrase human rights in the *New York Times* and the *Times*. The locations of possibly human rights stories for ABC and the BBC are also included in the table.

There are 10 locations reported in the *Times* and 21 in the *New York Times* that were not reported by either ABC or BBC as possibly human rights story locations. There is an entire world of human rights issues happening, many of which are gaining the attention of print journalists, but television news broadcasts in both the US and UK simply are not covering human rights. Not only did print news cover a wider universe of human rights, they covered them more in depth. The release of the US State Department's annual report on human rights, discussed earlier, is again illustrative. While the BBC didn't mention the report at all, the *Times* printed one story on February 22, explaining the findings of the

Table 4.2 Locations Featured in Print and Television News Human Rights
Stories, February 1990

Location of Possibly Human Rights Stories

Country	ABC	Country	BBC
South Africa	43	South Africa	60
US	20	UK	34
USSR	7	USSR	15
Romania	6	Lithuania	3
Nicaragua	2	Romania	3
UK	2	India	2
Ethiopia	1	Iran	2
Lithuania	1	PRC	2
Panama	1	US	2
PRC	1	Zambia	2
Vietnam	1	Czechoslovakia	1
Zambia	1	Egypt	1
Total	**86**	France	1
		Germany	1
		Iraq	1
		Lebanon	1
		Nicaragua	1
		Yugoslavia	1
		Total	**133**

Stories were coded for up to three locations that were added together, which is
why the totals for locations are greater than the number of possibly human
rights stories (television) or stories that contain the phrase human rights
(print). Germany includes both East and West Germany.

Location of Stories that Contained the Phrase Human Rights

Country	The Times	Country	The New York Times
UK	17	US	62
USSR	11	PRC	14
Germany	6	Germany	13
Israel & Palestine	4	USSR	10
Yugoslavia	4	Israel & Palestine	8

Country	The Times	Country	The New York Times
Hong Kong (British Dependent Territory)	3	South Africa	8
PRC	3	Czechoslovakia	6
South Africa	3	El Salvador	6
US	3	Cuba	4
Vietnam	3	UN	3
Czechoslovakia	2	Bangladesh	2
European Community	2	European Community	2
Iran	2	Hong Kong (British Dependent Territory)	2
Nicaragua	2	India	2
Cambodia	1	Myanmar	2
Cuba	1	Namibia	2
El Salvador	1	Nepal	2
Iraq	1	Nicaragua	2
Italy	1	Pakistan	2
Namibia	1	Poland	2
Thailand	1	Romania	2
Tibet	1	Turkey	2
Total	73	Afghanistan	1
		Bulgaria	1
		East Timor	1
Shaded locations did not appear in either ABC or BBC possibly human rights stories		Haiti	1
		Iraq	1
		Kenya	1
		Lithuania	1
		Mozambique	1
		Panama	1
		Philippines	1
		Sudan	1
		Thailand	1
		UK	1
		Vietnam	1

Table 4.2 (Continued)

Country	*The* Times	Country	*The* New York Times
		Zambia	1
		Zimbabwe	1
		Total	174

report in 623 words, which described violations committed by China, Israel, Cuba, Iraq, Burma, and Vietnam, as well as noting progress made by the Soviet Union. The *New York Times* went much further, printing eight full stories about the human rights report totaling 6088 words, as well as four news summary stories that included news about the human rights report along with summaries of the rest of the paper's news that day. The *New York Times's* coverage began early, with the first story appearing on February 3, two and a half weeks before the report would be officially released on February 21. The *New York Times* printed stories about the human rights report on February 3, 4, 9, 10, 21, 22, 23, and 27. The stories explored several of the countries named in the report in detail and included reactions from the states that were called out, including official responses from Chinese and Israeli officials. The *Times* deemed the report newsworthy enough for one story; the BBC ignored it completely. The *New York Times* covered the State Department's human rights report repeatedly over time from a wide variety of angles, while ABC only broadcast one short news brief when the report was officially released. Newsworthy human rights issues are occurring, as judged by print journalists, but television news still does not cover them.

What's In a Name?

Several print news stories only mentioned the phrase human rights in the title of an individual or organization, such as the five *New York Times* and the two *Times* stories that discussed the Initiative for Peace and Human Rights in East Germany. Including human rights in the name of an institution or group is an obvious way to get more attention to the idea of human rights, one that can have wide-reaching effects. For example, six *New York Times* stories in February 1990 included the phrase human rights solely because they mentioned the New York City Human Rights Commission. Since 1962,[15] New York City has incorporated human rights into city government right in the name of its Commission on Human Rights, which is responsible for nondiscrimination. The inclusion of human rights in the name of this institution means that the idea of human rights is automatically included in media coverage of city affairs.

Over time, people in New York have been regularly exposed to the phrase human rights and the repeated connection between nondiscrimination and human rights. At the federal level, discrimination claims are handled as civil rights issues or equal employment claims, often with no mention of human rights, though nondiscrimination is a bedrock human right enshrined in several international agreements, such as the UDHR, ICCPR, ICERD, and CEDAW, so media tends not to cover domestic human rights issues as human rights, so audiences are less exposed to human rights ideology. The United Kingdom adopted the Human Rights Act in 1998 to bring human rights standards into domestic legislation and the everyday lives of UK residents. The federal government in the US has yet to adopt similar legislation, preferring civil rights and constitutional rights language to human rights. Simple changes in the name of existing legislation or institutions could make American audiences much more comfortable with human rights at the domestic level, but until such changes occur, the vicious cycle is likely to continue. Television news in the US does not cover human rights domestically because other frameworks, such as constitutional and civil rights, are more familiar to audiences; but since the media does not cover these issues as human rights, audiences have no way of ever getting comfortable with human rights as an approach to domestic issues.

Conclusions

Closely examining one month of British shooting scripts, American transcripts, and print news from both countries provides evidence that concurs with several of the conclusions made in the previous chapter. Again, there is not much human rights content in television news, and what little there is often focuses on foreign countries. This is true for the UK as well as for the US, though to a lesser extent for the UK, as it broadcasts both more human rights stories and more domestic human rights stories than the US does. Major issues sometimes monopolize television news broadcast time, as happened during February 1990 with the hot topics of the release of Nelson Mandela in South Africa, German reunification, and political reform and liberation movements within the USSR. This analysis shows that even when a hot topic is an obvious human rights issue, such as apartheid in South Africa, human rights framing to coverage is not guaranteed. Human rights detail was lacking in most stories in the US and UK, though the BBC did include some stories with more extensive details. Both the nightly news's inability to spend too much time on background information and human rights being only one competing frame among many for stories help to explain the very small number of human rights and close to human rights stories. Comparison with quantitative rankings of human rights conditions around the world as well as with print news from the *New York Times* and the *Times* provides evidence that while there are many significant human rights issues happening throughout the world, television news simply is not covering them. The violations are not being televised.

To best way to account for the potential differences between using LexisNexis transcripts for the American case and BBC shooting scripts for the British case, as well as for the lack of publicly available shooting scripts after 1995, is to compare full broadcasts the way audiences would have seen them aired. Using full broadcasts as the data source means that for both cases, exactly what was broadcast to audiences is being evaluated, eliminating the possibility that errors were made in transcription or that changes were made during the broadcast that were not noted on the archived shooting scripts. Using full broadcasts makes the results more comparable. In addition, expanding the time frame from just one month in 1990 to one week per year from 1990 to 2009 simultaneously provides more depth and breadth to the story of how the violations do not get televised. It is to that large task that this study now turns.

Notes

1 Transcripts made after the broadcasts by LexisNexis were collected for the American news. Shooting scripts, or the pages that the BBC actually used to produce each evening broadcast, were collected for the British news. For simplicity, transcript and shooting script will be used interchangeably in this chapter. See Appendix I: Methodology for month selection and coding scheme.
2 See Appendix 1: Methodology for further information on selection criteria.
3 It is important to note that the American news transcripts preserved on Lexis-Nexis for this period did not include the text of broadcast introductions, teasers before commercials, and good-nights, which were included in the British shooting scripts and therefore in the analysis; this helps to explain why a larger number of stories were coded for the British news than for the American news.
4 This number excludes purely sports reports, general weather reports, stock market reports, and introductions and good-nights that have no story information, for both British and American broadcasts. See Appendix 1: Methodology for further explanation.
5 *BBC Nine O'Clock News*, February 9, 1990 and February 26, 1990.
6 *BBC Nine O'Clock News*, February 21, 1990.
7 Rosenthal, Andrew. "Bush, Citing Security Law, Voids Sale of Aviation Concern to China." The *New York Times*, February 3, 1990.
8 *World News Sunday*. February 21, 1990.
9 *World News Sunday*. February 21, 1990.
10 See Appendix 1: Methodology for further description of the coding scheme.
11 *World News Sunday*. February 1, 1990.
12 *BBC Nine O'Clock News*, February 11, 1990.
13 *World News Sunday*. February 11, 1990.
14 See Appendix I: Methodology for explanation of newspaper selection and the coding scheme.
15 "Commission's History." http://www.nyc.gov/html/cchr/html/about/commission-history.shtml

Bibliography

Abrajano, M., & Singh, S. (2009). Examining the link between issue attitudes and news source: The case of Latinos and immigration reform. *Political Behavior*, *31*(1), 1–30.

Beyer, A., & Matthes, J. (2015). Public perceptions of the media coverage of irregular immigration: Comparative insights from France, the United States, and Norway. *American Behavioral Scientist*, *59*(7), 839–857.

Caliendo, S., Gibney, M., & Payne, A. (1999). All the news that's fit to print? *Harvard International Journal of Press/Politics*, *4*(4), 48.

Cingranelli, D. L., & David, L. R. (2014). *The Cingranelli-Richards (CIRI) Human Rights Data Project Coding Manual Version 5.20.14*. Retrieved February 20, 2015 from http://www.humanrightsdata.com/p/data-documentation.html

Cingranelli, D. L., David, L. R., & Clay, K. C. (2014). *The CIRI Human Rights Dataset*. Version 2014.04.14. Retrieved February 20, 2015 from http://www.humanrightsdata.com

Figenschou, T. U., & Thorbjørnsrud, K. (2015). Faces of an invisible population: Human interest framing of irregular immigration news in the United States, France, and Norway. *American Behavioral Scientist*, *59*(7), 783–801.

Gibney, M., Cornett, L., Wood, R., & Haschke, P. *Political Terror Scale 1976–2012*. Retrieved February 20, 2015 from the Political Terror Scale website: http://www.politicalterrorscale.org/

Kim, S., Carvalho, J. P., Davis, A. G., & Mullins, A. M. (2011). The view of the border: News framing of the definition, causes, and solutions to illegal immigration. *Mass Communication & Society*, *14*(3), 292–314

Ovsiovitch, J. S. (1993). News coverage of human rights. *Political Research Quarterly*, *46*(3), 671.

Ramos, H., Ron, J., & Thoms, O. N. T. (2007). Shaping the northern media's human rights coverage, 1986–2000. *Journal of Peace Research*, *44*(4), 385–406.

5 Content Analysis III

Comparing Twenty Years of American and British Television News Coverage

Chapters 3 and 4 found that the violations are not televised. Looking either at stories containing the phrase human rights in US television news or in months of transcripts and shooting scripts analyzed from ABC and the BBC, there are very few human rights stories broadcast on television news, even though there are human rights issues occurring throughout the world. Chapter 5 continues the comparative approach by analyzing one week of television news broadcasts in the US and UK. Building on the work of Canino & Huston (1986), one week of news coverage was considered representative for the year. Again, the very small amount of human rights information available on television news must preclude any argument in favor of the CNN Effect.

Weeks for viewing were selected to maximize the likelihood of human rights coverage.[1] Summaries of *NBC Nightly News* were collected through the Vanderbilt Television News Archive (VTNA), and recorded broadcasts were viewed online through the VTNA's website. Weeks of British footage were viewed through the British Film Institute's research viewing service. Seven nightly broadcasts were collected for all years in the US case, excluding 1990, 1991, 1997, and 1998 where six broadcasts were collected; seven nightly broadcasts were collected for all years in the UK case, excluding 1999, where six broadcasts were collected. A total of 136 NBC and 139 BBC broadcasts were viewed. Excluding commercials, weather reports, local news reports, and stock market reports, 2,020 NBC stories and 1,878 BBC stories were viewed for an average of 13.5 BBC stories per broadcast and 14.5 NBC stories per broadcast.

All stories for the UK and the US were viewed at least once, and a quick review of the main stories of each week for each country helps to set the stage for the human rights analysis that is to come. Major news topics were deemed to be those that included multiple stories (at least three substantive stories in the week, excluding broadcast introduction, pre-commercial teasers, and good-night summaries) in the weeks under study. This is a holistic account, designed to give an idea of the most prominent issues from the week, the ones that viewers tuning in would be most likely to see. The main story is the story that received the most frequent, prominent coverage that week.

Table 5.1 Major and Main Stories for UK & US Television News

UK News Stories 1990	US News Stories 1990
• **Main story:** Poll tax protests	• **Main Story:** Lebanon hostage developments and relations with Iran
• South Africa–protests in Bophuthatswana	• USSR–local elections and developments of USSR's decreasing involvement in Eastern Europe
• MUN investigation on Skargill	• South Africa–death squads investigated, protests in Bophuthatswana
• Elections and reforms in USSR	• German Reunification plans
• German unification process–Polish border question, property question for reunification	

UK News Stories 1991	US News Stories 1991
• **Main story:** USSR dissolving	• **Main Story:** USSR dissolving
• Yugoslavia–fighting between Croat and Serb forces	• Yugoslavia–fighting between Croat and Serb forces
• Majors visits China for first time since Tiananmen	• Independence of Latvia, Lithuania, and Estonia
• Independence of Latvia, Lithuania, and Estonia	
• IRA attacks	

UK News Stories 1992	US News Stories 1992
• **Main Story:** Yugoslavia–UN asks NATO to plan more military action in Bosnia, prisoners released, Paddy Ashdown visit, calls for Serb leaders to be tried for war crimes, battle for Bosnia	• **Main Story:** Somalia–US military in Somalia, operations to deliver aid beyond the capital
• Somalia–US and French forces in Somalia, US troops going to interior	• Israel-Palestine–body of kidnapped Israeli border soldier discovered, 400 Palestinians deported, protests
• Teen girl found by side of road burned, investigation for torture and kidnapping, girl dies	• President-elect Clinton's economic summit in Little Rock
• IRA attacks, including bomb attack on Christmas shoppers in London	• Yugoslavia–possibility of US involvement in military action, atrocities in Bosnia, reactions to offer to use US planes to enforce no-fly zone
• Israel-Palestine–body of abducted Israeli soldier discovered, 400 Palestinians deported from Israel, protests over the deportations, deaths at the protests	

(Continued)

Table 5.1 (Continued)

UK News Stories 1993	US News Stories 1993
• **Main Story:** Northern Ireland–Majors reaches out to Sinn Fein and offers them a place if they renounce violence, new plan for peace, reactions of both sides, leaked document denied by Irish prime minister	• **Main Story:** NAFTA
• Former Yugoslavia–UN troops in Bosnia, hundreds of mentally ill people abandoned at hospitals, need for humanitarian aid	• APEC Summit, meetings with Asian leaders, discussion of US-Asia relations
• South Africa–new constitution lacks some key support, protests and reactions	• Israel-Palestine–Israel-PLO meetings, Arafat aide shot, violence in Israeli-occupied territories
• Economic indicators announced	
• NAFTA	
• James Bulger murder trial	
• APEC Summit	

UK News Stories 1994	US News Stories 1994
• **Main Story:** Former Yugoslavia–UN relief missions in Bosnia, football match in Sarajevo stadium, Serb weapons cache discovered, Tuzla airport reopened, UN aid convoy hijacked and looted	• **Main Story:** North Korea–nuclear weapons standoff after the US sends Patriot missiles to South Korea
• Northern Ireland–attacks and talks, conflict between prime minister and Northern Ireland minister rumored	• Whitewater scandal
• Europe–Britain and Spain trying to prevent dilution of their ability to block legislation, change in voting pattern looks set to pass	• Israel-Palestine–Israel-PLO talks
• Scott Inquiry–Hesseltine and Lyell at Matrix-Churchill trial	• Political assassination in Mexico
• South Africa–protests and unrest ahead of elections, particularly in prisons	
• Trial and sentencing of youths who beat a young man to death for interrupting their vandalism	

UK News Stories 1995	US News Stories 1995
• **Main Story:** Zaire–Expulsion of Rwandan refugees from Zaire, and the humanitarian crisis there	• **Main Story:** US and China–Harry Wu expelled from China, Hillary Clinton decides to attend Beijing Conference on Women
• Northern Ireland–offer to release IRA convicts rejected as an insult to the IRA	• Bosnia–memorials and return of bodies of three American diplomats killed
• Water shortages in UK prompt questions of regulator and individual meters	• O. J. Simpson murder trial
• US and China–Harry Wu expelled from China	• Iraq weapons inspections
• Water shortages in UK and responses of water companies	• Plane crash in Georgia
• Anglican priest who held Raves for Jesus up on sex abuse charges	
• India–hostages being held in Kashmir	
• Former Yugoslavia–UN troops use force, UN troops prepare to withdraw from Gorazde	

UK News Stories 1996	US News Stories 1996
• **Main Story:** BSE–European ban, mass slaughter of cattle, reaction of ministers and markets	• **Main Story:** Ron Brown's plane crash in Croatia, details of crash and victims, memorials
• Russia ceases fighting in Chechnya	• Standoff with anti-government Freeman group in Montana
• Government decides to hold a referendum on joining the European single currency	• New suspect in the Unabomber case, Theodore Kaczynski, arrested, evidence examined
• Northern Ireland–IRA issues Easter message, which is taken as a threat by the government, expansion of police powers to deal with terrorist suspects	• High-speed chase of illegal immigrants ending in videotaped beating of suspects in Riverside California
• Former Yugoslavia–UN War Crimes Tribunal investigations are ongoing, Bosnian Serbs missed deadline for releasing POWs	

UK News Stories 1997	US News Stories 1997
• **Main Story:** British au pair Louise Woodward trial and sentence	• **Main Story:** US-China summit with Jian Zemin visiting US
• Labour government spells out its stance on the euro single currency	• Stock market crash, reactions, and recovery

(Continued)

Table 5.1 (Continued)

UK News Stories 1997	US News Stories 1997
• Ziang Zemin goes to the US for official summit	• British au pair Louise Woodward trial and conviction
• Prince of Wales visit to Africa	
• Lead-up to and start of French lorry driver strike	

UK News Stories 1998	US News Stories 1998
• **Main Story:** Northern Ireland–lead-up to and elections for new assembly	• **Main Story:** Clinton visit to China
• World Cup in France–riots, hooligans	• Special prosecutor investigation into Clinton
• Investigation into disappearance, and discovery, of the body of 13-year-old Clare Hart	
• Clinton visit to China	

UK News Stories 1999	US News Stories 1999
• **Main Story:** Possible breakthrough in Northern Ireland Peace Process–statement from IRA saying they will decommission when Sinn Fein is in power	• **Main Story:** EgyptAir Flight 990 crash investigation
• French ban of British beef products, labeling of British beef	• Chechnya–escalation of Russian activity
• Russian troops moving in on Chechnya, problems for civilians and refugees	• Women on the Job–recurring feature with different aspects covered
• Question of who will run for London's mayor	• Texas A&M bonfire collapse
• EgyptAir flight 990 crash cause not known	
• Queen's speech with legislative agenda	
• Blairs announce they are having a baby	

UK News Stories 2000	US News Stories 2000
• **Main Story:** Trial of racially motivated London nail bomber begins	• **Main Story:** Campaign 2000–various campaigns and primary results followed
• Northern Ireland Assembly met for first time after being suspended four months ago	• D-Day Remembrances

UK News Stories 2000	US News Stories 2000
• Euro 2000 security concerns over hooligans	• Microsoft Anti-Trust Suit decision and follow-up
• Debate over hunting with dogs	• President Assad of Syria died
• Britain's military attaché in Greece murdered	
• Conservative party conference	
• President Assad of Syria died	
• Sierra Leone–British call to restrict conflict diamond trade, Robin Cooke visits Sierra Leone	

UK News Stories 2001	US News Stories 2001
• **Main Story:** Possible epidemic of foot and mouth disease–culling of sheep, stopping farm clean up	• **Main Story:** Chandra Levy disappearance and investigation
• G8 Summit–end of G8 Summit in Genoa where there was violence and accusations of police abuse of protestors, talks between Putin and Bush at G8 Summit on missile defense, release of arrested British protestors, Italian government promises investigation into police conduct	• Mount Etna erupting
• Indonesia throws out its president, who stays in the presidential palace initially, but then goes to the US for medical treatment	• China–arrest and release of two Chinese-born American scholars for espionage, Powell's visit to China
• 200 countries sign on to a watered down environmental treaty—the US did not sign	
• Mt. Etna erupting	
• US pulls out of germ warfare enforcement talks	
• Trial and sentence of parents whose child and a friend died on the railroad tracks	

UK News Stories 2002	US News Stories 2002
• **Main Story:** Bodies of Holly and Jessica, missing girls in Soham, found, mourning, investigation, and arrests	• **Main Story:** Iraq–possible chemical and biological weapons in Iraq, debate over invading Iraq examined
• Russian military helicopter crashed in Chechnya	• Israel-Palestine–security agreement for pullout, arrest of five Hamas members

(*Continued*)

Table 5.1 (Continued)

UK News Stories 2002	US News Stories 2002
• French declare they will close the Sangat refugee camp in Callais	• Terrorism–secret courts, arrest warrants for suspects issued, firing of a Florida professor for supporting terrorist groups, suspect detained in Saudi Arabia
• World summit in Johannesburg–expectations, leaders begin to arrive, clashes between protestors and police	

UK News Stories 2003	US News Stories 2003
• **Main Story:** Invasion of Iraq	• **Main Story:** Invasion of Iraq
• IRA handed government a statement on decommissioning but declines to clarify it	
• Local English election campaigns begin, stories on local government in Scotland and Wales ahead of local elections	
• Murderers of Holly and Jessica appeared in court	
• SARS–Is China hiding cases?	
• Report that RUC officers colluded in murder in the 1980s in Northern Ireland	

UK News Stories 2004	US News Stories 2004
• **Main Story:** Prisoner abuse in Iraq	• **Main Story:** Iraqi prisoner abuse scandal
• Pro-Russian president of Chechnya killed in an explosion	• Berg execution
• Glasgow factory exploded	• Campaign 2004
• Congress Party won election in India	
• Mirror fake abuse photos scandal, Piers Morgan sacked	
• Maxine Carr's release from prison and theft of documents relating thereto	

UK News Stories 2005	US News Stories 2005
• **Main story:** Iraq–president says British troops could leave in a year's time, US admits using deadly white phosphorus, Iraqi troops accused of abuse, suicide, car, and roadside bombings	• **Main Story:** Iraq prisoner abuse, rebuilding efforts, departure debate

UK News Stories 2005	US News Stories 2005
• Weeks of rioting continue in France, emergency powers extended	• Hurricane Katrina recovery updates
• Debates for Conservative Party Leadership–David Davis versus David Cameron	• Bombing of hotel in Jordan
• Trial of murderers of Antony Walker	• Tornadoes in Iowa
• Government changing licensing laws for pubs, bars, and clubs	
• Bird flu	
• Sri Lanka, presidential elections, ceasefire failing	
• Police woman shot and killed in an armed robbery in Bradford City center, investigation and arrests	

UK News Stories 2006	US News Stories 2006
• **Main Story:** World Cup–England goes through to quarter finals, English fans cause trouble in Germany, reaction to English loss	• **Main Story:** Iraq–troop withdrawal question, rape accusations, military tribunals ruling from Supreme Court
• Israel-Palestine–Palestinian kidnapping of Israeli soldier, Israel's hunt to get him back	• Warren Buffett's large donation to the Gates Foundation
• Former home secretary Kenneth Clarke criticizes Home Office and Blair, government hits back	• Israel-Palestine–Israeli soldier kidnapped, Israel's hunt to get him back
• Marking the 90th anniversary of the Battle of the Somme	• Secondhand smoke declared to be deadly
	• Flooding in northeast

UK News Stories 2007	US News Stories 2007
• **Main Story:** Massive security breach at the Revenue Service as a disc with the personal information of 25 million went missing, tales of other similar scandals	• **Main Story:** Holiday travel stories, Thanksgiving, and Black Friday shopping
• Duke and Queen's 60th wedding anniversary	• Campaigns for election in 2008
• Schemes to rescue Northern Rock bank	• Bangladesh cyclone

(*Continued*)

Table 5.1 (Continued)

UK News Stories 2007	US News Stories 2007
• Several teen girls' bodies found in the yard of a house in Margate • Aid programs to help cyclone victims in Bangladesh • Commonwealth meeting–Pakistan suspended	

UK News Stories 2008	US News Stories 2008
• **Main Story:** Olympics and Olympic Torch Relay, with protestors against China	• **Main Story:** Iraq war–US deaths, Petraeus report and reactions, war orphans, naturalization of foreign-born US soldiers
• Inquest verdict on the death of Princess Di	• Olympics and Olympic Torch Relay, with protestors against China
• Shannon Matthews disappearance investigation and arrests	• Raid in Texas on Yearning for Zion sect
• Zimbabwe election–government refuses to release results, opposition refusing a runoff, Southern African leaders hold a summit	• Campaigns for election in 2008
	• Food riots in Haiti and ousting of prime minister

UK News Stories 2009	US News Stories 2009
• **Main Story:** Government issues budget statement–trying to talk up economy before statement, opposition reaction after, report saying economic output dropped significantly, high level of borrowing and tax increases	• **Main Story:** Anti-terrorism policies–interrogation techniques, question of pursuing prosecutions of former administration officials,
• Criticism of policing at G-20 in London	• Swine flu
• Collapse and defeat of Tamil Tigers, final Sri Lankan government assault on rebel areas	• Iraq War–tourism, suicide bombings, Clinton visit
• MP expense scandal	• Economic downturn–housing crisis and credit card rate hikes from bailed-out banks
• Swine flu	
• Election in South Africa–campaigning, Zuma and ANC win	

There are more major stories listed for the UK than for the US each week, except in 2008. Based on these weeks, *NBC Nightly News* does not seem to do as many follow-up stories on most topics during the same wee, and so would have fewer major stories according to this measure. The major stories for the UK news also appear to include more foreign stories than for the US, and the major stories from both countries are consistent with communications literature that predicts broadcast news will cover its home country and its own "near neighbors"—for the UK, members of the Commonwealth, for the US, Latin American and Caribbean countries—more than other countries or regions. Despite concerns among academics about the Americanization of British broadcasting over the last 20 years, the average number of stories in both countries does not seem to be very far apart at any point during the period under review, nor does the number of stories seem to be changing; furthermore, there does not seem to be a tremendous amount of overlap in the major stories covered. The US has only one story about the Poll Tax, the main story British story in 1990 and few or none on major stories in other years, such as no American stories on IRA attacks in 1991 or 1992, only one US brief on Majors visit to Tiananmen in 1991, and one American story on Bosnia in 1993, during which week the temporary disappearance of Michael Jackson got two American stories. In 1995, NBC carried only one full package story on Rwandan refugees during the week under review, while the BBC covered it more than they covered any other story that week. In 1996, there was one American story each for BSE and the ceasefire in Chechnya, stories which dominated the BBC that week. Similarly, Chandra Levy's disappearance and the ensuing investigation was the primary NBC story for 2001, and it received no coverage on the BBC during the same week.

The idea that the BBC is converging with the American model of television news as evidenced by covering the same stories all but evaporates if the special relationship and frequent cooperation between the two countries is considered and if it is conceded that there are certain stories that are so big, any news outlet would have to cover them. Stories like the invasion, war, and abuse scandals in Iraq, in which both countries were involved, and the Olympic Torch Relay in 2008, which went through both countries, are the types of stories that both broadcasters would cover because they are both inherently newsworthy and involved their home country, not because either broadcaster is copying or converging with the other.

Finally, and most relevant to this study, very few of the main or major stories are even tangentially related to human rights issues, and this holds true of both countries. While the BBC has more potentially human rights–related stories as main and major stories, such as the expulsion of Rwandan refugees from Zaire in 1995 or the treatment of protestors at the G8 Summit in 2001, human rights–related stories are certainly not the majority of the main or major stories listed for either country.

How Many Stories? How Many Human Rights Stories?

In both the US and the UK, the majority of stories broadcast were domestic in nature, though the division was more exaggerated in the US case: 64 percent of NBC's total stories versus 48 percent of the BBC's stories were solely domestic. The amount of international coverage in both countries is consistent with comparative media studies literature: US media tends to cover more domestic and less international news, and international news primarily as it ties in to US interests (which in this coding would be "both"), while the UK media has both more purely international coverage (25 percent against the US 13 percent) and a comparable combination domestic and international stories (26 percent against 23 percent).

Stories were coded for whether they could possibly be human rights stories, and the results were surprising. In examining the human rights content of television news, the author had hoped to see what the audience could have learned about human rights from television news coverage. This question, however, rests on the assumption that there would be human rights coverage, and this turns out not to be the case most of the time in either country. First, very few stories out of the total in either country actually qualified as even a possible human rights story. Three hundred fifty-one NBC stories and 268 BBC stories (17.4 percent and 14.3 percent of the total stories viewed) were coded as either containing the phrase human rights or possibly being human rights stories, so they were viewed again and coded further. The author had further expected the UK media to have much more human rights content than the US

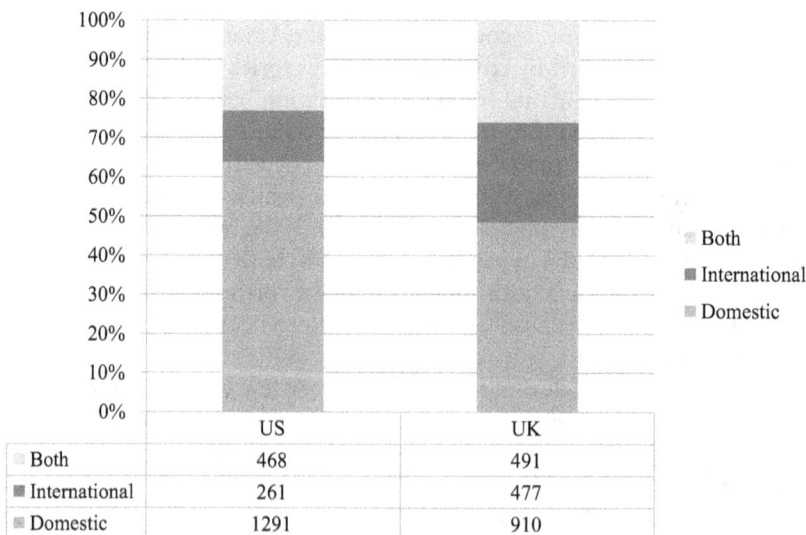

	US	UK
Both	468	491
International	261	477
Domestic	1291	910

Figure 5.1 Domestic Versus International Stories, UK & US

media, since the UK is more integrated into human rights mechanisms, the BBC is more insulated from commercial pressures than American commercial television news, and because the BBC has a specific mission to educate and inform. But this turned out not to be such a simple case, as there were more possible human rights stories selected for NBC than for the BBC. Figure 5.2 shows the number of stories for both countries that were coded as being possibly human rights stories and viewed again. The percentage of these stories that were coded as domestic stories dropped significantly for both countries, and the percentage of purely international stories doubled for both countries.

The possibly human rights stories were coded further for whether or not they contained the phrase human rights (1), were human rights stories without containing the phrase human rights (2), contained the phrase human rights in text without it being spoken audibly (5), or were not human rights stories (3). As the development of the coding instrument progressed, it became obvious that an additional category was needed—not just human rights or not, but something to represent the grey area in between. In these cases, stories were close to human rights stories but lacked the detail, description, or framing to qualify as a human rights story without the phrase human rights (code 2). Thus a final category (4) was created: close to human rights but not quite enough detail or framing to be a 2.[2] Overall, very few stories were found to actually be categorized as human rights stories in either country, as shown in Table 5.2.

The author's hypotheses about more UK human rights coverage were partially redeemed. In the time period under review, the BBC broadcast

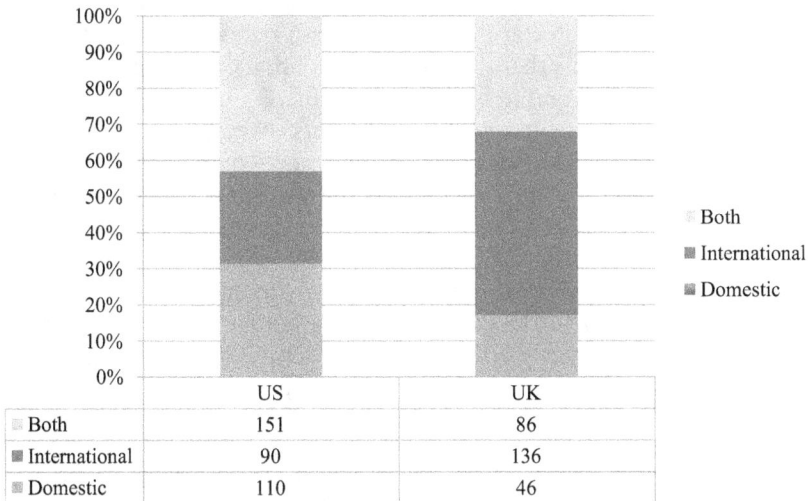

	US	UK
Both	151	86
International	90	136
Domestic	110	46

Figure 5.2 Domestic Versus International Stories of Human Rights & Possibly Human Rights Stories, UK & US

Table 5.2 Human Rights News Stories in the US & UK, 1990–2009

	US		UK	
	# of Stories	% of Possibly HR	# of Stories	% of Possibly HR
1. Contain HR Phrase	48	14%	53	20%
2. HR Story Without Phrase HR	28	8%	45	17%
3. Not HR Story	139	40%	90	34%
4. Close to HR Story	131	37%	79	29%
5. Contain HR Phrase in Text Only	5	1%	1	0%
Total # of Stories	**351**		**268**	

more actual human rights stories-: 53 stories with the phrase human rights against 48 US NBC stories with the phrase and 45 stories that were human rights stories without the phrase compared to 28 NBC stories. Counting these human rights stories with code 5, (stories that include the phrase in text but not audibly) means the BBC broadcast 99 human rights stories or 5.3 percent of the total stories broadcast, which is greater than the 81 stories NBC did, which accounted for only 4 percent of the total stories. This study did not count broadcast minutes of stories, but on average, BBC stories tend to be longer than NBC stories, despite the BBC's shorter broadcast lengths, because of the lack of commercials during the BBC broadcast and the lower average number of total stories per broadcast. So a greater number of human rights stories on the BBC most likely also means that there were more broadcast minutes spent on human rights stories on the BBC than on NBC.

The author had expected more human rights coverage in the UK than in the US for every year, but again, the results more complex than "more in the UK, less in the US." Table 5.3 shows the number of human rights stories annually broken down by domestic, international, and combination.

The UK does have more human rights stories overall, and it does have at least one human rights story in every week examined, while the US has two weeks, in 2001 and 2003, that have no human rights stories at all. Despite this larger number of stories, however, fully half the years have the US broadcasting more human rights stories than the UK, and two additional years tied with the same number of stories in both countries. Figure 5.3 compares both countries' human rights stories by year, showing that the UK has many more stories than the US in several years.

Figure 5.4 shows these human rights stories (codes 1, 2, and 5) for both countries, again divided by domestic versus foreign stories. The

Table 5.3 Human Rights Stories in the US & UK by Year (codes 1, 2, & 5)

Year	Human Rights Stories- US				Human Rights Stories- UK			
	Domestic	International	Both	Total	Domestic	International	Both	Total
1990		2	1	3		1	2	3
1991		3		3	1	1	5	7
1992	1	3		4		5	1	6
1993		1	7	8		3		3
1994			1	1		2		2
1995	1	1	3	4	1	8	1	10
1996	1	2	1	4		2		2
1997			9	9		3	2	5
1998			7	7		3	1	4
1999		3	1	4	1	2		3
2000	2	2		4	1	1	1	3
2001				0			3	3
2002	2		1	3	2	2		4
2003				0	4	2	4	10
2004			7	7	1	4	5	10
2005	2	1	2	5		3	1	4
2006	4	1	1	6	4			4
2007		1		1		1		1
2008		1	3	4	1	4	7	12
2009	4			4	1	2		3
Total	16	21	44	81	17	49	33	99

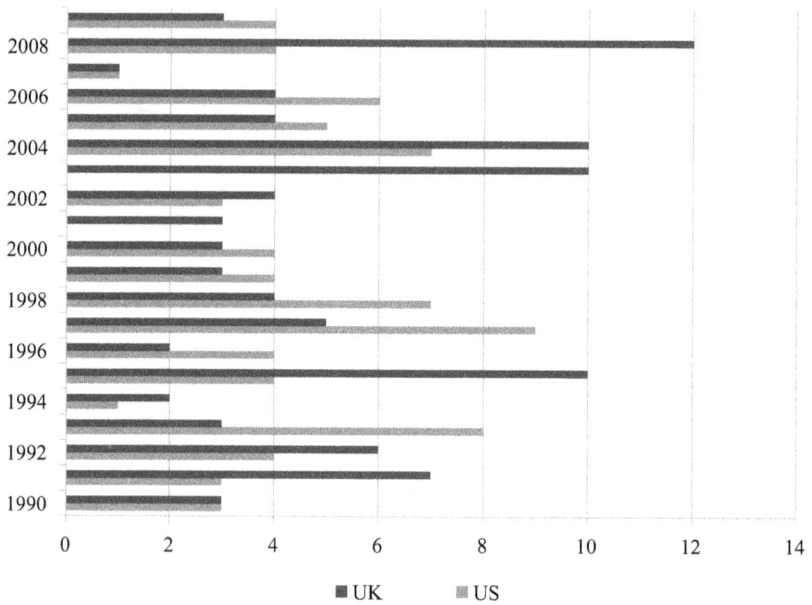

Figure 5.3 Human Rights Stories in the US & UK by Year (1, 2, & 5)

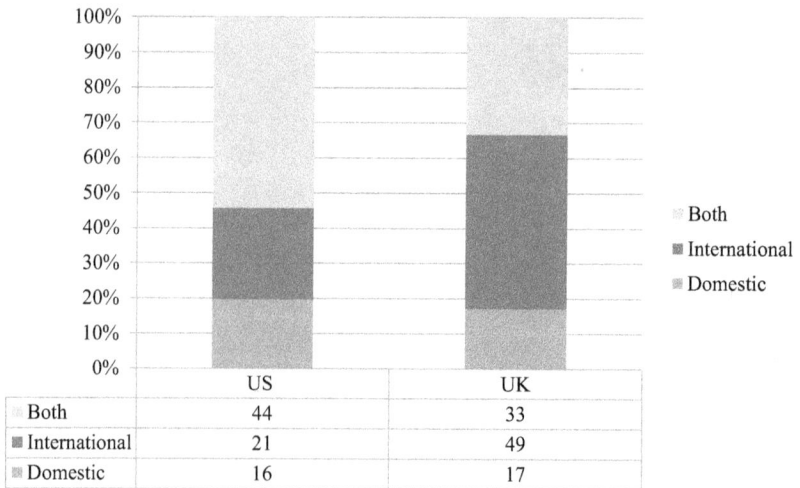

	US	UK
Both	44	33
International	21	49
Domestic	16	17

Figure 5.4 Domestic Versus International Stories Human Rights Stories (codes 1, 2, & 5)

BBC's percentages of domestic and foreign stories were essentially stable at the levels for the possibly human rights analysis in Figure 5.2, but the NBC domestic stories percentages again dropped, from 31 percent to

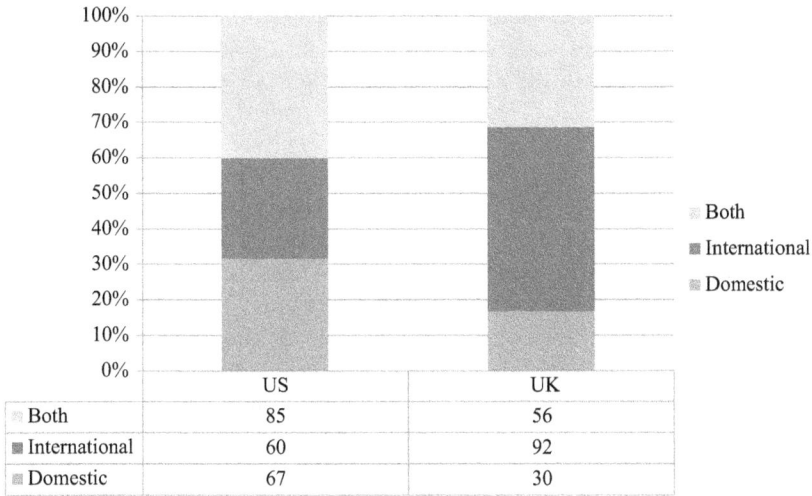

	US	UK
Both	85	56
International	60	92
Domestic	67	30

Figure 5.5 Domestic Versus International Stories: Human Rights Stories and Almost Human Rights Stories (codes 1, 2, 5, & 4)

20 percent. The British human rights stories included five stories about the Human Rights Act of 1998 (HRA), namely two stories on April 11, 2008, on a court ruling on soldiers' human rights under HRA and stories on June 25, 26, and 28 in 2006 on Conservative government's clashes over trying to get rid of the HRA. There is no comparable domestic human rights legislation in the US system and no similarly named initiatives at the federal level in the US, which could contribute to the lack of domestic human rights coverage.[3]

If code 4 stories are considered, as shown in Figure 5.5, the BBC percentages for domestic versus international stories stay essentially the same, while the NBC percentages shift back in the direction of domestic stories from 20 percent to 32 percent. In fact, if the code 4 stories are added to the human rights stories (codes 1, 2, and 5), the percentage of total stories more than doubles for the US from 4 percent to 10.5 percent of total stories. The percentage of total stories goes up for the UK as well, but not by as much—from 5.3 percent to 9.5 percent. This indicates that, more so than in the UK, there are several stories—particularly domestic ones—that are close to human rights stories but are framed differently for the US audience.

Non-Human Rights in the US

These results are consistent with the general US approach to the human rights framework. In the US, human rights are often thought of as a foreign affair; similar events and issues in the US itself are usually covered using a different frame, such as civil rights. To examine this phenomenon further, all US stories were coded for whether or not they included the phrase "right" (not in the context of left, right, or politically conservative). Of the 2,020 NBC stories that were viewed, 68 stories (3.4 percent) included the word right, while there were only 49 that included the phrase human rights (2.4 percent). Of those 68, 28 were not deemed to be even possibly human rights stories. These 28 included two stories on gun rights, five stories on abortion rights, six stories on Medicare or patient's rights, and three stories on the right to die. These stories are all domestic movements that have explicitly framed their issues using rights language, largely without reference to or relation with international human rights frameworks. There were also five stories that mentioned civil rights or constitutional rights issues without enough information to merit being coded "possibly human rights stories." Looking at the remaining 40 stories that were coded as possibly human rights stories, eight were human rights stories—seven contained the phrase and one on November 17, 1993, about the South African constitution that "gives blacks the right to vote for the first time," was coded a human rights story even though it did not use the phrase "human right"). Nine stories were coded as not human rights stories, of which five contained the phrase "civil right" or rights. The remaining 23 stories, those that were close to human rights stories but lacked either sufficient description or sufficient framing to be coded a human rights story, were most illustrative. These stories were not framed as human rights but were very close. Nine stories included the phrase civil rights explicitly, and seven additional stories covered topics that are typically considered civil liberties or constitutional rights, such as "the right to burn the flag," "the right to free speech," and "privacy rights."[4] Many if not most of these stories could have been reframed with minimal changes to be human rights stories but were not.

Contents of the Human Rights Stories

Having established the number of human rights stories broadcast in the US and UK in the period under review, it is time to examine those stories themselves. What human rights information could audiences viewing those 81 US and 99 UK stories obtain? The answer in both countries is not very much. The small number of human rights stories is compounded by the lack of information in most of the stories, and that is true in both countries, though more so in the US than in the UK. First, the type of story these human rights stories are sheds light on the amount of information that could possibly be transmitted. A short Video Over Sound On Tape (VOSOT) has less detail and information in it than a longer full package but more than a teaser before a program break, and live two-ways are often used for further analysis from the reporter as a way to follow up on a story. In addition to the amount of information each type of story can convey, story type can also indicate the priority of the story for producers. VOSOTs take fewer resources to produce, while full packages and live two-ways require more substantial planning and commitment. Placement in headline introductions and teasers before program breaks indicate that producers believe the story to be one of the major stories of the day and of sufficient interest to entice viewers to stay with the program. So what types occurred most in the human rights stories? Table 5.4 lists the story type of human rights stories in the US and UK.

Both countries have primarily full packages as the story type, which indicates some dedication of resources and program time to human rights stories. When human rights are covered, they are covered mostly in full-length stories, the most expensive type to produce. If story type is taken as a measure of dedication, then the BBC does edge out NBC. By using more full packages, live two-ways, and fewer VOSOTs they can deliver more details about the stories to their audience than NBC can in short VOSOTs. The BBC also had more human rights stories in their headline introductions than NBC and reiterated more human rights stories at the close of their broadcasts,[5] indicating that the BBC viewed those stories to be of importance and interest to the audience. Three of the seven BBC headline stories were about the 2008 human rights protestors along the Olympic Torch Relay routes in Paris, London, and San Francisco. Although NBC did cover these same stories and even included them in the headline program introductions, NBC did not mention human rights, merely nonspecific "protests."

In evaluating the human rights content of the stories coded as human rights stories, it is useful to look at whether the phrase was used substantively, and descriptively, or simply in a title. In 15 US stories and 11 UK stories, the only usage of the phrase human rights is in the official or unofficial title of a person, place, or group, such as "Tom Malinowski, Human Rights Watch," "human rights lawyers," or "human rights

Table 5.4 Story Type of Human Rights Stories (codes 1, 2, & 5)

Story Type	US	UK
VOSOT	11	5
Full Package	62	72
Live Two-Way	3	5
Headline/Intro	3	8
Restatement at End	0	7
Teaser Before Break	0	1
Commentary	2	0
Total	81	98

activists." That means that in 18.5 percent of the human rights stories for the US and 11 percent of those in the UK, the phrase that triggered the classification of the story as a human rights story at all was only used in a person, place, or group's title. To put it more starkly, consider these numbers as the percentage out of the total of stories with the phrase human rights audibly or in text (codes 1 and 5). That brings the number up to 28 percent for the US and 20 percent for the UK. Thus almost one-third and one-fifth of human rights stories are only so classified because of the inclusion of an official or unofficial title!

But a story could theoretically include the phrase human rights with either a lot, some, or no description of human rights issue; it could also theoretically omit the phrase human rights but still include a lot of human rights information, so the human rights stories were analyzed to see to what extent they could inform the audience. To put it another way: To what extent could these stories form the basis for a substantive discussion of human rights? Stories were coded for what amount of human rights detail, description, and focus they contained. Most of the stories coded as human rights stories were lacking in description or examples of human rights; this held true across both countries, although again more markedly for the US. Figure 5.6 breaks down the US and UK human rights stories by how much human rights description they included.

Only 16 of the 81 US human rights stories (20 percent of the total human rights stories) that were coded as human rights stories actually had clear descriptions or detailed illustrations of human rights concepts, while 22 stories (27 percent) had no description, examples, or

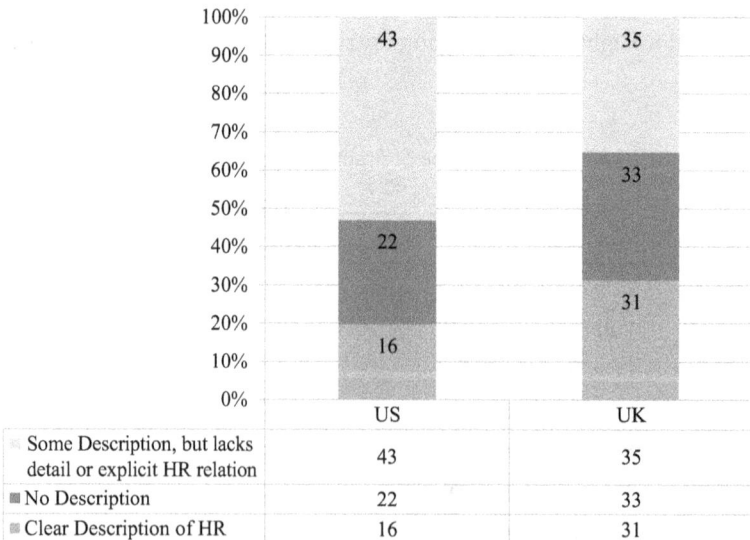

	US	UK
Some Description, but lacks detail or explicit HR relation	43	35
■ No Description	22	33
■ Clear Description of HR	16	31

Figure 5.6 Human Rights Description in Human Rights Stories (codes 1, 2, & 5)

illustrations of human rights issues. The UK had a more even divide, but still only 31 stories (31 percent) had clear definitions or illustrations while 33 stories (33 percent) had no description or examples. Whether or not human rights were the primary focus of the story showed more of a sharp distinction between NBC and the BBC. Most of the NBC stories coded as human rights stories did not include human rights as the primary focus or frame of the story but most of the BBC human rights stories did. Figure 5.7 shows the human rights focus of the human rights stories. Sixty-two of the BBC human rights stories (63 percent) had human rights as the primary focus of the story, while only 30 of the NBC stories (37 percent) did.

Interestingly, both the US and UK human rights stories included several stories (15 and 12, respectively) whose summaries would not have included human rights at all. These stories included fleeting references to "China's human rights record" in stories about protests or economic summits,[6] as well as stories that included a generic statement of support for human rights as part of an unrelated story.[7] Based on this data, it can be concluded that many of those few stories that are coded as being human rights stories have little information about human rights and, in the US, do not for the most part focus on human rights directly.

Human rights is a large framework, encompassing many different issues, so the human rights stories were coded for what kind of human right they covered, as shown in Table 5.5 and Figures 5.8 and 5.9.

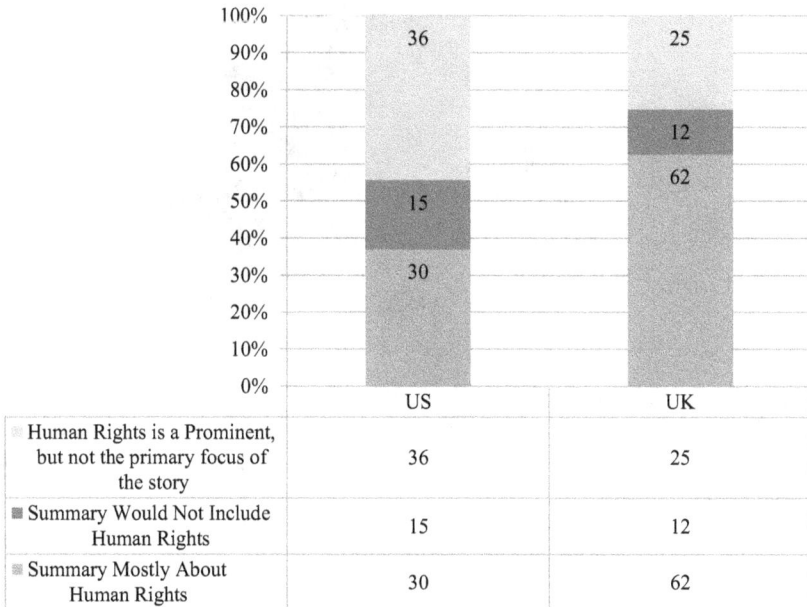

	US	UK
Human Rights is a Prominent, but not the primary focus of the story	36	25
▪ Summary Would Not Include Human Rights	15	12
▪ Summary Mostly About Human Rights	30	62

Figure 5.7 Human Rights Focus in Human Rights Stories (codes 1, 2, & 5)

Table 5.5 Human Rights Categories of Human Rights Stories (codes 1, 2, & 5)

Categories of Human Rights	US	UK
1. Racial Discrimination	3	1
2. Civil & Political Rights	22	27
4. Women's Rights	1	1
5. Torture and Other Cruel, Inhuman, or Degrading Treatment or Punishment	11	6
6. Children's Rights	0	2
9. Disabled Persons	0	1
10. Abolition of Death Penalty	0	1
11. Refugees & Asylees	4	8
12. Humanitarian Law, Laws of War, Crimes Against Humanity, War Crimes Tribunals	11	18
13. Genocide	2	2
15. Slavery	1	0
17. GLBTQ	1	0
18. Not Applicable/Not Specified/Unclear	25	32

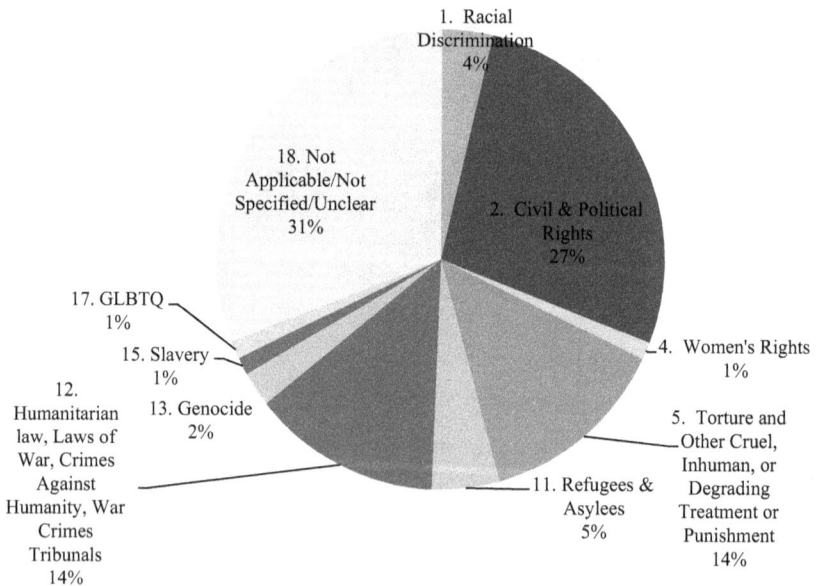

Figure 5.8 US Human Rights Stories Categories

1. Racial
Discrimination
1%

4. Women's
Rights
1%

18. Not
Applicable/Not
Specified/Unclear
33%

2. Civil & Political
Rights
27%

5. Torture
and Other
Cruel,
Inhuman, or
Degrading
Treatment
or
Punishment
6%

13. Genocide
2%

12. Humanitarian
law, Laws of War,
Crimes Against
Humanity, War
Crimes Tribunals
18%

6. Children's Rights
2%

9.
Disable
d
Persons
1%

10. Abolition of
Death Penalty
8%   1%

11. Refugees &
Asylees

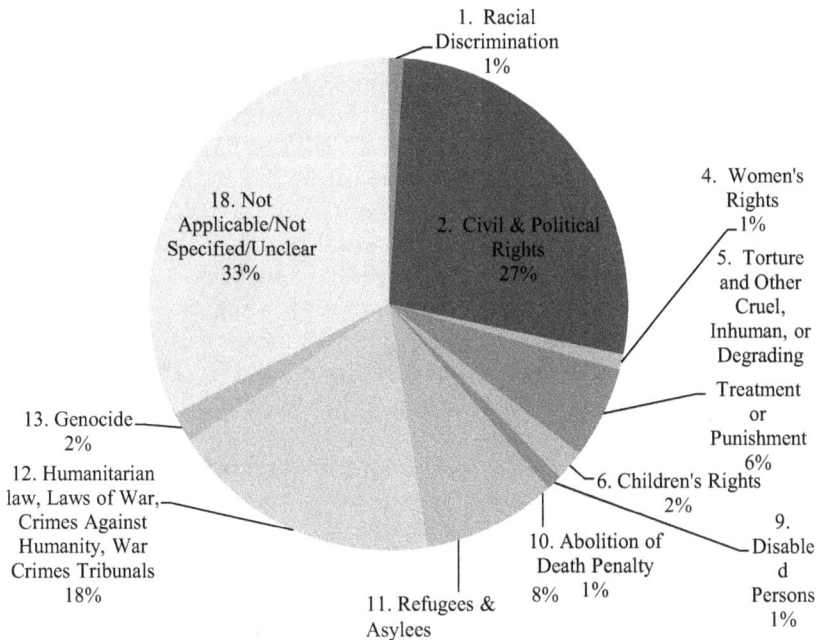

Figure 5.9 UK Human Rights Stories Categories

In both countries, the largest category is "18, Not Applicable/Not Specified/Unclear"—33 percent of British stories and 31 percent of American stories. That means that the plurality of both countries' human rights stories did not contain enough information to categorize the story as covering a specific human rights issue. The largest amount of stories that could be categorized as a specific human rights issue, Civil and Political Rights, was the same for both countries at 27 percent. This is in line with the long history of US focus on civil and political rights, as opposed to other types of human rights, such as economic, social, and cultural rights. It is interesting to note the same apparent bias toward civil and political rights in the British stories as in the American ones, despite the wider acceptance of economic, social, and cultural human rights by the British state.

The British stories did, however, cover a wider variety of rights categories than the US ones did, with children's rights, the rights of the disabled, and the abolition of the death penalty all receiving coverage as human rights in the UK. The category results are perhaps more revealing in what did not show up at all. From the coding list, which is based on all of the international human rights treaties and prominent nontreaty norms, several categories did not have even one story: Economic, Social, and Cultural Rights; Rights of Migrant Workers/Families; Protection Against

Enforced Disappearance; and Rights of the Elderly. Many of these issues were covered in stories that were viewed in both countries, but those stories did not cover the issues as human rights stories; they were framed in other ways, and so the stories were not coded as human rights stories. To that end, several of the issues whose categories did appear in human rights stories (Racial Discrimination and Civil and Political Rights stand out particularly) were also covered extensively in non-human rights stories, just not as human rights issues. American and British television news may be more open to human rights issues than this analysis is showing, but neither explicitly connects those issues to human rights.

The location of the human rights stories reveals important information about their content. Table 13 lists the top-12 locations and their Political Terror Scale, CIRI Physical Integrity Rights, and CIRI Empowerment Rights averages from 1990–2009 for both NBC and BBC human rights stories.

It is not surprising that the most frequent location for each country is the home country, as television news tends to cover stories involving its home country as a first priority. Consistent with the findings of Chapter 3's human rights phrase search, neither the US nor the UK features the worst human rights offenders (as measured by PTS, CIRI Physical Integrity rights, and CIRI Empowerment Rights averages) in their human rights stories. Also consistent with Chapter 3's findings, China is the most common location of human rights stories for both countries after the home country, even though it has far from the worst human rights record as ranked by PTS. China's 20-year average CIRI scores are low, yet there are still 12 countries with worse Physical Integrity averages than China from 1990–2009 and there are 4 countries with worse New Empowerment averages. The lists of locations covered by the BBC and NBC do overlap quite a bit. Only three countries covered by the US were not on the UK list at all (Tibet, North Korea, and Mexico had one story each). Based on these results, the BBC appears to cover a wider variety of countries in human rights stories than NBC does. Not only does it have more human rights stories covering more countries than NBC, but it is also both less home country and China obsessed than NBC. The US and China account for 70 percent of NBC's human rights story locations, while the UK and China account for only 46 percent of the BBC's human rights story locations. The top-three locations for human rights stories in the US, the US, China, and Iraq, represent 79 percent of the US human rights story locations, while the top three in the UK, the UK, China, and the US, make up only 59 percent of the UK human rights story locations.

One prominent frame found in some of the human rights stories turned out to be the Global War on Terror (GWOT), which was instituted after 2001. This was unsurprisingly more marked in the US case, as the concept originated in the US, but it is also very present in the UK stories, as shown in Table 5.7.

Table 5.6 Locations of Human Rights Stories (codes 1, 2, & 5)

Locations of Human Rights Stories, US	PTS Average, 1990–2009	CIRI Physical Integrity Rights Index, Average 1990–2009 (0–8)	CIRI New Empowerment (0–14)	Locations of Human Rights Stories, UK	PTS Average, 1990–2009	CIRI Physical Integrity Rights Index, Average 1990–2009 (0–8)	CIRI New Empowerment (0–14)
US	61 1.85	6.15	12.00	UK	42 1.6	6.55	12.20
PRC	31 3.83	1.6	0.80	PRC	24 3.83	1.6	0.80
Iraq	12 4.93	0.61	1	US	19 1.85	6.15	12.00
Bosnia	4 3	6.44	7.22	Iraq	17 4.93	0.61	1
Russia/USSR	4 3.89	2.6	4.85	Rwanda	7 3.93	2.25	5.70
South Africa	4 3.6	3.35	10.50	Zaire/DRC	5 4.6	1.00	3.10
Chechnya	3 –	–	–	Israel & Palestine	4 4.1	2.9 (Israel)	7.6 (Israel)
Lithuania	2 1.11	7.06	11.5	Russia/USSR	4 3.89	2.6	4.85
France	1 1.63	6.75	12.7	Bosnia	3 3	6.44	7.22
Israel & Palestine	1 4.1	2.9 (Israel)	7.6 (Israel)	Chechnya	2 –	–	–
Kosovo	1 2	6	9	Italy	2 1.7	6.55	12.75
Mexico	1 3.3	2.1	10.25	Nigeria	2 3.65	2.3	4.3
North Korea	1 4.5	0.2	0.1	Serbia	2 2	3.4	5.86
Rwanda	1 3.93	2.25	5.70	South Africa	2 3.6	3.35	10.50
Serbia	1 2	3.4	5.86	Bulgaria	1 2.5	4.95	9.35
Tibet	1 –	–	–	Croatia	1 2.25	5.83	9

(Continued)

Table 5.6 (Continued)

Locations of Human Rights Stories, US	PTS Average, 1990–2009	CIRI Physical Integrity Rights Index, Average 1990–2009 (0–8)	CIRI New Empowerment (0–14)
Turkey	1 3.83	1.85	6
UK	1 1.6	6.55	12.20
Zaire/DRC	1 4.6	1.00	3.10
Total	**132**		

Locations of Human Rights Stories, UK	PTS Average, 1990–2009	CIRI Physical Integrity Rights Index, Average 1990–2009 (0–8)	CIRI New Empowerment (0–14)
France	1 1.63	6.75	12.7
Ireland	1 1.05	7.4	12.8
Kenya	1 3.48	3.05	4.95
Lithuania	1 1.11	7.06	11.5
Turkey	1 3.83	1.85	6
Zimbabwe	1 3.05	3.2	5.25
Total	**143**		

Stories were coded for up to three locations that were added together, which is why the totals for locations (132 for the US and 143 for the UK) are greater than the number of human rights stories (81 and 99 respectively). Russia and the USSR were collapsed into one category to account for the transition that occurred during the time period under study.

Table 5.7 Global War on Terror in Human Rights Stories (codes 1, 2, & 5)[8]

Year	US			UK		
	Total HR Stories	*GWOT HR Stories*	*GWOT % of Year's HR Stories*	*Total HR Stories*	*GWOT HR Stories*	*GWOT % of Year's HR Stories*
2002	3	3	100%	4	1	25%
2003	0			10	2	20%
2004	7	6	86%	10	9	90%
2005	5	5	100%	4	3	75%
2006	6	5	83%	4	1	25%
2007	1			1		
2008	4			12		
2009	4	4	100%	3	3	100%
Total	30	23	77%	48	19	40%

In every year that the GWOT frame occurred in US human rights stories, it represented the overwhelming majority of stories for that year, amounting to 100 percent of the coverage in 2002, 2005, and 2009; it represented a majority of UK human rights stories in only three years (2004, 2005, and 2009). Once the GWOT concept gained ground in 2001, it accounted for 23 of the 30 human rights stories from 2002 to 2009, or 77 percent in the US. The UK GWOT human rights stories are a smaller number and a smaller share of the total stories from 2002–2009: 19 stories or 40 percent of the human rights coverage in the period were about the GWOT. Thus, though the issue was an important part of human rights coverage, it was not the only part. If the GWOT frame is considered as a share of the human rights stories from 1990–2009, 28 percent, or almost one-third, of US human rights stories use the GWOT frame, while only 19 percent of the UK human rights stories do.

Case Studies

The numbers tell an important part of the story about how the US and UK cover human rights, but they cannot tell the whole story. For that, coverage of individual human rights issues is needed. Four case studies have been selected from the stories covered during the week: conflict in the Balkans (this case spans several years), the expulsion of Rwandan refugees from Zaire in 1995, prisoner abuse in Iraq in 2004, and the protests leading up to the Beijing Olympics in 2008. All coverage of these stories from the weeks under study, whether it was coded as possibly human rights, human rights, or not, was reviewed, and all stories that were related to these issues were collected and analyzed together.

Conflict in the Balkans: The Breakup of Yugoslavia

The breakup of Yugoslavia in the 1990s was a long, bloody process that one could argue has still not finished as of today.9 It spawned several wars and resulted in the creation of at least six independent countries. Naturally, ongoing violent conflict within eight hundred miles would make it high on the newsworthiness scale for the British news media as a "near neighbor," and the BBC covered the breakup of Yugoslavia and the ensuing conflicts as major stories. In the weeks under review, it was a major story in the UK in six years: 1991–1996. It was only a major story in the US in 1991 and 1992.[10] As shown in Table 5.8, the BBC had more coverage of the conflicts in the Balkans than NBC did, both in total and in every week under consideration.

The difference can be addressed partly by geography, the UK is much closer to the Balkans and therefore would be more interested, and partly by active military presence, the UK had troops on the ground by 1992. But neither of these factors can fully explain the great discrepancy in coverage of the conflicts. For that, alternative priorities must be the answer. NBC was more interested in covering other stories during these weeks than they were the conflicts in the Balkans. In the week under review for 1992, for example, the US had troops on the ground launching a big movement to the interior of Somalia. This issue received much more coverage than the Balkans did, both in that year and in total: 24 Somalia stories in 1992 against 18 total US Balkans conflict-related stories. In 1993, NBC had more stories on Michael Jackson's temporary disappearance (2) than on the Balkans (1), although in fairness, the BBC had three Jackson disappearance stories in that week.

Table 5.8 Number of Stories on the Balkans Conflicts

	US	UK
1991	4	13
1992	8	24
1993	1	5
1994	1	11
1995	2	5
1996	2	3
Total	18	61

Rwandan Refugees Expelled from Zaire–1995

In August 1995, Zaire decided to evict the Rwandan refugees who had fled the genocide and civil war in Rwanda in 1994. Despite no troops from either home country being involved and a location that excludes the region from being the near neighbor of either country, this issue also received numerically more and more extensive coverage in the UK than in the US. NBC covered the story on one day, August 22, 1995, mentioning it as part of the program introduction, in a teaser before a commercial break, and as a full-package story. The BBC, in contrast, reported the issue in eight stories, broadcasting at least one each day from August 21–26, 1995. This included a full-package story every day of August 22–26, as well as inclusion in the headline program introduction and the main news restatement on August 22. The content of the BBC stories was also much more substantive and human rights focused than the NBC story, explicitly exploring and explaining issues such as forced repatriation, the possibility of prosecution for participation in the genocide, and the dire conditions in the refugee camps and forced return process. More stories and longer more detailed stories mean that the Rwandan refugee crisis in Zaire received much more coverage on the BBC than on NBC during that week.

Abu Ghraib and Iraqi Prisoner Abuse–2004

The prisoner abuse scandal in Iraq that broke in the spring of 2004 provides an excellent natural experiment for comparing human rights coverage between the US and the UK, since the same conditions for high-level newsworthiness would be triggered in both countries. Both countries had troops on the ground who were allegedly involved in abusing Iraqi prisoners, and there were gruesome pictures in abundance to feed the visual nature of the medium. The abuse scandal dominated the week's news in both countries and also represented all of the human rights stories for both countries (10 BBC, 7 NBC), as well as most of the near-human rights stories in both countries (all 11 BBC code 4 stories from 2004 and 13 out of the 15 NBC code 4 stories). At 35, there were three more stories about the abuse scandal aired in the UK than the 32 aired in the US. Both British and American television news devoted significant program time and resources to this issue, with 23 full-package stories and 6 headline introductions in the US and 19 full-package stories, 5 live two-ways, and 5 headline introduction in the UK.

Coverage on this issue did overlap significantly across the two countries. Both the BBC and NBC repeatedly showed the actual photographs of detained Iraqis being abused, used iterations of the phrase "allegations of abuse," and avoided the word torture in their reporting. Both countries pursued additional angles to the story with some overlap; for example, both investigated the potential political fallout of the revelations.

The BBC, however, did double duty on covering political fallout, with stories about the Blair administration's response, as well as the American response, possible trials, and the question of whether or not Secretary Rumsfeld should or would resign. NBC covered the American fallout, focusing particularly on hearings and committee meetings on Capitol Hill, but it did not have any stories on the UK's response to allegations of abuse. Media was a frame in common between the US and UK coverage of the abuse, though much more was utilized in the UK than in the US. While NBC broadcast two stories on the media on May 12, one on the advisability of broadcasting the photos and giving potentially too much coverage to the abuse and one on the reactions to the abuse in the media of the Arab world, the BBC was much more preoccupied with media as a frame, largely because of the accusations that abuse photos published by the *Daily Mirror* had been faked. The question of the authenticity of the photos and whether or not the *Mirror's* editor, Piers Morgan, would be sacked represent a significant amount of the BBC coverage of the abuse scandal in the week under review, and it is completely uncovered by NBC in this week. The BBC also pursued troop morale and the impact on the troops as an angle, including several stories from Basra and stories covering the reaction to the abuse by cleric Muqtada al-Sadr; the NBC coverage was largely focused in the US and did not pursue troop morale as a frame for follow-up stories. Overall, in both countries during this week, the abuse scandal was extensively covered and often in human rights terms.

Olympic Torch Relay and Protests–2008

In the lead-up to the Beijing Summer Olympics in 2008, the Olympic flame was paraded from Athens through many world capitals on its way to Beijing, carrying on the tradition that began in 1936. This relay was different, however, because it was besieged by human rights protestors at several of its European stops and its only North American stop. The protests along the relay were captured in this study from April 5–12, 2008, which, not coincidentally, also had the highest number of human rights stories for either country with the UK's 12 human rights stories for the week. The BBC again had more stories on this issue, more in-depth stories on this issue, and more of its stories on this issue framed with human rights as the primary lens of the story. The BBC covered the Olympics in 15 stories, while NBC had only 10 stories, which is partly inflated by the inclusion of three segments (a headline intro, teaser before commercial, and full package) of Ann Curry's interview with the Dalai Lama, which only mentioned the protests and relay in passing. The NBC stories were also mostly shorter types—only three were full packages and two were VOSOTs, while three were part of program introductions and two were teasers before commercial breaks. The BBC stories were predominantly substantial story types, with six full packages, three live two-ways, only one VOSOT, four inclusions in program introductions, and one in the restatement at the end of the broadcast. The BBC pursued more angles to the story than NBC did, broadcasting segments on how the relay was being covered in China and how the IOC was reacting to the protests and concerns over China's human rights record. NBC was silent on these issues and covered the story as straight reports from the scenes of the protests and with an interview with the Dalai Lama. NBC's coverage was primarily about the protests: showing some clashes between protestors and police but mostly the measures being taken to prevent interference with the relay in San Francisco. There was very little NBC coverage of what the protestors were actually protesting, only a few vague references to anti-China protests without elaboration or description. The BBC, on the other hand, had more information about what protestors were protesting, including multiple references to "violence in Tibet" and "torture, lack of human rights." The British stories included more footage of the relay itself than the American stories did, both in London and in San Francisco, and the attempts at stopping it, including several closeup shots of police and guards forcefully stopping protestors. Clashes were largely omitted from the NBC coverage, with most of the footage used being aerial shots from a great distance. The NBC stories only had one shot of pro-Chinese relay attenders, while the BBC stories included several, with comments from them about their pride in China hosting the Olympics. Overall, the BBC devoted more program minutes and more production resources to covering the Olympic Torch Relay and protests than NBC did and covered it in a more detailed and more human rights–focused way.

Twenty Years' Comparison Conclusion

After viewing one week of television news footage from the US and UK from 1990–2009, several conclusions can be drawn. There was overall very little coverage of human rights in either media system and no significant trend over time to either increasing or decreasing human rights coverage. The UK had more human rights coverage overall, though not by as much as might have been expected. There was, however, a decided advantage to the UK in terms of depth of coverage and human rights framing. Those stories that were covered as human rights stories in British television news were more likely to be both detailed and explicitly framed in human rights terms than American television news stories on human rights. Overall, however, in both media systems, arguments for a CNN Effect on human rights cannot be supported. There is simply too little coverage. The violations are not being televised.

Notes

1 See Appendix I: Methodology for an explanation of the week selection and coding scheme.
2 For further detail, please see Appendix 1.

3 See Chapter 4 for a discussion of how New York City's Human Rights Commission increases print news coverage of human rights in the US.

4 *NBC Evening News*, March 21, 1994, August 22, 2002, and April 21, 2009.

5 The Restatement at the end of the break is not exactly comparable between the BBC and NBC, as the BBC tended to do it more frequently in general with lots of different stories in the period under study, while NBC tended to have a simple good-night without any restatement of any stories, human rights or not. It is included in the data because, for different parts of the weeks under review, both programs did use substantive restatements.

6 *NBC Evening News* April 8, 2008, April 9, 2008, and November 20, 1993. *BBC 9 o'clock News* November 19, 1993 and November 20, 1993.

7 *NBC Evening News* August 19, 2002 and August 20, 2002. *BBC 9 o'clock News* September 4, 1991 and April 22, 2009.

8 Years with no GWOT stories have been blacked out for clarity.

9 The partial recognition of Kosovo as an independent state participating in several international institutions, but not as a full member in the UN, is evidence that the process has not completely finished yet.

10 The years1995 and 1996 both had major stories in the US that occurred in the Balkans: the memorials of American diplomats who died in Bosnia in 1995 and the plane crash and death of Commerce Secretary Ron Brown and 31 other Americans in 1996. Both of these stories related only to the deaths of the Americans and the memorials for them, and neither included any information about the conflicts in the Balkans, so they are not included in the analysis here.

Bibliography

Canino, G. J., & Huston, A. C. (1986). A content analyses of prime-time TV and radio news in Puerto Rico. *Journalism Quarterly*, *63*(1), 150–154.

Cingranelli, D. L., Richards, D. L., & Clay, K. C. (2014). *The CIRI Human Rights Dataset*. Version 2014.04.14. Retrieved February 20, 2015 from http://www.humanrightsdata.com.

Gibney, M., Cornett, L., Wood, R., & Haschke, P., *Political Terror Scale 1976–2012*. Retrieved February 20, 2015 from the Political Terror Scale website: http://www.politicalterrorscale.org/

6 Case Studies
China, Somalia, and Sudan

Chapter 3 looked at the universe of stories that included the phrase human rights and found an extremely limited number of stories. Chapters 4 and 5 used cross-national comparison of the US and UK and expanded the search parameters to months and weeks where news coverage would be reasonably expected to include human rights stories to see if there were any human rights stories that did not use the phrase human rights in the text of the story. All three chapters so far have found so little human rights coverage on television news that a CNN Effect argument cannot be sustained. Human rights violations are simply not televised in either the US or the UK. Yet there is still one more path to pursue. Inspired by the case study methodology in Caliendo, Gibney, & Payne (1999), this chapter flips the previous chapters' approach by examining the total television news coverage of three countries with known human rights concerns to see how these countries are covered and what share of the media coverage that each country receives involves human rights issues. China, Somalia, and Sudan were selected as case studies because they all have widely known human rights issues. Table 6.1 lists the Political Terror Scale (PTS) averages, CIRI Physical Integrity Index Averages, and CIRI New Empowerment Index for the three case studies from 1990–2009.

All three of these countries have widely known and documented human rights concerns, yet the amount their human rights issues that have been covered on US television news has varied significantly. Table 3.5 lists China as the most frequently featured non-US country in human rights stories with 221 mentions, while Sudan is the eleventh most frequently reported on location in human rights stories, with 19 stories, and Somalia only had 2 mentions in stories that contain the phrase human rights from 1990–2009. So while Chapter 3 has explored the amount of human rights stories that cover these countries, Chapter 6 looks at the other side of the same picture: What portion of these countries' total television news coverage actually deals with human rights? The results here are consistent with the earlier analyses in this book. There is very little overall coverage of human rights issues and very little human rights information—far too little to support arguments for the CNN Effect, and

Table 6.1 Political Terror Scale, CIRI Physical Integrity, and CIRI New
Empowerment Averages, 1990–2009

Country	PTS Average, 1990–2009 (1–5)	CIRI Physical Integrity Rights Index, 1990–2009 (0–8)	CIRI New Empowerment Index, 1990–2009 (0–14)
China	3.8	1.6	0.8
Somalia	4.3	3	5
Sudan	4.8	0.6	0.65

yet more evidence that the violations will not be televised much at all and certainly not explicitly as human rights issues.

China: Espionage, Trade, and Pandas

As has already been shown, China is the most frequently mentioned non-US country when it comes to television news coverage of human rights, but most of that coverage is hollow—not a lot of human rights information or substance for the frequency of coverage. China receives a steadily high level of television news coverage in the US, and this is not surprising. China is a nuclear power with geostrategic importance and a large population representing a big chunk of the world's economy. These reasons reinforce another reason for the high level of coverage of China: news production capacity. Because China is seen to be important and newsworthy, news outlets have continued to maintain multiple outposts in China, even as they have closed or consolidated their overseas operations in other areas of the world, which makes it easier to cover China, since the news organizations have boots (and cameras) on the ground already. Examining 20 years of television news coverage of China, with an initial search yield of 6,880 stories, is beyond the scope of this project, so 1999–2002 were selected as the four consecutive years with the highest number of stories returned from the initial search. In total, 502 stories were coded to see what issues were covered and what share of the television news coverage on China is actually about human rights.

The purpose of using China for the case study approach here was twofold: to see what percentage of China news is devoted to human rights and to discover human rights stories that might have been missed by performing the narrower search for the phrase human rights. The case study approach reveals that for China, the phrase search approach was very accurate: only two stories were uncovered that did not include the phrase human rights but were actually human rights stories. The May 8, 2000, story about human trafficking and the June 5, 2000, story about the international conference following up on the Beijing 1995 Women's conference

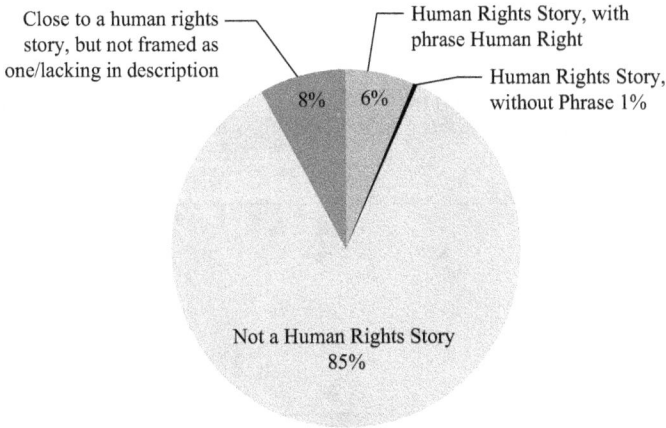

Close to a human rights
story, but not framed as
one/lacking in description

Human Rights Story, with
phrase Human Right

Human Rights Story,
without Phrase 1%

8% 6%

Not a Human Rights Story
85%

Figure 6.1 China Stories About Human Rights, 1999–2002

are the only stories that were sufficiently detailed and descriptive enough to qualify as human rights stories without using the phrase human rights. Figure 6.1 shows the distribution of human rights stories versus non-human rights. Consistent with the other results from this study, there are overall very few stories about human rights. An overwhelming number of stories, 428 or 85 percent, had nothing to do with human rights.

The other purpose for doing a broad case study approach to collecting stories about China was to see what percentage of China stories are actually about human rights. The phrase search conducted in Chapter 3 showed that from 1990–2009, 27 percent of human rights stories featured China, but that said nothing about what the other China stories covered. What percentage of China stories are about human rights? In the phrase search from 1999–2002, 19 percent (32 of 165) of human rights stories featured China, while during the same time period, an average of 7 percent of China stories covered human rights. Table 6.2 displays the number and percentage of China stories that are human rights stories per year, along with the annual PTS average, CIRI Physical Integrity Index, and CIRI New Empowerment Index for the year. The high PTS scores and low CIRI scores indicate that the human rights situation in China is not good, yet television news is not covering China's human rights stories in large amounts, even relative to the amount of other China coverage.

Examining the topics that did get covered in the China stories gives a fuller picture of where human rights ranks in the news agenda for coverage in China. Each story was coded for its primary topic. Table 6.3 displays the topics that had five or more stories from 1999–2002.

This list includes all stories, whether or not they were also human rights stories. The list of most frequent topics holds few surprises. China is a major trading partner of the US that was seeking permanent normal

Table 6.2 Human Rights Stories as a Percentage of all China Stories, 1999–2002

Year	Total Stories	Human Rights Stories	Human Rights Share of Total China Stories	PTS Average (1–5)	CIRI Physical Integrity Rights Index (0–8)	CIRI New Empowerment Index (0–14)
1999	115	8	7%	4	2	1
2000	81	7*	9%	4.5	3	1
2001	198	14	7%	4	2	1
2002	108	5	5%	4	1	1
Total	**502**	**34**				

*Includes the two stories from 2000 that were coded as human rights stories but do not include the phrase human rights.

Table 6.3 Topics of China Stories, 1999–2002

Topic		Number of Stories	Percentage of Total China Stories
1	Spy Plane Incident	82	16.30%
2	Trade/Investment	43	8.60%
3	Sports	26	5.20%
4	Espionage	22	4.40%
5	Pandas	20	4.00%
6	Natural Disaster	17	3.40%
7	Taiwan	15	3.00%
8	Belgrade Bombing	13	2.60%
9	Falun Gong	13	2.60%
10	High-Profile Prisoner	13	2.60%
11	US National Security	13	2.60%
12	Nuclear Weapons	13	2.60%
13	Global War on Terror	11	2.20%
14	Population	11	2.20%
15	High-Level Visit	10	2.00%
16	Immigration/Emigration	9	1.80%
17	Iraq	9	1.80%
18	Plane Crash	8	1.60%
19	AIDS	7	1.40%
20	Tiananmen Square	7	1.40%

Topic		Number of Stories	Percentage of Total China Stories
21	50th Anniversary of China	6	1.20%
22	Agriculture/Fish	5	1.00%
23	Environment	5	1.00%
24	Execution	5	1.00%
25	General Human Rights	5	1.00%
26	US Elections	5	1.00%
Total		393	78.30%

trade relations during the period under review, so the fact that trade and investment is a major topic of China news coverage makes sense. The April 2001 crash of a US spy plane on Chinese soil, subsequent holding of the crew and plane, and reactions after the crew was returned, as well as the investigation of and subsequent arrest of a Chinese-American scientist for leaking nuclear secrets to the Chinese government seem tailor-made for getting the attention of television news producers. The US accidentally bombing the Chinese Embassy in Belgrade garnered a lot of coverage for the same reason.

There is little evidence that human rights are a high priority in television news coverage of China. Human rights are not covered in American television news stories because news producers decide to broadcast stories about other topics, some of which are intrinsically newsworthy, while others are decidedly less so. The five most frequently occurring topics account for 38 percent of the total China stories for this time period and have nothing to do remotely with human rights. The coverage of pandas is telling. The list of topics that received less coverage than panda bears is extensive, including everything except espionage, trade, and sports. From 1999–2002, 20 stories about panda bears were broadcast, either covering conservation efforts in China or the process for several American zoos to lease panda bears from China.

The few explicitly human rights stories in the China news coverage were analyzed in greater detail in Chapter 3, but exploring the almost human rights stories in the China stories reveals further insights about the lack of human rights focus on television news. Table 6.4 shows the topics of possibly human rights stories.

The 502 China stories broadcast from 1999–2002 contained 13 Falun Gong Stories, of which two contained the phrase human rights, while 10 were close-to-human-rights stories. These stories were very close-to-human-rights stories but lacked sufficient detail or human rights framing to qualify as a human rights story, such as the November 11, 1999, story:

Table 6.4 Possible China Human Rights Stories 1999–2002

Topic	Number of Possible Human Rights Stories
Falun Gong	10
Population	6
Tiananmen	5
High-Profile Prisoner	4
Spy Plane incident	2
Religion	2
Immigration/Emigration	2
AIDS	2
Tibet	1
Sports	1
Internet Access	1
High-Level Visit	1
Environment	1
Corruption	1
Anniversary of Mao's Death	1
Total	**40**

"In China, a group of foreign journalists is complaining about harassment by the government. They say that China is pressuring reporters to stop covering an enormous spiritual movement called the Falun Gong."[1] The story hints at religious repression and even press censorship but stops short of providing further detail, description, or an explicit rights claim against the government's actions. Eleven of the 502 China stories were classified as stories about population, of which six were about sex-selective abortions and the preference for male children under the One Child Policy. This topic could easily be framed as a human rights issue generally, and with very minimal changes to the broadcasts, these six stories could easily have been human rights stories, but instead they are simply reported as the way things are without any reference to the idea of human rights as minimal standards for the way things should be. In total, 40 stories were coded as almost human rights but lacking in either detail or human rights framing and so falling short of being full human rights stories. Not only are there very few human rights stories in the case of China, on stories journalists have decided to cover, they do not reach for the human rights frame even when it would easily fit. With such evidence, it is clear to see that human rights violations will not be televised.

Somalia: Starvation, Soldiers, and Pirates on the High Seas

For the entirety of the period 1990–2009, the human rights situation in Somalia was dire. In only two years, 1997 and 1998, the country's average Political Terror Scale (PTS) dipped below four. Yet despite the conditions in the country, it received very little television news coverage. From 1990–2009 there were 512 stories broadcast that included the word Somalia, the majority of which were broadcast in 1992 and 1993. Figure 6.2 shows the number of stories per year that included the word Somalia and Somalia's average Political Terror Scale score per year.

As might be expected by the timing of the large number of stories in 1992 and 1993, the majority of the stories about Somalia cover the famine and UN/military intervention in the famine. Yet even though the PTS score remains high, the average number of stories mentioning Somalia drops precipitously after 1994. Figure 6.3 shows the number of stories for each subject and the percentage of the total stories that subject represents.

Three hundred sixteen stories, or 62 percent of the Somalia stories, were about the famine and military intervention. The only other subjects that come close are the 67 stories that covered so many topics they could not be individually categorized. Piracy also featured prominently as a subject of 5 percent of Somalia stories, accounting for 28 of the 512

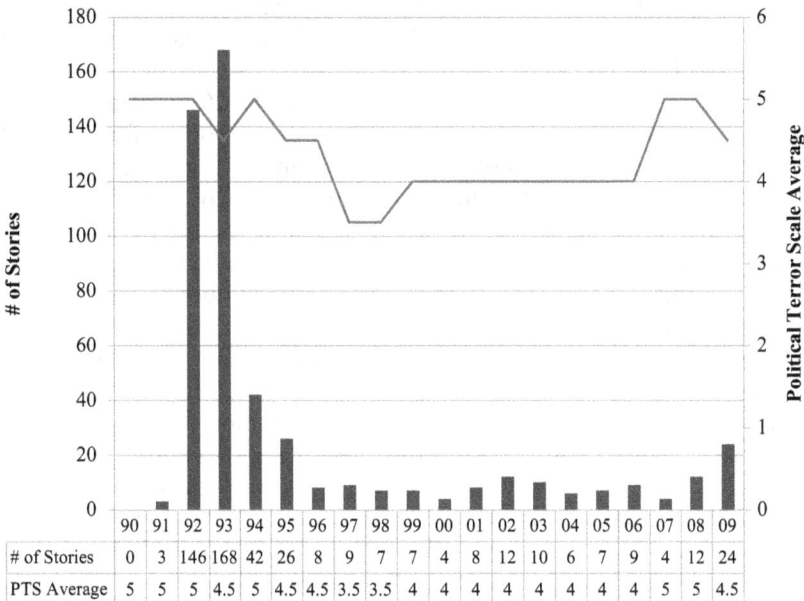

	90	91	92	93	94	95	96	97	98	99	00	01	02	03	04	05	06	07	08	09
# of Stories	0	3	146	168	42	26	8	9	7	7	4	8	12	10	6	7	9	4	12	24
PTS Average	5	5	5	4.5	5	4.5	4.5	3.5	3.5	4	4	4	4	4	4	4	4	5	5	4.5

Figure 6.2 Somalia Stories and PTS Average per Year

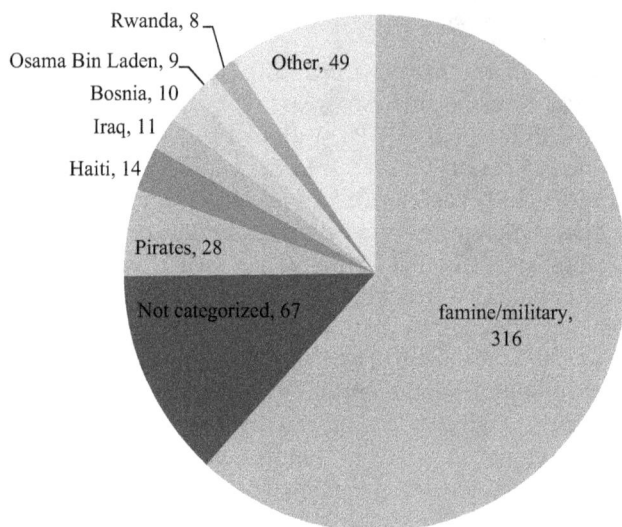

Figure 6.3 Subject of Somalia Stories by Number of Stories

total stories. The bulk of these stories, however, do not focus on Somalia, except occasionally mentioning it as a failed government incapable of stopping piracy off its shores. The stories about piracy are more focused on the ships, international reaction to cases of piracy, and extensive coverage of the hijacking of the ship *Maersk Alabama*, whose captain was rescued by US Navy Seals.

Examining the coverage of Somalia from 1990–2009 yields not just a small number of news stories but also an extremely small number of human rights stories. In a country where famine and significant extrajudicial violence threaten the rights of so many every day, 89 percent (455) of the stories including the word Somalia were definitely not human rights stories. Only two of the 512 Somalia stories included the phrase human rights, and neither of them was actually about Somalia! The December 9, 1993, story about the release of the annual human rights report from Human Rights Watch was primarily about Bosnia, with only one brief reference to "the madness and murder of Somalia," while the September 11, 1994, story covered Haiti and mentioned Somalia only as a previous deployment for the troops then heading to Haiti. Two other stories had such detailed information about human rights issues that they qualified as human rights stories, even though they did not use the phrase human rights. Both the August 13, 1992, and July 28, 2001, stories featured extensive descriptions of famine and human suffering with such detail that they actually crossed over into being human rights stories. But these two were glaring exceptions.

Given the nature and scope of the crisis in Somalia from 1990–2009, it is surprising that more stories were not framed as human rights stories. Fifty-three of the Somalia stories were close to being human rights stories and could have been reframed as human rights stories with minimal changes to the stories. Sixty percent of these 53 were the 32 stories about the famine and military intervention in Somalia. These stories included some human rights issues but were not framed as human rights issues and were not the primary focus of the stories, which usually focused more on the logistics of aid delivery, troop movements, or the evolution of military strategy. Several stories about piracy hinted at the poverty and starvation in Somalia that may have made piracy an appealing career opportunity, but the stories did not explore or develop that possible angle, so the stories were coded as non-human rights stories. The April 8, 2009, story with the first officer of the hijacked *Maersk Alabama* is one such example. "They're ruled by the law of the gun in that country now, and the stem of the problem is the collapse of the government in Somalia. Anyone with a weapon and means can go out. And when these people come back, they're heroes in their town."

Overwhelmingly, stories from Somalia are not framed as human rights issues, even when they easily could be. Human rights are simply not a frame journalists reach for when working on Somalia. Therefore, it is difficult to argue in favor of the influence of television news on human rights policy, because there is so little coverage of human rights.

Somalia in the early 1990s is often put forward as the example that proves the CNN Effect. Television news coverage of starving children is credited with having forced the United States into sending aid and then providing military support for aid delivery. "Television is singled out as the main stimulus in the process, supposedly triggering Washington's military intervention and then its abrupt withdrawal" (Minear, Scott, and Weiss 1996 53). Comparing a time line of events in Somalia with the actual television news coverage does not actually prove this point. Jonathan Mermin (1997) carefully examines broadcast news coverage leading up to American intervention in Somalia and finds that it could not have forced the government to act because coverage only begins in significant amounts after several government officials are already pushing for action. Mermin's study only covers the beginning of American involvement, but his argument is supported by the data collected here. While the number of stories about Somalia increase following the October 3, 1993, downing of a Blackhawk helicopter that resulted in the deaths of 18 American soldiers, the wounding of 73 others, and 1 soldier being taken captive, the television coverage can hardly be considered the causal mechanism for US withdrawal from Somalia, as several stories had already been covering US government officials' demands for withdrawal plans. A month prior to the incident, the story on September 10, 1993, includes calls from multiple senators for an exit strategy, including

Senator Larry Pressler saying, "I believe we should get our troops out of Somalia now, lock, stock, and barrel." By a week before the event on September 28, 1993, even President Clinton's emphasis had shifted toward getting American troops home soon:

> BRIT HUME: Mr. Clinton insisted he's not changed his policy on Somalia. But it was clear, nonetheless, that he now has a new emphasis on getting American troops out of there.
> PRES. BILL CLINTON: In the end, every peacekeeping mission or every humanitarian mission has to have a date certain when it's over.[2]

One last point this data reveals is the so-called ghost of Somalia. One hundred forty-eight of the 512 stories including Somalia are actually not about Somalia the country. Eleven reference a person from Somalia in a story that is unrelated to the country, but the other 137 are largely unconnected to the country, and many stories that mention Somalia only do so as an example or a warning about the potential dangers of American military intervention. Stories about Haiti, Afghanistan, Iraq, Rwanda, and Liberia, as well as other countries, all reference Somalia as a common example of how wrong military intervention can go. Somalia is held up as a cautionary tale: "U.S. forces in Haiti would not become entangled in the nation-building that led to such trouble in Somalia." "There's a lot of memory of what happened in Somalia eight years ago." "Still, what happened in the aftermath of today's attack was reminiscent of Somalia 11 years ago, when American soldiers were dragged through the streets of Mogadishu." ""The President insisted this will not be another Somalia." "The specter of the 1993 US intervention in Somalia, which ended in the deaths of 18 US soldiers, haunts US policy in Africa."[3] The cautionary tales of Somalia, mainly mission creep and casualty aversion, may be the lasting legacy of television news coverage of Somalia, both for journalists and policy makers, as the warnings come from both reporters and official sources. The data collected here about television news coverage of Somalia cannot definitively prove that television news has no influence on government policy. The explicit lack of coverage of human rights issues, however, goes a long way to discrediting the idea that television news coverage of human rights issues in Somalia had a definitive influence on policy.

Sudan: Darfur, Terrorism, Iraq, and Famine

From 1990–2009, human rights conditions in Sudan were severe, to say the least. The period 1990–2009 spans not one but two separate civil wars in Sudan: the ongoing war between North and South Sudan, which ultimately led to the secession and creation of a new country, South Sudan, as well as the ongoing conflict in the western region of

Darfur. The Political Terror Scale (PTS) average never goes below 4 for the entirety of this period, and the 20-year average for this period is 4.8. Despite this, however, there was relatively little coverage of Sudan on television news during this period. Two hundred fifty-one total stories on ABC that mentioned Sudan or Darfur, which works out to an average of 12.5 stories per year is hardly a lot of coverage. The American Progress Action Fund reported that the three major networks and cable stations "aired a combined 8,303 segments on the 'runaway bride', the Michael Jackson trial and Tom Cruise" in June 2005, while only airing 126 segments on Sudan (Eke 2008 283). Figure 6.4 shows the number of stories that contained Sudan or Darfur along with the PTS average of each year for Sudan.

The limited number of total stories is only part of the issue. Three years had spikes in coverage due to coverage of specific events, including terror attacks and responses in 1998 and Darfur in 2004 and 2007. These three years account for 44 percent of the Sudan/Darfur stories from 1999–2009.

The topics of these stories are even more revealing, and the most frequently covered topics are listed in Table 6.5.

The most frequently covered topics in Sudan/Darfur stories are the crisis in Darfur followed closely by terrorism. These two topics together account for more than half of all of the Sudan/Darfur stories from 2008, and this holds true whether measuring all of the Sudan/Darfur stories, as in Figure 6.5, or excluding stories that mention Sudan/Darfur only as geographic locations and nationalities, shown in Figure 6.6, or measuring

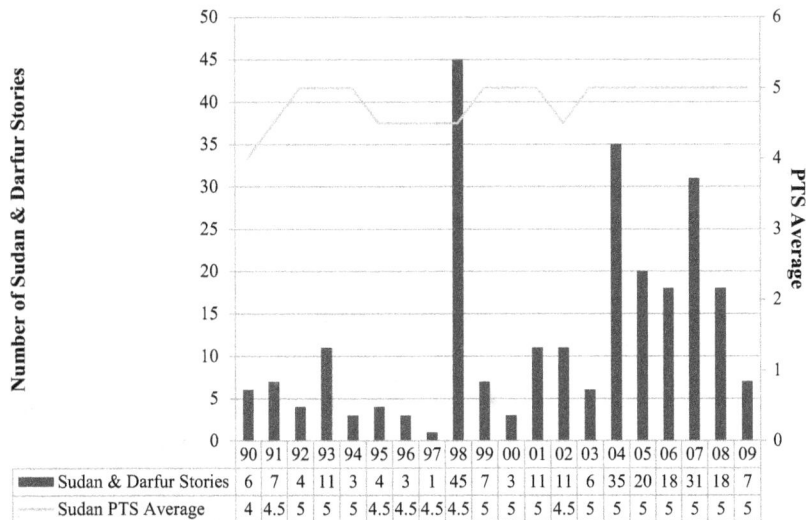

	90	91	92	93	94	95	96	97	98	99	00	01	02	03	04	05	06	07	08	09
Sudan & Darfur Stories	6	7	4	11	3	4	3	1	45	7	3	11	11	6	35	20	18	31	18	7
Sudan PTS Average	4	4.5	5	5	5	4.5	4.5	4.5	4.5	5	5	5	4.5	5	5	5	5	5	5	5

Figure 6.4 Sudan and Darfur Stories and PTS Average, 1999–2009

Table 6.5 Topics of Sudan and Darfur Stories, 1990–2009

Topic- All Sudan/Darfur Stories	Number of Stories	Topic- About Sudan/Darfur, About Sudan/Darfur and Another Issue, & Mentions Sudan/Darfur in Passing	Number of Stories	Topic- About Sudan/Darfur & About Sudan/Darfur and Another Issue	Number of Stories
Darfur	73	Darfur	73	Darfur	73
Terrorism	71	Terrorism	59	Terrorism	37
Iraq	18	Starvation	11	Starvation	10
Starvation	11	Iraq	9	Iraq	4
Olympics	9	Olympics	9	Lost Boys/ Girls	4
Human Rights	6	Human Rights	6	Sports- Olympics 2008	4
WMD	5	Lost Boys/Girls	4	Teddy Bear Scandal	4
Lost Boys/ Girls	4	Teddy Bear Scandal	4	Human Rights	3
Teddy Bear Scandal	4	US Presidential Election	3	Other	21
Israel- Palestine	3	WMD	3	**Total**	160
US Presidential Election	3	Other	42		
Other	44	**Total**	223		
Total	251				

just those stories that are about Sudan/Darfur or about Sudan/Darfur and another issue or country, shown in Figure 6.7.

As the parameters become more focused on Sudan and Darfur progressively through Figures 6.5–6.7, the most repeated topics stay largely the same, with the exception of Darfur, which becomes a bigger and bigger piece of the total coverage, which is understandable given the data collection of searching for stories that include the phrase "Darfur." [4]

Looking at the entire 20-year period together obscures some detail. Looking more closely at just the two most frequent story topics, terrorism and Darfur, a clearer picture emerges. While these are the two most

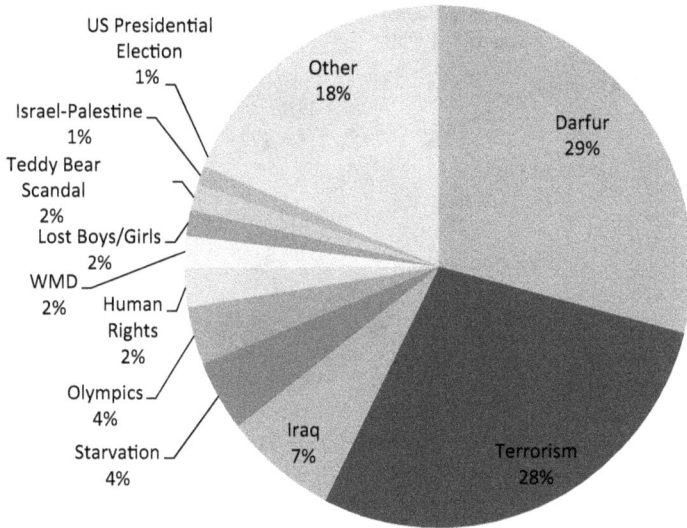

Figure 6.5 Topics of All 251 Sudan/Darfur Stories, 1990–2009

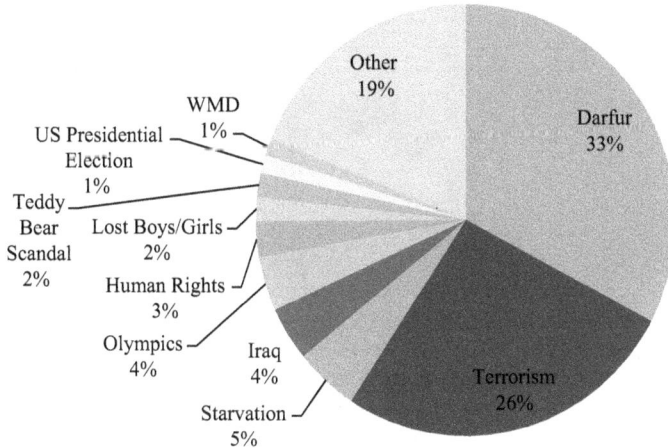

Figure 6.6 Topics of 223 Stories About Sudan/Darfur, Stories About Sudan/Darfur and Another Issue and Stories that Mention Sudan/Darfur in Passing, 1990–2009

common story topics in the time period, they do not overlap. Largely, Sudan stories prior to 2004 are terrorism stories. Darfur becomes the dominant topic of all Sudan/Darfur stories broadcast after 2004. Figure 6.8 shows the change in time from Sudan/Darfur stories about terrorism to those about the crisis in Darfur.

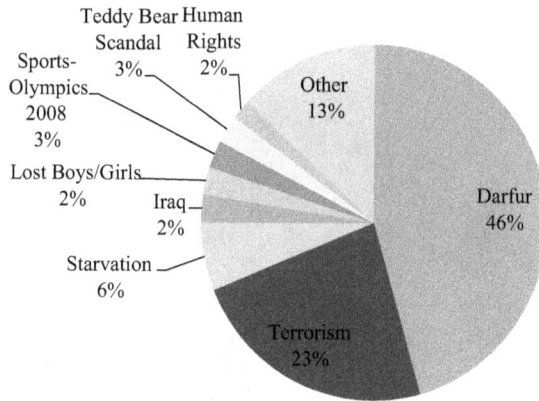

Figure 6.7 Topics of 160 Stories About Sudan/Darfur and Stories About Sudan/
Darfur and Another Issue, 1990–2009

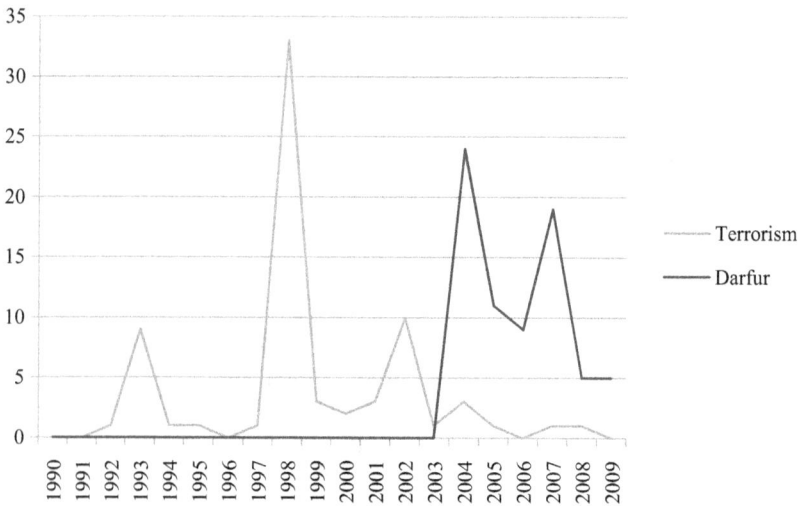

Figure 6.8 All Sudan/Darfur Stories About Terrorism and Darfur, 1990–2009

The 1998 terrorist attacks against US embassies in Tanzania and Kenya, stories about the alleged mastermind behind the attacks, Osama bin Laden, and the American response of air strikes against Sudan and Afghanistan are responsible for the large number of stories in 1998. Thirty-three of the 45 stories from that year (73 percent) are about terrorism.

The television news coverage of Darfur latched on quickly to a frame of humanitarian crisis, which is repeated frequently and formulaically.

Darfur's brand as "the world's worst humanitarian disaster" is firmly established and often repeated using almost identical phrasing:

> April 27, 2006: "There's major news, tonight, about what *some are calling the worst crisis on the planet.*"
>
> May 23, 2006: "The United Nations warned today that *the world's worst humanitarian crisis*, the fighting in the Darfur region of Sudan, is getting worse."
>
> May 8, 2006: "Overseas, a potential breakthrough in the effort to end *the world's worst humanitarian crisis*, the violence in the Darfur region of Sudan."
>
> May 16, 2007: "We're going to turn next to *the world's worst humanitarian crisis*, the Darfur region of Sudan."
>
> May 17, 2007: "Next, we turn to *the world's worst humanitarian crisis* and how one person can make a difference."
>
> May 29, 2007: "President Bush launched a new push to end *the world's worst humanitarian crisis.*"
>
> July 31, 2007: "What the UN calls *the worst humanitarian crisis in the world* today."
>
> March 7, 2009, starts with "We turn now to *the world's worst humanitarian crisis* in the Darfur region of Sudan"[5]

More evidence for American television journalists' avoiding taking a position to maintain neutrality is that the reporters do not argue genocide is occurring. But such an operationalization of neutrality while reporting on massive refugee problems, extrajudicial killings, violence against women and children is hard to maintain. The journalists do not themselves say genocide is occurring, but they take every opportunity to repeat that the Bush administration is labeling Darfur as genocide:

> September 9, 2004: "The secretary of state, Colin Powell, said for the first time today, that genocide is taking place in the western Darfur region of Sudan."
>
> September 19, 2004: "No mention that the US accuses Sudan of genocide."
>
> May 29, 2005: "President Bush has called this a genocide."
>
> June 6, 2005: "And the US has called it genocide."
>
> December 8, 2005: "The Bush administration has accused the Sudanese government of committing genocide against its own people."
>
> April 27, 2006: "The Bush Administration has called it genocide."
>
> May 8, 2006: "It was almost two years ago that the Bush Administration labeled the killing in Darfur genocide. But today, the President made his most passionate promise to do something about it.
>
> PRESIDENT GEORGE W. BUSH (UNITED STATES): America will not turn away from this tragedy. We will call genocide by its rightful name."

May 29, 2007: "A crisis, Mr. Bush, again called genocide."

June 3, 2007: ". . . what he calls genocide in Darfur."

September 25, 2007: "PRESIDENT GEORGE W. BUSH (UNITED STATES) In the Darfur region, many are losing their lives to genocide."

October 7, 2007: "The Bush administration says the Sudanese government is complicit in the genocide there."

January 4, 2009: "President Bush called this a genocide."[6]

This represents an evolution from Rwanda, where journalists and officials danced around whether a genocide, or acts of genocide, or genocide-like acts were occurring. ABC journalists, having obtained a presidential label of genocide, used the frequent repetition to highlight the importance of the issue, even while American journalistic ethics prevented them from more overtly advocating for or against one party of a story.

This stretch of neutrality does not extend toward covering more human rights issues as human rights, however. Despite the steady existence of major human rights concerns throughout this period, television news coverage of Sudan and Darfur included extremely little human rights information. Only six stories were coded with the topic human rights from 1990–2009, where the subject of the story was completely dedicated to human rights, each of these stories included the phrase human rights. Twenty-five other Sudan/Darfur stories were coded as being human rights stories either containing the phrase "human right" or by having so much focus on human rights issues that they were human rights stories, for a total of 31 human rights stories. Figure 6.9 shows the breakdown of human rights stories and non-human rights stories out of all of the Sudan and Darfur stories.

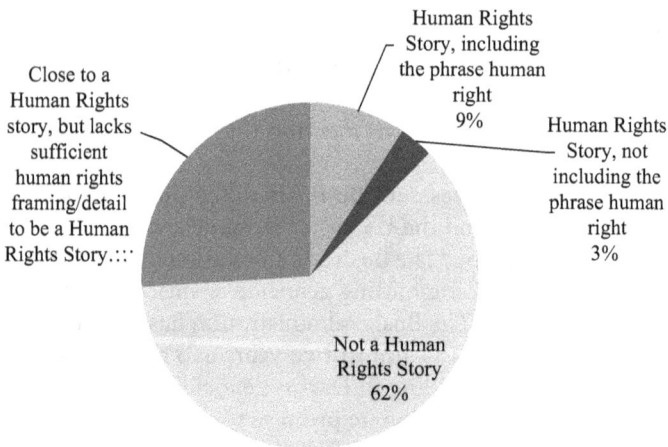

Close to a Human Rights story, but lacks sufficient human rights framing/detail to be a Human Rights Story.:::

Human Rights Story, including the phrase human right 9%

Human Rights Story, not including the phrase human right 3%

Not a Human Rights Story 62%

Figure 6.9 Human Rights Stories in Sudan/Darfur Television News Coverage, 1999–2009

Sixty-two percent, or 154 of the 251 total Sudan and Darfur stories, were coded as clearly not human rights stories. One quarter of the total stories were not human rights stories, but with very minimal reframing or editing they could have been. And 47 of these 65 close-to-human-rights stories were about the crisis in Darfur, a clear human rights issue that was repeatedly not framed as a human rights story but covered in another way. Stories coded as close-to-human-rights stories were not coded as human rights stories for two main reasons: first, the story might be too brief to provide any real human rights content, or second, they might not provide enough framing and focus on a human rights issue to make it about the actual human rights issue, instead of including it as one of several ideas in a story. The teaser and full story on August 25, 2007, about children's drawings depicting violence they had witnessed are examples of both reasons for not qualifying as an actual human rights story. The teaser is extremely short, and only alludes to general violence without a human rights connection, "Still ahead on World News this Saturday, the power of art. How the children who have survived Darfur's terrible violence may help bring their attackers to justice. We'll take 'A Closer Look.'"[7] The full story from that same day does not frame the description of the children's artwork in human rights terms, offering minimal details on what human rights violations occurred and none of the advocacy or claims against the state commonly associated with human rights. The American journalism approach to neutrality may be at play here again. Even in the stories about violence and mistreatment that could be framed as human rights issues, American television journalists report based on their operationalization of neutrality. They scrupulously try to avoid taking sides or placing blame and only report on the blame placed by others. Two of the stories that give the most detailed human rights information and human rights framing, July 21, 2004, and August 26, 2004, are actually full packages done by BBC reporters. These stories differ from those produced by American television journalists as a result of the depth and richness of the human rights focus in the stories, which are much harder to find in the ABC journalists' stories.

Overall, human rights coverage represents such a tiny fraction of the very small amount of television news coverage of Sudan and Darfur that a CNN Effect for human rights cannot be supported in the case of Sudan and Darfur.

Case Study Conclusion

When examining the total coverage of countries to see how much of their television news coverage is about human rights, it is again clear that very little of television news coverage is about human rights or provides significant information about human rights. This is true both in cases such as Somalia and Sudan, which have little besides their extremely high levels of human rights concerns to make them appealing to American news broadcasters, as well as in the case of China, which has broad relevance to American news broadcasters. In all three cases, there is so little coverage of human rights issues that any idea of a CNN Effect on human rights must be rejected, as the violations have not been televised.

Notes

1 ABC *World News Tonight*. November 11, 1999.
2 ABC *World News Tonight*. September 28, 1993.
3 ABC *World News Tonight*. September 13, 1994, October 17, 2001, March 31, 2004, July 29, 1994, and July 21, 2003.
4 It may seem redundant to point out that in a search that included collecting all stories containing "Darfur" the crisis in Darfur would be the major topic, but in fact, this added only 18 stories to the total number of stories, 9 of which were classified as stories being about other topics. Of the 73 stories coded as being about Darfur, 55 of them mentioned both Darfur and Sudan, 9 mentioned only Sudan, and 9 mentioned only Darfur.
5 ABC *World News Tonight*. April 27, 2006, May 23, 2006, May 8, 2006, May 16, 2007, May 17, 2007, May 29, 2007, July 31, 2007, March 7, 2009. Emphasis added.
6 ABC *World News Tonight*. September 9, 2004, September 19, 2004, May 29, 2005, June 6, 2005, December 8, 2005, April 27, 2006, May 8, 2006, May 29, 2007, June 3, 2007, September 25, 2007, October 7, 2007, and January 4, 2009.
7 ABC *World News Tonight*. August 25, 2007.

Bibliography

Apsel, J. (2009). The complexity of destruction in Darfur: Historical processes and regional dynamics. *Human Rights Review*, 10(2), 239–259.
Caliendo, S., Gibney, M., & Payne, A. (1999). All the news that's fit to print? *Harvard International Journal of Press/Politics*, 4(4), 48.
Cingranelli, D. L., Richards, D. L., & Clay, K. C. (2014). *The CIRI Human Rights Dataset*. Version 2014.04.14. Retrieved February 20, 2015 from http://www.humanrightsdata.com.
Eke, C. (2008). Darfur: coverage of a genocide by three major US TV networks on their evening news. *International Journal of Media and Cultural Politics* 4(3), 277–292.
Friedland, L. A., & Mengbai, Z. (1996). International television coverage of Beijing spring 1989: A comparative approach. *Journalism & Mass Communication Monographs*, (156), 1–56.
Gibney, M., Cornett, L., Wood, R., & Haschke, P., (2015), *Political Terror Scale 1976–2012*. Retrieved February 2015 from the Political Terror Scale Web site: http://www.politicalterrorscale.org/
Heinze, E., & Freedman, R. (2010). Public awareness of human rights: Distortions in the mass media. *International Journal of Human Rights*, 14(4), 491–523.
Huang, J. (2012). THE ICC AND DARFUR. *Eyes on the ICC*, 9(1), 63–93.

Hubbert, J. (2014). The Darfur Olympics: Global Citizenship and the 2008 Beijing Olympic Games. *Positions*, 22(1), 203–236.

Mermin, J. (1997). Television news and American intervention in Somalia: The myth of a media-driven foreign policy. *Political Science Quarterly (Academy Of Political Science)*, 112(3), 385.

Minear, L., Scott, C., & Weiss, T. G. (1996). *The News Media, Civil War, and Humanitarian Action*. Boulder, CO: L. Rienner.

Ricchiardi, S. (2005). Dèjá Vu. *American Journalism Review*, 27(1), 34–41.

Tsan-Kuo, C., Jian, W., & Chi-Hsien, C. (1998). The social construction of international imagery in the post-Cold War era: A comparative analysis. *Journal of Broadcasting & Electronic Media*, 42(3), 277.

Xuan, L., Jiun-Yi, T., Mattis, K., Konieczna, M., & Dunwoody, S. (2014). Exploring attribution of responsibility in a cross-national study of TV news coverage of the 2009 United Nations climate change conference in Copenhagen. *Journal of Broadcasting & Electronic Media*, 58(2), 253–271.

7   Conclusion

This study conducted four different types of content analysis on American television news broadcasts and two different types on British television news broadcasts, all with the goal of determining how much and which human rights issues do and do not get covered to see whether or not the CNN Effect exists on human rights issues. As it turns out, there is very little human rights coverage on television news, period. Most human rights issues do not make the cut for evening television news broadcasts, so the CNN Effect cannot be said to exist. Caliendo, Gibney, and Payne (1999) concluded their analysis of *New York Times* stories with the same finding:

> If no information about human rights violations is accessible, it is unlikely that people will judge such issues to be important, and if human rights are not important to the public, political elites are unlikely to devote considerable time to the issue.
>
> (49)

In short, the violations will not be televised and stories that are never broadcast can have no effect.

Even though there is very little coverage of human rights on television news in either the US or UK, there is still a lot to learn from what does and does not make the cut as human rights for television news coverage in both the US and UK. For both American and British television news, the gravity of the human rights situation in a given country does not necessarily translate into television news coverage, as the human rights stories that do get broadcast seem not to be coming from the countries with the worst human rights violations. Heinze and Freedman (2010) found this to be true for print news from 2006, and it has held true in every chapter of this study, whether looking at stories containing the phrase "human rights," transcripts from one month, footage spanning 20 years, or case studies of individual countries. In fact, Heinze and Freedman could easily have been writing about the evidence in this book when they concluded their article by saying

> We can understand that a Western military presence heightens interest in Afghanistan, Iraq or, prospectively, Darfur. We must regret, however, the dearth of reporting before such involvement, or in places, such as DR Congo, where no such involvement is imminent, as well as any tendency to focus more on harm to Western forces as on local victims. We can welcome critical coverage of violations in Iran, but must regret the absence of similar reporting on Saudi Arabia.
>
> (514)

There is more human rights coverage in the UK than in the US but not as much more as might have been expected given the states' differing approaches to human rights and differing television media systems. This is both surprising and disappointing. The UK is party to more international human rights treaties and is a more integrated participant of a more powerful supranational human rights body than the US is. The UK even has a piece of legislation entitled "The Human Rights Act," whose purpose is to explicitly incorporate human rights standards into domestic law in Britain, yet despite all of these facts, the UK did not have a significantly higher level of coverage of human rights than the US.

Additionally, the BBC has an explicit Charter-based mission to educate and inform, and its license fee funding makes it more insulated from commercial pressures than American television stations are, yet the UK only has a little more human rights coverage than the US and very little human rights coverage overall. This could support claims of the decline in the quality of the BBC's hard news coverage in favor of more soft news and infotainment coverage, with quality broadcast journalism succumbing to decreasing regulation and increasing competition in the domestic media market from satellite and digital channels. The evidence here is far from conclusive, however, as this study also offers evidence in the difference in the depth of coverage of human rights stories in the US and UK to support the contrary argument that the BBC still covers hard news better and more than its US counterparts do. Although the BBC is almost as unlikely to cover a human rights issue as its American counterparts are, once the BBC does cover a human rights issue, it tends to do it more thoroughly, from more angles, and with more explanation than either NBC or ABC does. So the British audience is able to learn more about human rights in the rare event when they are covered on British television than the American audience is able to in the even rarer event when human rights are covered on American television.

Just a Third of Young People Watched Any TN News Yesterday			
Watched news on television yesterday...	2006 %	2012 %	Change
Total	57	55	-2
18-29	49	34	-15
30-49	53	52	-1
50-64	63	65	+2
65+	69	73	+4
PEW RESEARCH CENTER 2012 News Consumption Survey. Q13			

Figure 7.1 Decline in Television News Viewership by Age

Overall, a viewer would be hard pressed to learn anything from nightly television news about human rights as it is currently covered in either the US or UK. This does not necessarily resign human rights issues to academics, activists, and the bureaucrats they seek to influence. For one, television news, while still the overall most popular source of news, is losing ground against Internet sources, as shown in Figure 7.1. The decline of television news is particularly sharp among young people,[1] as shown in Figure 7.1, and the downward trend in television viewership among younger people looks set to continue.

Avenues for Future Research

It is not only the decline of television news as the primary source of news but also the rise of Internet sources as a place to read and share news that is important to the future of human rights news coverage. A growing number of people look to the Internet in addition to or even instead of television for their news; this is most true for younger people but in increasing proportions across all demographics. Internet news outlets and social media allow for the possibility of citizen journalism and citizen activism in ways that can create more outlets for human rights–minded individuals to connect, share information, and spread their message. This is an unproved area. For every scholar claiming that Internet communications and social media have played a major role in a social movement, there are several who say these technological advances are not the real mechanism at work. One such essay, "Small Change: Why the Revolution Will Not Be Tweeted," takes its title from the same pop culture phrase that inspired the title of this book. In it, Malcolm Gladwell argues that social media is not actually a magic tool that can change the world as was argued in the case of the Moldovan "Twitter Revolution" or the Iranian protests in 2009.[2] However, Gladwell's essay has garnered several reactions offering counter-examples with compelling evidence where social media specifically and Internet communication more broadly are playing important roles in creating social change, and both Gladwell and most of his critics on this issue are writing as public intellectuals, not digging deep into the empirical and historical evidence to find out whether the social web is actually the explanatory variable in a given social movement's success or failure. Whether or not human rights violations will be tweeted, and what, if any impact those tweets might have, is by no means settled, and challenging research needs to be done to answer these questions. It is very possible that human rights are being more fully integrated in newer Internet news and social media platforms, which raises several additional important questions for further research: Are there other media, outside of television, with wide audience penetration where human rights are being covered? What is the nature and effect of human rights coverage on the Internet and social media? What human rights issues do and do not get covered? Why do some human rights stories go viral and not others? And what, if any, effect do these new means of creating and sharing information have on policy makers? If the CNN Effect refers to the possibility of television news influencing government policy, is there possibly a Net Effect of Internet coverage influencing state policy? In a multilayered media environment where print, broadcast, and Internet news all interact, what influence does Internet coverage have on mainstream traditional news outlets? The powers of Internet connectivity and social media are particularly notable in the wake of the Arab Spring movements and Kony 2012 campaign. In both cases, stories that started on social media and Internet platforms gained so much momentum they became mainstream news that were picked up by television news. These means of communication are still new enough that scholars are struggling to develop methodologies for studying them, even while new technologies and new ways of using existing technology are developed every day. Exploring the amount and nature of human rights topics and what if any effects Internet coverage of human rights issues might have on state policies is an essential next step in research, for the fields of both political communication and human rights.

Exploring Internet coverage of human rights is not, however, the only next step in research on this topic. Television news in both the US and UK do not cover human rights frequently or in much depth, which leads to several further research questions. First, where does this level of coverage come from? Is it reflective of official policy makers' disinterest in the topic, which would support the government-leading-media direction of causality, the opposite of the CNN Effect? Or is it a failure of human rights advocates to get their issues onto the news media agenda, meaning that the CNN Effect could actually have some effect on human rights issues if only the media were to cover them? Saying that human rights advocates have failed to get their issues on television implies effort. Are human rights advocates even seeking television news coverage? If so, why have they been unsuccessful? How can human rights violations get more coverage on American and British television news? If, on the other hand, human rights advocates are not seeking television news coverage, what is their reason? Do they prefer more inside strategies of direct lobbying for influencing policy makers? None of these questions can be answered by the present research, and all of them are fruitful directions for further research as a complement to the present study, particularly using interviews or other qualitative methods with policy makers, journalists, news producers, and human rights organizations.

There are potential areas for improvement in the methodology of this study's approach as well. This study has shown four different ways of cutting television news data—as a phrase search, a country search, or a cross-national comparison of transcripts or taped broadcasts—all of which found that there is very little television news coverage of human rights. Without television news coverage, there can be no CNN Effect, so the CNN Effect cannot be said to exist on human rights issues. One type of data analysis that was not conducted in this project was using data mining software to conduct word cloud analysis from extremely large pools of data. It is possible that such a big data approach might identify human rights coverage patterns that were not evident to human coders, which could then be explored by human coders in further detail, as mixed methods provide richer data than either purely robotic or purely human coding.

The challenges in pursuing television research in the British system, due to the lack of publicly available transcripts, is one faced by all researchers, not just this one. Despite the difficulty of achieving change in a large public organization such as the BBC, digitizing and making public the transcripts of BBC news broadcasts is a worthwhile long-term project to pursue, and recent developments in the availability of BBC Radio schedules,[3] sound and video archives[4] inspire hope in the possibility of wider access to television news archives in time. Richard Hewitt's report summarizes the results of what academics would like to have available (digitally searchable summaries and transcripts, along with digitally playable media) along with the piecemeal availability of BBC materials produced prior to 1989 in various places and formats.[5] One possible solution might be utilizing a time limit, such as is the current practice with declassifying most British government documents after 30 years according to the Public Records Act. Such a plan could balance protecting the BBC's independent operations while still making footage, shooting scripts, or transcripts both digitally searchable and available for academics, which would be useful in both British and cross-national settings.

The results of this study prove that it is very difficult for the average viewer in either the US or the UK to learn anything about human rights from television news. It is perhaps all the more important then to revitalize other means of learning about human rights. National general education curricula in both the US and UK should be revised to include more human rights starting in kindergarten all the way through college as an essential part of a well-rounded civic education, not as extra fluff about "sad things that happen somewhere else." Human rights organizations can help by developing standards and curricular units at multiple grade levels that are integrated with national learning standards. Once audiences are more knowledgeable about human rights more generally, they may be more interested in human rights, which would make their increasingly competition-driven news broadcasters provide more human rights stories. This might actually result in the violations being televised after all.

Notes

1 In Changing News Landscape, Even Television is Vulnerable," Pew Research Center, Washington, DC (September 27, 2012). http://www.people-press.org/2012/09/27/in-changing-news-landscape-even-television-is-vulnerable/.
2 "Small Change: Why the Revolution will not be tweeted," Gladwell, Malcolm, *The New Yorker*. October 4, 2010. http://www.newyorker.com/magazine/2010/10/04/small-change-malcolm-gladwell.
3 The BBC Radio Genome project lists the scheduled broadcast information printed in Radio Times from 1923–2009, http://genome.ch.bbc.co.uk/.
4 Notable resources include the British Library's Listening Service (http://www.bl.uk/reshelp/inrrooms/stp/sound/listening.html) and the British University Film and Video Council (http://bufvc.ac.uk/tvandradio).
5 "Academic Requirements for pre-1989 BBC Archive content," Richard Hewitt, Retrieved July 4, 2015 from http://repository.jisc.ac.uk/5659/

Bibliography

Caliendo, S., Gibney, M., & Payne, A. (1999). All the news that's fit to print? *Harvard International Journal of Press/Politics*, 4(4), 48.
Heinze, E., & Freedman, R. (2010). Public awareness of human rights: Distortions in the mass media. *International Journal of Human Rights*, 14(4), 491–523.

Appendix I
Methodology

This appendix outlines the methodology and coding schemes that were used in this project. First, one flagship evening news program from each country was selected. The *Ten O'Clock News* is the BBC's flagship news program (formerly the *Nine O'Clock News* prior to October 2000), with the largest audience of any evening news program in the UK.[1] *World News* is ABC's flagship national news program and had the highest ratings of ABC, CBS, and NBC from the period 1990–1995,[2] so it was used for the month transcript content analysis that covers that period. The overlap between US network news programs has been well established in media studies literature, which, combined with the fact that from1990–2009, ABC's *World News Tonight* and NBC's flagship *Nightly News* split the number of years for which they had higher ratings and market shares, which made using both networks an easy choice. ABC was used for the phrase month search, while NBC was used for the visual content analysis.

Coding Instrument[3]

Each story was assigned a unique identifier based on its date (dates with multiple stories were coded with the date and a sequential letter) (I). The coder read the story once completely then coded for eleven categories. First, stories were coded for domestic versus international news (I). Domestic stories were those that were primarily concerning the home country (either the US or UK) and were scored 1,[4] while stories primarily about foreign news were coded 2, and stories that included both domestic and foreign components were coded 3. For example, BBC stories from August 1995 about hostages taken in Malaysia were coded a 2 when the nationality of the hostages were not mentioned, but a 3 when the two British hostages' nationality was not mentioned.[5] Increasingly, stories take place outside of specific geographic dichotomy of domestic/foreign; for example, the June 26, 2006, NBC story (#11) about Warren Buffett's large financial donation doesn't mention the US location, though he is an American and the story also fleetingly references several other countries. Another example comes from the June 25, 2006, NBC story of actress

Nicole Kidman's wedding to American singer Keith Urban in Australia. Both of these stories could be argued to be either national or foreign, as well as international. They were both coded as both (3).

Stories were then coded (II) for whether they included the phrase right or rights to refer to other rights besides human rights, such as in civil rights, right to freedom, etc. Use of the word "right" to refer to conservative political tendencies was not included, nor was the word to mean correct.

The type of story (III) was coded as one of eight possibilities:

1. **VOSOT,** or voice-over sound on tape of five lines or less
2. **Full Package,** or complete story of more than five lines including taped feature
3. **Live Two-Way,** or major story featuring live substantive conversation between an anchor or another person in the studio and a correspondent (more than just "Thanks, John") as part of a full package.
4. **Headline/Intro** at beginning of newscast
5. **Restatement** at end of newscast
6. **Teaser** before commercial
7. **Weather or Stock Market Report**
8. **Commentary,** opinion from one or more talking heads with no additional video

Stories were coded for the primary subject location (IV) of the story, being careful to record the location of the subject of the story, which may deviate from the location of the anchor or the correspondent. The following abbreviations were used as necessary: US, UK, DRC, PRC, and Israel and Palestine is used for stories that are primarily about Israel and/or the territories administered by Israel and not claimed as part of another currently existing state. The coder wrote in the subject of the story as a short phrase (V).

Stories were coded as to whether "human right!" was used as an informal introduction/description for a person, group, or place or as part of an official title for a person, group, or place(VI), and if they were, coders copied and pasted the relevant phrase(s) into a column in the row recording specifics of introduction or title. Stories were also coded as to whether the only use of "human right!" was in an informal introduction or official title (VII).

Coders determined whether a description, explanation, or clear example of human rights was included in the story (VIII), coding either 1 for yes, 2 for no, or 3 for the story including some description or information included but not being explicit, specific, detailed, or directly related to human rights as such. Coders then determined whether human rights was the primary focus of the story, answering yes, no, or that human rights is a prominent but not the primary focus of the story (IX) using the question "To what extent is the story a discussion or more in-depth analysis of human rights?" to guide their decision.

Coders then classified the story as one of 17 possible categories of human rights, or as 18, not applicable/not given/not specified (IX). The first fourteen categories are derived from international treaties, while fifteen through seventeen are from international norms that are currently widely prominent, despite lack of enshrinement in multilateral treaties. While most of the categories could be covered by either 2, Civil and Political Rights, as derived from the International Covenant on Civil and Political Rights (ICCPR) or 3, Economic, Social, and Cultural Rights, as derived from the International Covenant on Economic, Social and Cultural Rights (ICESCR), additional categories were included to investigate more specifically exactly what types of human rights were covered in television news. For example, protection against torture is clearly included as a civil and political right under Article 7 of the ICCPR, but is significantly expanded under the Convention Against Torture and Other Cruel, Inhuman, and Degrading Treatment (CAT). Torture was included as its own category to allow more fine-grained analysis. Additionally, there is a question of overlap, as several treaties and issue areas overlap with each other; for example, most treaties include a prohibition against excluding the rights and privileges contained therein against persons for reasons of race, ethnicity, or gender. But the International Convention on the Elimination of All Forms of Racial Discrimination (ICERD) and the Convention on the Elimination of All Forms of Discrimination against Women (CEDAW) expand and cover these areas more directly, and so racial discrimination and women's rights were included as separate categories. Coders were then able to select the narrowest category that was supported by the story. During reliability testing, it was discovered that the distinctions originally in place, that listed the categories in #12 as two different categories, one for Humanitarian Law and the Laws of War and one for Crimes Against Humanity and War Crimes Tribunals, were unnecessary distinctions, as stories that mentioned something from one almost always mentioned at least one part of the other, and the subjects are so intricately tied that making them one category made much more sense logically and to the coders.

If the relevant section had not been copied into the file previously (as part of V or VII), then the coder pasted the phrase including "human right!" into the file (X). Coders then determined whether the use of the phrase "human right!" was a purely rhetorical reference in a story unrelated to human rights issues (XII) and whether the primary frame of the story is the Global War on Terror (GWOT) (XIII).

Reliability

The majority of the coding was conducted by the author, but to test the reliability of the coding scheme, 40 stories were coded by a team of coders.[6] Ninety-five percent or better intercoder reliability between two coders was achieved for the type of story, location, if human rights was used in an introduction or title, whether it was used only in the introduction or title, if the reference was purely rhetorical, and if the story was framed primarily as a GWOT story. Eighty percent intercoder reliability was achieved for categorizing the human right, with slightly lower (60 percent and 65 percent respectively) reliability for whether a description or example of human rights was given and if human rights was the primary focus of the story. In conjunction with the coders, the coding scheme was revised to make clearer definitions for the categories and to clarify distinctions between the answers of whether a story gave a human rights description or had human rights focus, after which test-retest reliability from the primary coder was 100 percent. The tested and revised codebook was used for the monthly content analysis and the visual content analysis, with only minor changes.[7]

Monthly Content Analysis

To address the possibility that human rights stories were being covered without the use of the phrase "human rights," as well as to allow for valid selection and comparison of US and UK television coverage, one month of broadcast transcripts for 1990 (February) was selected for including the most human rights coverage, based on a search of the BBC Motion Gallery's[8] Archive. Using the Motion Gallery's search function, instead of a Vanderbilt Television News Archive search or a LexisNexis transcript search,[9] was deemed most appropriate, as the same metrics for classifying stories would be applied to both the BBC and CBS news stories, yielding the most comparable data.[10]

Scripts from the *Nine O'Clock News* were collected from the BBC Written Archives in Reading, UK, where they are stored on microfilm. Transcripts of ABC's 6:30 p.m. *World News Tonight with Peter Jennings* were collected from the LexisNexis online database. LexisNexis does not include introductions, good-nights, or teasers before commercials in their transcripts for this period, so they were omitted from this study.

Scripts/transcripts of stories were analyzed to see what, if any, use of the phrase human rights was included. The coding instrument is largely duplicative of the coding instrument used in the phrase analysis explained earlier and is included in Appendix I. The week/visual coding instrument is largely duplicative of the month/transcript instrument, so the following points of explanation apply to both sets of analysis, except where noted. For both the month/transcript and week/visual codes in both the US and UK analyses, commercials, stock market, and (regular) weather reports were coded as 4 for location, "no story information," so they would not be included in the count of stories. Where stock market reports are included as part of another story, they are not disaggregated for story counts (since they wouldn't be counted anyway). Where the stock market report is part of a general economic report, even if it's just the Consumer

Price Index figures given, as on NBC on May 14, 2004, the package is coded as 1 for location so it would be counted as a story. Local London news broadcasts and the teasers for them were not viewed and were coded as 4 so they would not be included in the overall number of stories.

Sports stories note: For the month/transcript analysis, sports stories were coded as a 4/non-story for location, so they are not included in the general count; stories involving professional athletes that were not accounts of specific sporting events, such as the February 9, 1990, US profile of golfer Lee Trevino as person of the week and the coverage in the UK of the rebel cricket tour in South Africa in February 1990 were viewed and coded according to the contents of the story; they were therefore also included in the general story count. For the week analysis, sports reports were viewed as a single story, not disaggregated into individual stories, counted into the general story count as one story, and coded as one segment.

To see if the US and UK news covered certain issues in a similar fashion, all month/transcript stories were coded for whether they involved South Africa, the reforms and independence movements within the USSR, or the reunification of Germany. To be coded for the USSR, a story had to deal with party reforms or independence movements within the USSR itself, stories about US-USSR arms reduction negotiations, stories about the Warsaw Pact but not formally Soviet countries such as Romania, Hungary, Bulgaria, and Czechoslovakia, and nonreform-related topics were not coded as USSR for this category.

In addition to the coding applied from the phrase search code, month/ transcript stories and week/visual stories were also analyzed to see if they covered a human rights–related topic without using human rights as a phrase. It is important to note that the decision of whether the story is human rights, possibly, or not is made based on the contents of the story alone, as someone just tuning in for that story would view it. For example, protests against Chinese president Ziang Zemin speaking at Harvard in the intro story to the NBC November 1, 1997, broadcast does not qualify, because nothing about what the protests are against is mentioned. Item III on the coding sheet scores a 1 if the story includes the phrase "human right!" and a 2 if it does not include the phrase but nevertheless is a human rights story, by covering a clear human rights issue with focus and framing on the human rights issue (even if it is not named as such). A 3 was entered if the story is not a human rights story, as it neither contains the phrase "human right!" or substantially covers a human rights issue as such. A fourth category was added to cover a large number of stories that could have been human rights stories but both lacked the phrase "human right!" and were not framed as human rights issues. To clarify, a story coded 4 is close to a human rights issue but is not covered as such; the focus is not on the human right. A 3 is not a human rights story; if it does cover a human rights issue, it does so tangentially and does not in any way illuminate or focus on the human right. For example, the BBC's coverage of the former Yugoslavia on December 14, 1992, included a story (#8) of Muslim and Croat prisoners released that was coded a 4, because it mentions (in passing) possible abuse of the detainees while in prison, while the #6 and #7 stories of that same day, about Paddy Ashdown's visit to Bosnia and the US pressing for permission to use force against violators of the no-fly zone, are both coded 3 because they are framed as war stories about troop movement and armed attacks with no link to human rights whatsoever. Another illustrative case is the second BBC story from June 25, 1998, on need for food aid in Southern Sudan, which was coded a 4 because it discusses famine and the hardships the people and children face but with no mention/relation/frame to human rights (even though there easily could be). If there had been some connection to a state cause or some kind of government action or inaction then it might have been a 2—as in the case of the third BBC story on July 26, 2001, on protestors at the G8 claiming abuse by Italian police. The extensive description of violence and inhumane treatment with attribution to the state actor (police) makes it a 2, a human rights story even though the phrase human rights was not mentioned. The bright line can be shown by the ninth BBC story on August 19, 2002, about a Nigerian woman sentenced to death for having a baby out of wedlock. There was absolutely no explicit human rights frame to the story, but it was on a topic so close to several human rights issues (women's rights; civil and political rights; and economic, social, and cultural rights) it was coded a 4 instead of a 2 or 3. A further example comes from NBC coverage of Somalia in 1992. Stories on Somalia famine that focus on troop movements and only mention/show footage of starving Somalis (without expanding on human rights–related issues), such as NBC December 13, 1992, #2 are coded as a 3. If the story is only about starving Somalis (not troops) but without additional details, such as NBC December 14, 1992 #1, it's a 4. So #4 on December 14, 1992, is a 4 for its extensive coverage of the dire condition of the famine, while #3 and #5 on that same day are coded 3 because they focus more on fighting and the trip into Baidoa. The December 15, 1992, #8 story focuses on famine, starvation, and disease; there is no explicit reference to human rights, but there is enough detail to be coded a 4. Items that received a 3 or 4 were not coded further, while stories that received a 1 and 2 on Item II were fully coded.

Print Analysis for February 1990

Selecting a newspaper to analyze as a paper of record in the US system is fairly straightforward. The *New York Times* has a reputation for high quality journalism along with a consistently large circulation, which makes it an obvious choice for review. Caliendo et al. (1999) references the Ovsiovitch study as proving that the *New York Times* has more human rights stories than other print outlets in the US (52), thereby making the *New York Times* a good choice for this study to create a baseline of what journalists consider to be newsworthy human rights issues in February 1990. In contrast, selecting a British newspaper for comparison was slightly more complicated because of the greater diversity in the print news market in the UK. National newspapers in Britain are stratified into quality newspapers, which have a reputation for high quality journalism, and tabloids, which are more oriented toward popular entertainment; the tabloids are further divided into middle-market and mass-market varieties. (Hallin and Mancini 2004 206). Of the five quality press national daily newspapers listed by Kuhn (3), two papers, the *Daily Telegraph* and *Financial Times* do not have transcripts available for February 1990 on LexisNexis, while there is no Sunday edition of the *Guardian* for that month. As the *Times* has been around longer and has a higher circulation than the *Independent*, both in 1990 and on average, the *Times* was selected for review.

Comparing Twenty Years Analysis

Several methods for selection for which weeks of footage to view were considered. First, the "human rights" phrase search of *World News Tonight* was tried, but the number of stories for each year is relatively small (an average of 40 per year), so a larger number of stories was needed to better select the month of transcript analysis and the week of visual coding. To provide that larger number, and to increase the likelihood that major human rights stories that might not have been caught in the initial *World News Tonight* search would have a chance to be included, the *New York Times* online archive of stories from 1980–present[11] was searched for the phrase "human rights." The results for 1990–2009 were an unmanageably large number of stories, 31,082, so front-page stories were used to narrow the focus to consider only those stories that were of the highest prominence and news values, yielding 2,466 stories. These stories were arranged chronologically and merged with the ABC stories (an average of 162 total stories per year) to determine which week of footage should be analyzed. The week from the combined ABC and *New York Times* stories each year that had the most references to the phrase human rights was selected for analysis using the 2011 Microsoft Excel default WEEKNUM function, where week one starts on January 1 and week two the Sunday after that.[12] Table A.1 displays the selected weeks.

In several years, there were several weeks where the combined number of ABC and *New York Times* stories was the same as the selected week; in those cases, the week with the higher number of ABC stories was selected for analysis, as this seemed the best way to include the types of stories that television news coverage would deem most important to cover. In some cases, full weeks were not available due to broadcasts being interrupted

Table A.1 Human Rights Mentions in Weeks Selected

Year	Week #	Date	Combined	ABC	New York Times
1990	10	Mar 4–Mar 10, 1990	8	2	6
1991	36	Sep 1–Sep 7, 1991	7	4	3
1992	51	Dec 13–Dec 19, 1992	6	2	4
1993	47	Nov 14–Nov 20, 1993	7	2	5
1994	13	Mar 20–Mar 26, 1994	9	4	5
1995	34	Aug 20–Aug 26, 1995	10	5	5
1996	14	Mar 31–Apr 6, 1996	6	3	3
1997	44	Oct 26–Nov 1, 1997	12	7	5
1998	26	Jun 21–Jun 27, 1998	15	10	5
1999	47	Nov 14–Nov 20, 1999	11	2	9
2000	24	Jun 4–Jun 10, 2000	10	8	2
2001	30	Jul 22–Jul 28, 2001	7	2	5
2002	34	Aug 18–Aug 24, 2002	8	2	6
2003	16	Apr 13–Apr 19, 2003	9	3	6
2004	20	May 9–May 15, 2004	11	6	5
2005	47	Nov 13–Nov 19, 2005	10	3	7
2006	26	Jun 25–Jul 1, 2006	6	2	4
2007	47	Nov 18–Nov 24, 2007	10	1	9
2008	15	Apr 6–Apr 12, 2008	12	9	3
2009	17	Apr 19–Apr 25, 2009	9	1	8

by sporting events or preempted by local (Tennessee) coverage. The year 1996 had two weeks with identical combined *New York Times* and ABC story counts, so a random coin flip was used to select the week for analysis.[13] Where possible, weeks with identical combined scores that had the full week's broadcasts available were selected, but for the years 1990, 1991, 1997, 1998, 1999, and 2005, only six nights of broadcasts were visually analyzed. Broadcast transcripts for the missing days were sought, but LexisNexis does not possess any NBC transcripts before 1994, and LexisNexis had no NBC evening news transcripts for the days missing in 1997 and 1998, as evening news broadcasts were preempted nationally. Transcripts were analyzed for the missing dates in 1999 and 2005, as it was the local broadcast that was preempted. Additionally, the BBC aired no news programs in the evening of November 14, 1999, so only six programs are analyzed for that year for the UK. BBC stories were divided and numbered by the author. NBC stories were divided according to the titles and divisions provided by the VTNA but subdivided by the author when the VTNA heading contained discreet stories.[14]

Initial Viewing: All stories were viewed once and given a preliminary code for domestic versus foreign or combined domestic/foreign, whether the phrase "right" was included, and whether the story was a human rights story.[15] Stories that had no news content to them, such as promos for other shows, weather forecasts, and introductions and good-nights from the newscasts that did not include any references to the stories did not receive a domestic or foreign code, allowing them to be excluded from counts of actual news stories. For example, the good-night message from the BBC's broadcasts for the early 1990s did not include any summaries of the stories from the newscasts, while toward the end of the period they did include reviews of the major story or stories of the night.

If the story contained the phrase "human right!" then it was coded HR. If the story had any possibility of being related to human rights issues whatsoever, it was coded "possibly." Stories with even the remotest possible connection to human rights were coded "possibly" to ensure that no stories that cover human rights even tangentially would be missed. For example, in 2006, the BBC did a series of stories following up on the report of the racist murder of a juvenile prisoner by his mentally disturbed roommate. These stories were all coded "possibly" because they might include information on human rights as they pertain to children, prisoners, and racial discrimination. Stories did, however, need to have some possibility of connection to human rights content to be rated "possibly." NBC stories such as the March 23, 1994, story on the Clinton healthcare plan, the March 24, 1994, story on the ceasefire in Somalia, the April 20, 2009, story about women making less money than men, and the stories from November 2007 about the cyclone in Bangladesh were not rated "possibly" because they were not framed in any way remotely connected to human rights issues.

Full Coding: Stories that were coded HR or "possibly" were viewed a second time and given a fuller code. The coding for the full visual code was largely duplicative of the coding sheet for the monthly transcript analysis and can be found in Appendix I. For codebook item III, the code was the same as item III for the monthly transcript code, with the addition of a possible score of 5, for if the story contained the phrase "human right!" in text only, not mentioned audibly.

Non-human rights stories (3 and 4) were not coded further. Human rights stories (1, 2, and 5) were further coded similarly to the month code analysis, with the addition of items that, following Hoskins & O'Loughlin (2009), coded for references to past and/or current events (56), use of tickers or banners (71), and premediation and/or remediation (91).

Case Study Analysis

To explore further whether there were other human rights stories or stories that were very close to human rights stories that had not been discovered in the initial phrase search, case studies were selected. China, Sudan, and Somalia were chosen as case studies to see what the overall television media coverage of these countries could reveal about human rights coverage beyond a simple phrase search for human rights, including what stories are close to human rights or what issues are being covered in conjunction with these countries, human rights stories, or other topics. ABC evening news broadcast transcripts from *World News Tonight* were collected from LexisNexis searching the body of stories for "China!", "Somalia!", "Sudan!", and "Darfur!" from 1990–2009. Because China returned so many story results from 1990–2009, 1999–2002 were selected for full coding. These years are in the middle of the 1990–2009 span and had the highest number of stories for four consecutive years. To ensure that stories collected were actually about the case study countries under investigation and not just about those with that nationality, the search terms were selected carefully: "China!" instead of "Chin!" and "Somalia!" instead of "Somali!"[16] Care was taken to sort and verify[17] the LexisNexis results to remove other ABC news broadcasts as well as duplicates of stories in each case study while disaggregating stories that were included in one LexisNexis transcript but were actually two (or more) stories. The data collected is summarized in Table A.2.

China stories were coded for whether they are about China (1) or about China and another issue (1A), such as coverage of the US spy plane that crashed in China or the US bombing of the Chinese embassy in Belgrade. Stories that are not about China substantively, but refer to China in passing as an example or as a short comparison, were coded 3. Stories could also be coded 2 for not being about China but referring to a person who is from China. Stories were coded 4 if they included China

Table A.2 Case Study Data Collection

	LexisNexis Results	World News Tonight *Stories (excluding duplicates)*	World News Tonight Stories *(excluding duplicates & including disaggregated stories)*
China 1999–2002	2233	484	502
Somalia	1119	383	512*
Sudan/Darfur	866	307	251
Totals	4218	1174	1265

*December 13, 2008, story excluded from Somalia because it was not about the country but returned by LexisNexis because a teenager's name in the US was "Somalia."

as a geographical reference point, such as "on the border with China" or "as far away as China," and 7 if they included China as part of the name of a place that has nothing to do with China in a story that is not about China, such as China Beach in Vietnam. Finally, homonym stories that referred to china dishes were coded as 5.

Somalia stories were coded for whether they were actually about Somalia (1) or about Somalia and another issue (1A), such as the story profiling the International Commission of the Red Cross and its work in Somalia on August 14, 1992, or the preview aired on July 23, 1994, about Rwanda, Somalia, and Haiti; stories that provided some detail that was actually about Somalia while the rest of the story was not, such as the December 18, 2001, story about finding Osama Bin Laden, were also coded 1A. Stories that were not really about Somalia and provided little detail or information about Somalia but referred to Somalia as a reference or example were coded 3, while stories that mentioned Somalia only as a geographical reference, such as the May 28, 1991, story that referred to the border between Ethiopia and Somalia, were coded 4, and those that referred to Somalia as the place of origin or name of someone in a story not about Somalia were coded as 2. Stories that only included Somalia in text on the screen and not in the audio were coded 5.

Sudan stories were coded according to the same logic, with an extra question to determine whether the story included Sudan, Darfur, or both. All stories were coded for a topic, the general subject of the article, as well as whether terrorism was mentioned specifically. If a story mentioned terrorism specifically using terrorism, terrorist, acts of terror, or another variation, it was coded 1 for stories before September 11, 2001, and 2 for stories after September 11. If a story did not mention terrorism or did not do so explicitly, the story was coded a 3. For example, the July 21, 2003, story that referred to "having encouraged Osama bin Laden to attack" was coded a 3 for terrorism, because it did not use terror or terrorism in the story.

If a story mentioned the United Nations, it was coded a 1, and if not, the story received a 2. Only stories that included the phrase United Nations or UN qualified for a 1. For example, July 29, 1994, received a 2 for this category because it did not include the words UN or United Nations, even though it included footage of a colonel involved in Operation Turquoise, which was a UN-mandated operation, because the story did not provide that information to the viewer.

Several coding questions were included for each case that are specific to the case with straightforward yes or no coding schemes, so they are not explained here in further detail. Please see the following appendix for the full coding instruments.

Because all stories about the case study countries were analyzed, the coding for whether a story was a human rights story or not has evolved somewhat to be able to see what share of a case study country's stories are clearly not human rights stories versus those stories that could be human rights stories with minimal reframing. A story is coded 1 for human rights if it includes the phrase for human rights, 2 if it is clearly a human rights story that does not include the phrase human rights, and 3 if it has nothing to do with human rights. The coding for category 4, however, has become more lenient than in the other content analyses in this study. Stories that with minimal changes could easily be reframed to be about human rights but are not currently framed in that way are coded as 4. For example, stories about starvation in Somalia that were not framed as human rights stories were coded as 4, starvation being a violation of (at least) the rights to life, to food, and to a minimum standard of living. The UN High Commissioner for Human Rights has urged moving from approaching hunger as a humanitarian issue to a human rights issue.[18] If, however, a story mentions hunger or starvation only in passing, and the story would have to be significantly lengthened or changed to make the story a human rights story, such as in August 21, 1992-A, then it is classified as 3, not a human rights story.

Bibliography

Caliendo, S., Gibney, M., & Payne, A. (1999). All the news that's fit to print? *Harvard International Journal of Press/Politics, 4*(4), 48.

Hallin, D. C., & Mancini, P. (2004). *Comparing Media Systems: Three Models of Media and Politics.* Cambridge; New York: Cambridge University Press.

Hoskins, A., & Loughlin, B. (2009). *Television and terror: Conflicting Times and the Crisis of News Discourse.* Basingstoke: Palgrave Macmillan.

Kuhn, R. (2007). *Politics and the Media in Britain.* Houndmills, Palgrave Macmillan.

Ovsiovitch, J. S. (1993). News coverage of human rights. *Political Research Quarterly, 46*(3), 671.

Appendix II
Coding Instruments

A. Coding Instrument–Phrase Search Content Analysis[19]

Read story once. Then read story and code for the following:
   Unique Identifier–use date of story, for dates with multiple stories use the date and a sequential letter.

I. Is the Story Primarily About Domestic or International News?

1.   Domestic (including local)
2.   International
3.   Both (ex: a story that covers protests at the Egyptian Embassy in New York would be both)

II. Does the Story Use Right or Rights Besides HR (As in Civil Right, Right to Freedom, etc., NOT as in Conservative)

1.   Yes
2.   No

III. Type of Story

1.   **VOSOT**, or voice-over sound on tape of five lines or less
2.   **Full Package**, or complete story of more than five lines including taped feature
3.   **Live Two-Way**, or major story featuring live substantive conversation between an anchor or another person in the studio and a correspondent (more than just "Thanks, John")
4.   **Headline/Intro** at beginning of newscast
5.   **Restatement** at end of newscast
6.   **Teaser** before commercial
7.   **Weather or Stock Market Report**
8.   **Commentary**, opinion from one or more talking heads with no additional video

IV. Primary Location of Story

Coder writes in the country that is the primary subject of the story (what the story is about, not necessarily the location of the correspondent or anchor). Abbreviations used include US, UK, and DRC. Palestine-Israel is used for stories that are primarily about Israel and/or the territories administered by Israel and not claimed as part of another currently existing state.

V. Topic of Story

Coder writes a short summary (1 phrase) of what the story is about.

VI. Is HR Used as Introduction or as Part of Title for Person, Group, or Place?

Nota Bene (NB): If 1 or 2 is used, then coder copies the phrase in Column G, "Specific I/T"

1.   HR is part of an unofficial title, as in an introduction or description (ex: X, a fierce champion of human rights, or "pressure from human rights groups")
2.   HR is part of the official title of a person, group, or place (ex: Human Rights Watch issued the report, the State's Office of Human Rights was attacked)
1, 2.   HR is part of both a formal and an informal title
3.   HR is neither part of the formal or informal title

VII. Is HR Used Only in the Formal or Informal Title?

1. Yes
2. No, it is used elsewhere as well
3. N/A, as HR is not in the title or introduction (**NB:** can only use code 3 if 3 is coded in previous category)
4. Yes, it's used only in the formal or informal title in the heading of an individual, not spoken

VIII. Is a Description or Example of HR Given?

NB: If 1 or 3 is used, then coder copies the phrase(s) that support the classification into Column J, "Specific D/E"

1. Yes
2. No
3. Some description, but not explicit, specific, detailed, or related to Human Rights as such

IX. Is HR the Primary Focus of Story? To What Extent is the Story a Discussion or More In-Depth Analysis of Human Rights?

1. Yes
2. No
3. HR is prominent but not the primary focus of the story

X. Human Rights Categories (From Treaties With 15–17 From Prominent Non-Treaty Norms)

1. Racial Discrimination
2. Civil and Political Rights (code for subset, if possible, as 2-A, 2-C, etc.)

   a. Press Freedom/Freedom of Speech/Freedom of Information
   b. Voting/Political Participation/Freedom of Assembly
   c. Prison Conditions/Rights of the Accused
   d. State Violence/Extrajudicial Killings
   e. Freedom of Conscience/Religious Practice

3. Economic, Social, and Cultural Rights (code for subset, if possible, as 3-A, 3-D, etc.)

   f. Minimum Standard of Living
   g. Worker's Rights
   h. Food, Water Rights
   i. Housing

4. Women's Rights/Sexual Violence
5. Torture and Other Cruel, Inhuman, or Degrading Treatment or Punishment
6. Children's Rights
7. Migrant Workers/Families
8. Protection Against Enforced Disappearance
9. Disabled Persons
10. Abolition of the Death Penalty
11. Refugees, Asylees, Nationality, Statelessness
12. Humanitarian Law, Laws of War, Crimes Against Humanity, War Crimes Tribunals
13. Genocide
14. Elderly
15. Slavery, Slavery-Like Practices
16. Indigenous Groups
17. GLBTQ Rights
18. Not Applicable or Not Given or Not Specified or Unclear

XI. If Not Already in the File, Copy and Paste in the Phrase Including HR

XII. Is HR Used Only as a Rhetorical Reference in a Story Completely Unrelated to Human Rights? (ex: "Environmental Issues Now Have Reached That Stage Much Like Human Rights or Peace, That It's Not Something That's Episodic")

1. Yes
2. No

XIII. Is the Primary Frame of the Story Terrorism or the Global War on Terror?

1. Yes
2. No

XIX. Does the Story Mention a Written Report from the US State Department?

1. Yes
2. No

XX. Does the Story Mention a Report from an NGO (ex: Amnesty International, Human Rights Watch, ICRC)?

NB: Only actual written reports get this code, not "X says," "X claims," or "X Accuses."

1. Yes
2. No

B-1 Coding Sheet–Month Content Analysis, Television Coding[20]

Read story once. Then read story and code for the following:
   Unique Identifier–record story date and number of story in the broadcast.

I. Is the Story Primarily About Domestic or International News?

1. Domestic (including local)
2. International
3. Both (ex: a story that covers protests at the Egyptian Embassy in New York would be both)
4. Non-story (sports, simple stock market report)

II. Does the Story Use Right or Rights Besides HR (As in Civil Right, Right to Freedom, etc., NOT as in Conservative)

3. Yes
4. No

III. Is the Story a HR Story?

1. Yes, it includes the phrase HR
2. Yes, it does not include the phrase HR but still covers a clear HR issue with focus and/or framing on the HR (even if it is not named as such)
3. No, it neither includes the phrase HR, nor covers a HR issue
4. No, it could be a HR story but is not framed as one, and the primary focus of the story is not on the HR

NB: If answer is 3 or 4, then proceed to next story. If answer is 1 or 2, then continue coding story.

IV. Type of Story

1. **VOSOT,** or voice-over sound on tape of five lines or less
2. **Full Package,** or complete story of more than five lines including taped feature
3. **Live Two-Way,** or major story featuring live substantive conversation between an anchor or another person in the studio and a correspondent (more than just "Thanks, John")
4. **Headline/Intro** at beginning of newscast
5. **Restatement** at end of newscast
6. **Teaser** before commercial
7. **Weather or Stock Market Report**
8. Commentary, opinion from one or more talking heads with no additional video

V. Primary Location of Story

Coder writes in country that is the primary subject of the story (what the story is about, not necessarily the location of the correspondent or anchor). Abbreviations used include US, UK, and DRC. Palestine-Israel is used for stories that are primarily about Israel and/or the territories administered by Israel and not claimed as part of another currently existing state.

VI. Topic of Story

Coder writes a short summary (1 phrase) of what the story is about.

VII. Is HR Used as Introduction or as Part of Title for Person, Group, or Place?

NB: If 1 or 2 is used, then coder copies the phrase in Column G, "Specific I/T."

1. HR is part of an unofficial title, as in an introduction or description (ex: X, a fierce champion of human rights, or "pressure from human rights groups")
2. HR is part of the official title of a person, group, or place (ex: Human Rights Watch issued the report, the State's Office of Human Rights was attacked)
1, 2. HR is part of both a formal and an informal title
3. HR is neither part of the formal or informal title

VIII. Is HR Used Only in the Formal or Informal Title?

1. Yes
2. No, it is used elsewhere as well
3. N/A, as HR is not in the title or introduction (**NB:** can only use code 3 if 3 is coded in previous category).

IX. Is a Description or Example of HR Given?

NB: If 1 or 3 is used, then coder copies the phrase(s) that support the classification into Column J, "Specific D/E."

1. Yes
2. No
3. Some description but not explicit, specific, detailed, or related to Human Rights as such

X. Is HR the Primary Focus of Story? To What Extent is the Story a Discussion or More In-Depth Analysis of Human Rights?

1. Yes
2. No
3. HR is prominent but not the primary focus of the story

XI. Human Rights Categories (From treaties With 15–17 From Prominent Non-Treaty Norms)

1. Racial Discrimination

2. Civil and Political Rights (code for subset, if possible, as 2-A, 2-C, etc.)

    a. Press Freedom/Freedom of Speech/Freedom of Information
    b. Voting/Political Participation/Freedom of Assembly
    c. Prison Conditions/Rights of the Accused
    d. State Violence/Extrajudicial Killing
    e. Freedom of Conscience/Religious Practice

3. Economic, Social, and Cultural Rights (code for subset, if possible, as 3-A, 3-D, etc.)

    a. Minimum Standard of Living
    b. Worker's Rights
    c. Food, Water Rights
    d. Housing

4. Women's Rights/Sexual Violence
5. Torture and Other Cruel, Inhuman, or Degrading Treatment or Punishment
6. Children's Rights
7. Migrant Workers/Families
8. Protection Against Enforced Disappearance
9. Disabled Persons
10. Abolition of the Death Penalty
11. Refugees, Asylees, Nationality, Statelessness
12. Humanitarian Law, Laws of War, Crimes Against Humanity, War Crimes Tribunals
13. Genocide
14. Elderly
15. Slavery, Slavery-Like Practices
16. Indigenous Groups
17. GLBTQ Rights
18. Not Applicable or Not Given or Not Specified or Unclear

XII. If Not Already in the File, Copy and Paste in the Phrase Including HR

XIII. Is HR Used Only as a Rhetorical Reference in a Story Completely Unrelated to Human Rights? (ex: "Environmental Issues Now Have Reached That Stage Much Like Human Rights or Peace, That It's Not Something That's Episodic")

1. Yes
2. No

XIV. Major Stories: Is the Story About South Africa, German Reunification, or Political Reform or Independence Movements in the Soviet Union?

1. South Africa
2. None of these
3. Political reform or independence movements in the Soviet Union
4. German Reunification

B-2 Coding Sheet–Month Content Analysis, Print Coding[21]

Read story once. Then read story and code for the following:

Unique Identifier–use date of story, for dates with multiple stories use the date and a sequential letter.

I. Section and Page number: Record section of article. If available, record page number

I. Length: Record the Length of the Story

1. 1–50 words
2. 51–100 words
3. 101–200 words
4. 201–300 words
5. 301–400 words
6. 401–500 words
7. 501–600 words
8. 601–800 words
9. 801–1000 words
10. 1001 or more words

III. Is the Story Primarily About Domestic or International News?

1. Domestic (including local)
2. International
3. Both (ex: a story that covers protests at the Egyptian Embassy in New York would be both)

VI. Does the Story Use Right or Rights Besides HR (As in Civil Right, Right to Freedom, etc., NOT As in Conservative)

1. Yes
2. No

V. Primary Location of Story

Coder writes in country that is the primary subject of the story (what the story is about, not necessarily the location of the correspondent or anchor). Abbreviations used include US, UK, and DRC. Palestine-Israel is used for stories that are primarily about Israel and/or the territories administered by Israel and not claimed as part of another currently existing state.

VI. Title of Story

Coder copies headline of story; if headline is not included, then coder writes a short summary (1 phrase) of what the story is about.

VII. Is HR Used as Introduction or as Part of Title for Person, Group, or Place?

NB: If 1 or 2 is used, then coder copies the phrase in Column G, "Specific I/T."

1. HR is part of an unofficial title, as in an introduction or description (ex: X, a fierce champion of human rights, or "pressure from human rights groups")
2. HR is part of the official title of a person, group, or place (ex: Human Rights Watch issued the report, the State's Office of Human Rights was attacked)
1, 2. HR is part of both a formal and an informal title
3. HR is neither part of the formal or informal title

VIII. Is HR Used Only in the Formal or Informal Title?

1. Yes
2. No, it is used elsewhere as well
3. N/A, as HR is not in the title or introduction (**NB:** can only use code 3 if 3 is coded in previous category)

IX. Is a Description or Example of HR Given?

NB: If 1 or 3 is used, then coder copies the phrase(s) that support the classification into Column J, "Specific D/E."

1. Yes
2. No
3. Some description but not explicit, specific, detailed, or related to Human Rights as such

X. Is HR the Primary Focus of Story? To What Extent is the Story a Discussion or More In-Depth Analysis of Human Rights?

1. Yes
2. No
3. HR is prominent but not the primary focus of the story

XI. Human Rights Categories (From Treaties With 15–17 From Prominent Non-Treaty Norms)

1. Racial Discrimination
2. Civil and Political Rights (code for subset, if possible, as 2-A, 2-C, etc.)

    j.   Press Freedom/Freedom of Speech/Freedom of Information
    k.   Voting/Political Participation/Freedom of Assembly
    l.   Prison Conditions/Rights of the Accused
    m.   State Violence/Extrajudicial Killings
    n.   Freedom of Conscience/Religious Practice

3. Economic, Social, and Cultural Rights (code for subset, if possible, as 3-A, 3-D, etc.)

    o.   Minimum Standard of Living
    p.   Worker's Rights
    q.   Food, Water Rights
    r.   Housing

4. Women's Rights/Sexual Violence
5. Torture and Other Cruel, Inhuman, or Degrading Treatment or Punishment
6. Children's Rights
7. Migrant Workers/Families
8. Protection Against Enforced Disappearance
9. Disabled Persons
10. Abolition of the Death Penalty
11. Refugees, Asylees, Nationality, Statelessness
12. Humanitarian Law, Laws of War, Crimes Against Humanity, War Crimes Tribunals
13. Genocide
14. Elderly
15. Slavery, Slavery-Like Practices
16. Indigenous Groups
17. GLBTQ Rights
18. Not Applicable or Not Given or Not Specified or Unclear

XII. If Not Already in the File, Copy and Paste in the Phrase Including HR

XIII. Is HR used only as a Rhetorical Reference in a Story Completely Unrelated to Human Rights? (ex: "Environmental Issues Now Have Reached That Stage Much Like Human Rights or Peace, That It's Not Something That's Episodic")

1. Yes
2. No

XIV. Does the Story Mention a Written Report From the US State Department?

1. Yes
2. No

XV. Does the Story Mention a Report From an NGO (ex: Amnesty International, Human Rights Watch, ICRC)?

NB: Only actual written reports get this code, not "X says," "X claims," or "X accuses."

1. Yes
2. No

XVI. Major Stories: Is the Story About South Africa, German Reunification, or Political Reform or Independence Movements in the Soviet Union?

1. South Africa
2. None of these
3. Political reform or independence movements in the Soviet Union
4. German Reunification

C–Coding Sheet for Comparing Twenty Years Analysis

Watch the story once. Then watch the story and code for the following:
   For US stories, code the name of the story, using the VTNA title

I. Is the Story Primarily About Domestic or International News?

1. Domestic (including local)
2. International
3. Both (ex: a story that covers protests at the Egyptian Embassy in New York would be both)

II. Does the Story Use Right or Rights Besides HR (As in Civil Right, Right to Freedom, etc., NOT As in Conservative)

1. Yes
2. No

III. Is the Story a HR story?

1. Yes, it includes the phrase HR
2. Yes, it does not include the phrase HR but still covers a clear HR issue with focus and/or framing on the HR (even if it is not named as such)
3. No, it neither includes the phrase HR, nor covers a HR issue
4. No, it could be a HR story but is not framed as one, and the primary focus of the story is not on the HR
5. Yes, it includes the phrase HR but only in text, not audibly

NB: If answer is 3 or 4, then proceed to next story.

IV. Type of Story

1. **VOSOT**, or voice-over sound on tape of five lines or less
2. **Full Package**, or complete story of more than five lines including taped feature
3. **Live Two-Way**, or major story featuring live substantive conversation between an anchor or another person in the studio and a correspondent (more than just "Thanks, John")
4. **Headline/Intro** at beginning of newscast
5. **Restatement** at end of newscast
6. **Teaser** before commercial
7. **Weather or Stock Market Report**
8. **Commentary**, opinion from one or more talking heads with no additional video

V. Primary Location of Story

Coder writes in country that is the primary subject of the story (what the story is about, not necessarily the location of the correspondent or anchor). Abbreviations used include US, UK, DRC, and PRC.

VI. Is HR Used as Part of Title for Person, Group, or Place or as Introduction to a Person, Group, or Place?

1. **HR is part of an unofficial title, as in an introduction or description** (ex: X, a fierce champion of human rights, or "pressure from human rights groups")

2.   HR is part of the official title of a person, group, or place (ex: Human Rights Watch issued the report, the State's Office of Human Rights was attacked)

1, 2. **HR is part of both an unofficial title and an official title**

3.   HR is neither part of the formal or informal title

VI. Is HR Used Only in the Formal or Informal Title of a Person, Group, or Place?

1. Yes
2. No, it is used elsewhere as well
3. N/A, as HR is not in the title or introduction (**NB:** can only use code 3 if 3 is coded in previous category).

VII. Is a Description or Example of HR Given?

1. Yes (there is a clear description of human rights that is detailed and/ or explicitly linked to human rights)
2. No (there is no description, example, illustration or elaboration)
3. There is some description, but it is not explicit, specific, detailed, or related to Human Rights as such

VIII. Is HR the Primary Focus of Story? To What Extent is the Story a Discussion or More In-Depth Analysis of Human Rights?

1. Yes (if a summary of the story would be mostly about human rights)
2. No (if a summary of the story would not include human rights)
3. **HR is prominent but not the primary focus of the story** (if a summary of the story would include a bullet point about human rights but bullet points about other things as well)

IX. Is HR Used Only as a Rhetorical Reference in a Story Completely Unrelated to Human Rights? (ex: "Environmental Issues Now Have Reached That Stage Much Like Human Rights or Peace, That It's Not Something That's Episodic")

1. Yes
2. No

X. Is the Primary Frame of the Story Terrorism or the Global War on Terror?

1. Yes
2. No

XI. Does Story Use Comparison to Past or Current Events?

1. Relates current story to past events only
2. Relates current story to current events only
3. Relates current story to both past and current events
4. Relates current story to neither past nor current events

XII. Does Story Premediate or Remediate?

1. Story premediates–makes predictions about the future
2. Story remediates–tries to change conclusions from the past
3. Story both premediates and remediates
4. Story neither premediates nor remediates

XIII. Does the Story Use Split Screen?

1. Yes
2. No

If yes, then describe the screens.

XIV. Does the Story have a Banner Running Underneath it?

1. Yes
2. No

If yes, then record the banner.

XV. Does the Story Use Graphics?

1. Yes
2. No

If yes, then describe the graphics.

XVI. Human Rights Categories (From Treaties With 15–17 From Prominent Non-Treaty Norms)

1. Racial Discrimination
2. Civil and Political Rights (code for subset, if possible, as 2-A, 2-C, etc.)

    A. Press Freedom/Freedom of Speech/Freedom of Information
    B. Voting/Political Participation/Freedom of Assembly
    C. Prison Conditions/Rights of the Accused
    D. State Violence/Extrajudicial Killings
    E. Freedom of Conscience/Religious Practice

3. Economic, Social, and Cultural Rights (code for subset, if possible, as 3-A, 3-D, etc.)

   A. Minimum Standard of Living
   B. Worker's Rights
   C. Food, Water Rights
   D. Housing

4. Women's Rights/Sexual Violence
5. Torture and Other Cruel, Inhuman, or Degrading Treatment or Punishment
6. Children's Rights
7. Migrant Workers/Families
8. Protection Against Enforced Disappearance
9. Disabled Persons
10. Abolition of the Death Penalty
11. Refugees, Asylees, Nationality, Statelessness
12. Humanitarian Law, Laws of War, Crimes Against Humanity, War Crimes Tribunals
13. Genocide
14. Elderly
15. Slavery, Slavery-Like Practices
16. Indigenous Groups
17. GLBTQ Rights
18. Not Applicable or Not Given or Not Specified or Unclear

D. Coding Instrument–Case Study Content Analysis: China

Read story once. Then read story and code for the following:

Unique Identifier–use date of story, for dates with multiple stories, use the date and a sequential letter.

I. *Type of Story*

1. **VOSOT,** or voice-over sound on tape of five lines or less
2. **Full Package,** or complete story of more than five lines including taped feature
3. **Live Two-Way,** or major story featuring live substantive conversation between an anchor or another person in the studio and a correspondent (more than just "Thanks, John")
4. **Headline/Intro** at beginning of newscast
5. **Restatement** at end of newscast
6. **Teaser** before commercial
7. **Weather or Stock Market Report**
8. **Commentary,** opinion from one or more talking heads with no additional video
9. **Preview** for another show

II. Is the Story About China?

1.   Yes

    1A. Yes, about China and another country/issue

2.   No, it's about a person from China, but the story isn't about China
3.   No, the story refers to China in passing, as an example or as a short comparison (1 line) but is not about China
4.   No, the story refers to China as a geographic location in a story that is not about China (ex: Bhutan shares a border with China, as far away as China)
5.   No, the story refers to china, the fancy plates, not the country
7.   No, the story refers to China as part of a place name/work of art in a story that is not about China (ex: China Beach in Vietnam, the South China Sea, Chinatown the movie, etc.)

III. Topic: Write the Primary Topic of the Story in 1–3 words

IV. Does the Story Mention

1. Democracy only (or democratic)
2. Communism only (or Communist)
3. Both democracy and communism
4. Neither democracy nor communism

V. Does the Story Frame China as a Threat (Current or Rising) to the US or Something to be Feared by the US?

1. Yes
2. No

VI. Does the Story Use Right or Rights Besides HR (As in Civil Right, Right to Freedom, etc., NOT As in Conservative)

1.   Yes
2.   No

VII. Does the Story Explicitly Mention Terrorism?

1.   Yes, pre-9/11/01
2.   Yes, post-9/11/01
3.   No

VIII. Does the Story Mention a Written Report from the US State Department?

1.   Yes, human rights report
2.   Yes, Terror Report

3. Yes, Terror Report State department not mentioned
4. No
5. Yes, another State Department report

VIX. Does the Story Mention a Report From an NGO (ex: Amnesty International, Human Rights Watch, ICRC)

NB: Only actual written reports get this code, not "X says," "X claims," or "X Accuses."

1. Yes
2. No

X. Is the Story a HR Story?

1. Yes, it includes the phrase HR
2. Yes, it does not include the phrase HR but still covers a clear HR issue with focus and/or framing on the HR (even if it is not named as such)
3. No, it neither includes the phrase HR, nor covers a HR issue
4. No, it could be a HR story but is not framed as one, and the primary focus of the story is not on the HR

NB: If answer is 3 or 4, then proceed to next story.

XI. Is HR Used As An Introduction or As Part of Title for Person, Group, or Place?

NB: If 1 or 2 is used, then coder copies the phrase in Column G, "Specific I/T."

1. **HR is part of an unofficial title, as in an introduction or description** (ex: X, a fierce champion of human rights, or "pressure from human rights groups")
2. **HR is part of the official title of a person, group, or place** (ex: Human Rights Watch issued the report, the State's Office of Human Rights was attacked)
1, 2. **HR is part of both a formal and an informal title**
3 **HR is neither part of the formal or informal title**

XII. Is HR Used Only in the Formal or Informal Title?

1. Yes
2. No, it is used elsewhere as well
3. N/A, as HR is not in the title or introduction (**NB:** can only use code 3 if 3 is coded in previous category)
4. Yes, it's used only in the formal or informal title in the heading of an individual, not spoken

XIII. Is a Description or Example of HR Given?

NB: If 1 or 3 is used, then coder copies the phrase(s) that support the classification into Column J, "Specific D/E."

1. Yes
2. No
3. Some description but not explicit, specific, detailed, or related to Human Rights as such

XIV. Is HR the Primary Focus of Story? To What Extent Is the Story a Discussion or More In-Depth Analysis of Human Rights?

1. Yes
2. No
3. HR is prominent but not the primary focus of the story

XV. Human Rights Categories (From Treaties With 15–17 From Prominent Non-Treaty Norms)

1. Racial Discrimination
2. Civil and Political Rights (code for subset, if possible, as 2-A, 2-C, etc.)

   a. Press Freedom/Freedom of Speech/Freedom of Information
   b. Voting/Political Participation/Freedom of Assembly
   c. Prison Conditions/Rights of the Accused
   d. State Violence/Extrajudicial Killings
   e. Freedom of Conscience/Religious Practice

3. Economic, Social, and Cultural Rights (code for subset if possible, as 3-A, 3-D, etc.)

   a. Minimum Standard of Living
   b. Worker's Rights
   c. Food, Water Rights
   d. Housing

4. Women's Rights/Sexual Violence
5. Torture and Other Cruel, Inhuman, or Degrading Treatment or Punishment
6. Children's Rights
7. Migrant Workers/Families
8. Protection Against Enforced Disappearance
9. Disabled Persons
10. Abolition of the Death Penalty

11. Refugees, Asylees, Nationality, Statelessness
12. Humanitarian Law, Laws of War, Crimes Against Humanity, War Crimes Tribunals
13. Genocide
14. Elderly
15. Slavery, Slavery-Like Practices
16. Indigenous Groups
17. GLBTQ Rights
18. Not Applicable or Not Given or Not Specified or Unclear

XVI. If Not already in the file, copy and Paste in the Phrase Including HR.

XVII. Is HR used only as a rhetorical reference in a story completely unrelated to human rights? (ex: "Environmental Issues Now Have Reached That Stage Much Like Human Rights or Peace, That It's Not Something That's Episodic."

1. Yes
2. No

E. Coding Instrument- Case Study Content Analysis- Somalia

Read story once. Then read story and code for the following:
  Unique Identifier– use date of story, for dates with multiple stories use the date and a sequential letter.

I. Type of Story

1. **VOSOT,** or voice-over sound on tape of five lines or less
2. **Full Package,** or complete story of more than five lines including taped feature
3. **Live Two-Way,** or major story featuring live substantive conversation between an anchor or another person in the studio and a correspondent (more than just "Thanks, John")
4. **Headline/Intro** at beginning of newscast
5. **Restatement** at end of newscast
6. **Teaser** before commercial
7. **Weather or Stock Market Report**
8. **Commentary,** opinion from one or more talking heads with no additional video
9. **Preview/Promo** for another show

II. Is the story Primarily about Somalia?

1. Yes

    1A. Yes, story is about Somalia and another issue that is related in equal measure (such as Somalia and the ICRC in 1992–08–14-B)

2. No, story is about someone from Somalia mentioned tangentially in a story that is not about Somalia
3. No, story is about something else, with little description/info about Somalia, and only refers to Somalia as an example or comparison (ex: "like Somalia", "another Somalia," "mission creep like in Somalia")
4. No, story mentions Somalia as a geographic location in a story that is not about Somalia (ex: May 28, 1991 "border between Ethiopia and Somalia")
5. No, story only has Somalia in text, not audio
6. No, story is about a girl in the US named Somalia in a story unrelated to Somalia

III. Does the story mention any part of the Former Yugoslavia?

1. Yes
2. No

IV. Is the Story Primarily About A Natural Disaster (flood, earthquake, tsunami, etc.

NB: Not drought or general crop failure, unless it's a specific phenomenon and the focus of the story, and not just famine, unless specifically attributed to a specific natural disaster.

1. Yes
2. No

V. Does the Story use Right or Rights Besides HR (as in Civil Right, Right to Freedom, etc., NOT As in Conservative)

1. Yes
2. No

VI. Does the Story use the Word Warlord?

1. Yes
2. No

VII. Does the Story Explicitly Mention Terrorism?

NB: Only 1 or 2 if terrorism/terror/terrorists are explicitly noted.

1. Yes, pre-9/11/01
2. Yes, post-9/11/01
3. No

VIII. Does the Story Explicitly Mention Civil War?

1. Yes
2. No, but it does mention failed state or failed government or war (not civil). **NB:** Warring factions is not enough for 2
3. No

IX. Does the Story Mention the UN

1. Yes
2. No

X. Does the Story Mention a Written Report from the US State Department?

1. Yes, HR report
2. Yes, Terror List
3. Terror List, State department not mentioned
4. No

XI. Does the Story Mention a Report From an NGO or IGO (ex: Amnesty International, Human Rights Watch, ICRC, UN)?

NB: Only actual written reports get this code, not "X says," "X claims," or "X accuses."

1. Yes
2. No

XII. Is Foreign Assistance Mentioned in the Story?

1. Yes, a call for it is in the story
2. Yes, the story includes an assistance plan in place/in progress
3. No

XIII. Topic: Write the Primary Topic of the Story in 1–3 words

XIV. Are US Military Casualties Mentioned?

1. Yes, injured service person
2. Yes, KIA/death of service person
3. No
4. Both injury and death of service people are in the story
5. Captive military are mentioned in story
6. Captive, dead, and injured military are reported in the story

XV. Is the Story a HR story?

1. Yes, it includes the phrase HR
2. Yes, it does not include the phrase HR but still covers a clear HR issue with focus and/or framing on the HR (even if it is not named as such)
3. No, it neither includes the phrase HR, nor covers a HR issue
4. No, it could be a HR story but is not framed as one, and the primary focus of the story is not on the HR

NB: If answer is 3 or 4, then proceed to next story.

XVI. Is HR Used As Introduction or As Part of Title for Person, Group, or Place?

NB: If 1 or 2 is used, then coder copies the phrase in Column G, "Specific I/T."

1. **HR is part of an unofficial title, as in an introduction or description** (ex: X, a fierce champion of human rights, or "pressure from human rights groups")
2. **HR is part of the official title of a person, group, or place** (ex: Human Rights Watch issued the report, the State's Office of Human Rights was attacked)
1, 2. **HR is part of both a formal and an informal title.**
3. **HR is neither part of the formal or informal title**

XVII. Is HR Used Only in the Formal or Informal Title?

1. Yes
2. No, it is used elsewhere as well
3. N/A, as HR is not in the title or introduction (**NB:** can only use code 3 if 3 is coded in previous category)
4. Yes, it's used only in the formal or informal title in the heading of an individual, not spoken

XVIII. Is a Description or Example of HR Given?

NB: If 1 or 3 is used, then coder copies the phrase(s) that support the classification into Column R "Specific D/E."

1. Yes
2. No
3. Some description but not explicit, specific, detailed, or related to Human Rights as such

XIX. Is HR the Primary Focus of Story? To What Extent is the Story a Discussion or More In-Depth Analysis of Human Rights?

1. Yes
2. No
3. HR is prominent but not the primary focus of the story

XX. Human Rights Categories (From Treaties With 15–17 From Prominent Non-Treaty Norms)

1. Racial Discrimination
2. Civil and Political Rights (code for subset if possible, as 2-A, 2-C, etc.)

    a. Press Freedom/Freedom of Speech/Freedom of Information
    b. Voting/Political Participation/Freedom of Assembly
    c. Prison Conditions/Rights of the Accused
    d. State Violence/Extrajudicial Killings
    e. Freedom of Conscience/Religious Practice

3. Economic, Social, and Cultural Rights (code for subset if possible, as 3-A, 3-D, etc.)

    a. Minimum Standard of Living
    b. Worker's Rights
    c. Food, Water Rights
    d. Housing

4. Women's Rights/Sexual Violence
5. Torture and Other Cruel, Inhuman, or Degrading Treatment or Punishment
6. Children's Rights
7. Migrant Workers/Families
8. Protection Against Enforced Disappearance
9. Disabled Persons
10. Abolition of the Death Penalty
11. Refugees, Asylees, Nationality, Statelessness

12. Humanitarian Law, Laws of War, Crimes Against Humanity, War Crimes Tribunals
13. Genocide
14. Elderly
15. Slavery, Slavery-Like Practices
16. Indigenous Groups
17. GLBTQ Rights
18. Not Applicable or Not Given or Not Specified or Unclear

XXI. If Not Already in the File, Copy and Paste in the Phrase Including HR

XXII. Is HR used only as a rhetorical reference in a story completely unrelated to human rights? (ex: "Environmental Issues Now Have Reached That Stage Much Like Human Rights or Peace, That It's Not Something That's Episodic")

1. Yes
2. No

F. Coding Instrument–Case Study Content Analysis: Sudan

Read story once. Then read story and code for the following:

   Unique Identifier– use date of story, for dates with multiple stories use the date and a sequential letter.

I. Type of Story

1. **VOSOT,** or voice-over sound on tape of five lines or less
2. **Full Package,** or complete story of more than five lines including taped feature
3. **Live Two-Way,** or major story featuring live substantive conversation between an anchor or another person in the studio and a correspondent (more than just "Thanks, John")
4. **Headline/Intro** at beginning of newscast
5. **Restatement** at end of newscast
6. **Teaser** before commercial
7. **Weather or Stock Market Report**
8. **Commentary,** opinion from one or more talking heads with no additional video
9. **Preview/Promo** for another show

III. Does the Story Use Right or Rights Besides HR (As in Civil Right, Right to Freedom, etc., NOT As in Conservative)

1. Yes
2. No

IV. Is the Story About Sudan/Darfur?

1. Yes, the story is primarily about Sudan/Darfur

   1A. Yes, the story is about Sudan and another country or issue

2. No, the story is about a person from Sudan (ex: "a Sudanese," or "from Sudan")
3. No, the story is about something else and mentions Sudan/Darfur briefly as an example or in passing, in one line
4. No, the story mentions Sudan/Darfur as a point of geography
5. No, the story is about someone whose name contains "Sudan" but is not Sudanese

V. Does the Story Mention

1. Sudan
2. Darfur
3. Both Sudan & Darfur

VI. Does the Story Mention

1. The US
2. China
3. The UN
4. The US & China
5. The US & China & the UN
6. The US & the UN but not China
7. The UN & China but not the US
8. Somalia
9. Somalia & the US
10. Somalia & China
11. Somalia & China & US
12. None of these
13. Somalia and the UN

VII. Is the Story Primarily About a Natural Disaster (Flood, Earthquake, Tsunami, etc.)

NB: Not drought or general crop failure, unless it's a specific phenomenon and the focus of the story.

1. Yes
2. No

VIII. Is the Story About Terrorism?

1. Yes, pre-9/11/01
2. Yes, post-9/11/01
3. No

IX. Does the Story Mention Osama bin Laden?

1. Yes
2. No

X. Does the Story Mention a Written Report from the US State Department?

1. Yes, Human Rights report
2. Yes, Terror Report
3. Yes, Terror Report but State Department not mentioned
4. No
5. Yes, Travel Advisory issued by State department

XI. Does the Story Mention the Olympics?

1. Yes
2. No

XII. Does the Story Mention Slavery?

1. Yes
2. No

XIII. Does the Story Explicitly Mention Civil War?

1. Yes
2. No
3. No, but it does mention a war that is a civil war (just as "war," not including civil)

XIV. Does the Story Mention a Report From an NGO (ex: Amnesty International, Human Rights Watch, ICRC)?

NB: Only actual written reports get this code, not "X says," "X claims," or "X accuses."

1. Yes
2. No

XV. Topic: Write the Primary Topic of the story in 1–3 words

XVI. Is the story a HR story?

1. Yes, it includes the phrase HR
2. Yes, it does not include the phrase HR but still covers a clear HR issue with focus and/or framing on the HR (even if it is not named as such)

3. No, it neither includes the phrase HR, nor covers a HR issue
4. No, it could be a HR story but is not framed as one, and the primary focus of the story is not on the HR

NB: If answer is 3 or 4, then proceed to next story.

XVII. Is HR Used As Introduction or As Part of Title for Person, Group, or Place?

NB: If 1 or 2 is used, then coder copies the phrase in Column G, "Specific I/T."

1.	**HR is part of an unofficial title, as in an introduction or description** (ex: X, a fierce champion of human rights, or "pressure from human rights groups")
2.	**HR is part of the official title of a person, group, or place** (ex: Human Rights Watch issued the report, the State's Office of Human Rights was attacked)
1, 2.	**HR is part of both a formal and an informal title.**
3.	**HR is neither part of the formal or informal title.**

XVIII. Is HR Used Only in the Formal or Informal Title?

1. Yes
2. No, it is used elsewhere as well
3. N/A, as HR is not in the title or introduction (**NB:** can only use code 3 if 3 is coded in previous category)
4. Yes, it's used only in the formal or informal title in the heading of an individual, not spoken

XIX. Is a Description or Example of HR Given?

NB: If 1 or 3 is used, then coder copies the phrase(s) that support the classification into Column J, "Specific D/E."

1. Yes
2. No
3. Some description but not explicit, specific, detailed, or related to Human Rights as such

XX. Is HR the Primary Focus of Story? To What Extent is the Story a Discussion or More In-Depth Analysis of Human Rights?

1. Yes
2. No
3. HR is prominent but not the primary focus of the story

XXI. Human Rights Categories (From Treaties With 15–17
From Prominent Non-Treaty Norms)

1. Racial Discrimination
2. Civil and Political Rights (code for subset if possible, as 2-A, 2-C, etc.)

    a.   Press Freedom/Freedom of Speech/Freedom of Information
    b.   Voting/Political Participation/Freedom of Assembly
    c.   Prison Conditions/Rights of the Accused
    d.   State Violence/Extrajudicial Killings
    e.   Freedom of Conscience/Religious Practice

3. Economic, Social, and Cultural Rights (code for subset if possible, as 3-A, 3-D, etc.)

    a.   Minimum Standard of Living
    b.   Worker's Rights
    c.   Food, Water Rights
    d.   Housing

4. Women's Rights/Sexual Violence
5. Torture and Other Cruel, Inhuman, or Degrading Treatment or Punishment
6. Children's Rights
7. Migrant Workers/Families
8. Protection Against Enforced Disappearance
9. Disabled Persons
10. Abolition of the Death Penalty
11. Refugees, Asylees, Nationality, Statelessness
12. Humanitarian Law, Laws of War, Crimes Against Humanity, War Crimes Tribunals
13. Genocide
14. Elderly
15. Slavery, Slavery-Like Practices
16. Indigenous Groups
17. GLBTQ Rights
18. Not Applicable or Not Given or Not Specified or Unclear

XXII. If Not Already in the File, Copy and Paste in the Phrase
Including HR.

XXIII. Is HR used only as a Rhetorical Reference in a story
Completely Unrelated to Human Rights? (ex: "Environmental
Issues Now Have Reached That Stage Much Like Human
Rights or Peace, That It's Not Something That's Episodic"

1.   Yes
2.   No

Appendix III

All Countries Featured in Human Rights Stories, 1990–2009

Country	Stories
US (international)	398
PRC (216) & Hong Kong (5)	221
US (domestic)	115
Iraq	68
Yugoslavia(2) & Successor States: Bosnia (31), Kosovo (10), Serbia (6), Croatia (2) Macedonia(1)	52
Haiti	39
Israel & Palestine	37
Russia & USSR & Chechnya	35
Afghanistan	23
Vatican	23
Sudan	19
Cuba	18
UK & Northern Ireland	17
Indonesia & East Timor	15
Mexico	13
Kuwait	13
Rwanda	10
Chile	9
South Africa	8
Pakistan	7
El Salvador	6
Colombia	6
Iran	5
DRC & Zaire	5

(*Continued*)

Country	Stories
UN	4
Saudi Arabia	4
Romania	4
Nigeria	4
Canada	4
Jordan	4
Egypt	4
Cambodia	4
Australia	4
Myanmar & Burma	4
Vietnam	3
Poland	3
Peru	3
Italy	3
India	3
France	3
Zimbabwe	2
UAE	2
Turkey	2
South Korea	2
North Korea	2
Netherlands	2
Germany	2
Brazil	2
Somalia	2
Sierra Leone	2
Austria	2
Czechoslovakia & Czech Republic	2
Uzbekistan	1
Uganda	1
Tajikistan	1
Spain	1
San Marino	1
Philippines	1
Panama	1

Country	Stories
Norway	1
Moldavia	1
Malawi	1
Lithuania	1
Libya	1
Liberia	1
Lebanon	1
Kenya	1
Japan	1
Ireland	1
Finland	1
Benin	1
Bangladesh	1
Algeria	1
Singapore	1
Greece	1
Hungary	1
Total	**1268**

Notes

1 The BBC's evening news broadcast has been and remains the most viewed television news broadcast in the UK, sometimes averaging more than twice as many viewers as its competitors on ITV and Sky. "BBC's 10pm news audience is double ITV's." The *Guardian* online, April 17, 2008. http://www.guardian.co.uk/media/2008/apr/17/tvnews.television. BBC Press Release, December 17, 2007. http://www.bbc.co.uk/pressoffice/pressreleases/stories/2007/12_december/17/news.shtml

2 Dataset downloaded from The Pew Research Center's Center for Excellence in Journalism's website at http://stateofthemedia.org/2012/network-news-the-pace-of-change-accelerates/network-by-the-numbers/ February 8, 2013 and available from the author.

3 All codebooks available in Appendix II. Roman numerals in parentheses refer to the item in the codebook.

4 The same rubric was applied to all three code sheets. For the UK analyses, domestic was of or pertaining to the UK and included all stories about Scotland, Wales, and Northern Ireland as domestic stories unless there was additional story information that would make them both domestic and international, such as the involvement of another country, as was often the case with Northern Ireland stories. Similarly, stories about Puerto Rico and the Marianas Trench were coded as domestic for the US, as they are both under the US federal government.

5　Please contact the author for further documentation of the decision process.

6　The team of coders consisted of the author, Brian Hasbrouck, and John McMahon, all of whom are native speakers of English with at least a bachelor's degree and one class in international human rights.

7　The major change was adding an extra category for whether the story is a human rights story to account for stories that did not include the phrase "human right!" but where nevertheless human rights stories. See below for a description of the added categories.

8　BBC Motion Gallery is the BBC's footage sales and licensing arm. The Motion Gallery maintains summaries of news broadcasts for BBC News and CBS News to which it also holds licensing rights.

9　A search of both ABC and CBS evening news was conducted on Vanderbilt, but the results for the sample 1990–1995 appeared less subject-focused, only turning up stories that had "human right" in the title or summary and therefore less comparable to the BBC selection mechanism. A transcript search was deemed incomparable to the Motion Gallery search; for an analysis of US transcripts including the phrase "human right!" see Chapter 3.

10　This method of selection has several unfortunate drawbacks. First, no information on the manner of search and retrieval is available from the Motion Gallery. Second, the search conducted on the Motion Gallery in February 2010 is not replicable, as the Motion Gallery has subsequently unveiled a new search platform, which does not allow disaggregation of CBS and BBC News holdings. PDFs of the original search are available from the author.

11　Available at http://www.nytimes.com/ref/membercenter/nytarchive.html. Final data verification on September 1, 2010.

12　For more on the default WEEKNUM function in Excel and how it differs from the ISO date system, see http://www.rondebruin.nl/weeknumber.htm

13　More specific explanations for week selections are available. Please contact the author.

14　Disaggregated stories list available from the author.

15　See Appendix 1 for the complete Coding Instrument.

16　This means that stories that only use the reference to ethnic nationality instead of the country name for China and Somalia would not get picked up, and in at least a few cases, that seems to have occurred. The introduction to the broadcast on June 13, 1993, mentions Somalis but not Somalia; one story on December 4, 1992, discusses the Somali capital of Mogadishu without using the word Somalia in the story; and a news brief on September 9, 2000, discusses the Chinese President Ziang Zemin's meeting with President Bill Clinton without using the word China. This limitation is minimal, as it does not exclude many stories and is acceptable for the greater benefits of focusing on the coverage of the case study countries and of being consistent across all case study search operations.

17　In addition to duplicates and aggregates, LexisNexis had some missing stories, such as the October 27, 1997, teaser story on the China File that has no accompanying full story for that day, as well as some mislabeled stories, such as the broadcast for June 10, 1994, being labeled as January 21, 1994, for both the Somalia and China searches. The incorrectly labeled stories have been counted as duplicates for June 10, 1994, but represent a cautionary tale for those using LexisNexis. Wherever possible additional verification, such as the Vanderbilt Television News Archive, should be consulted.

18　http://www.ohchr.org/EN/NewsEvents/Pages/DisplayNews.aspx?NewsID=8335&LangID=E

19　HR used as abbreviation for "human right!"

20　HR used as abbreviation for "human right!"

21　HR used as abbreviation for "human right!"

Index

For Product Safety Concerns and Information please contact our EU
representative GPSR@taylorandfrancis.com
Taylor & Francis Verlag GmbH, Kaufingerstraße 24, 80331 München, Germany